CURATORS'
CHOICE

CURATORS' CHOICE

*An Introduction to
the Art Museums
of the U.S.*

BY BABBETTE BRANDT FROMME

PB 38   19

CROWN PUBLISHERS, INC.   NEW YORK

R708.14

FOR BRIAN FORMATO

Fromme

Copyright © 1981 by Babbette Brandt Fromme

Inquiries should be addressed to Crown Publishers, Inc., One Park Avenue, New York, New York 10016
Printed in the United States of America
Published simultaneously in Canada by General Publishing Company Limited

Library of Congress Cataloging in Publication Data
Fromme, Babbette Brandt.
    Curators' choice—Northeastern edition.

    1. Art—Northeastern States.   2. Art museums—
Northeastern States.   I. Title.
N510.5.N6F76   1981   708.14   80-17771
ISBN: 0-517-541917

Design by Deborah B. Kerner   CFAd

10 9 8 7 6 5 4 3 2 1
First Edition

CONTENTS

NEW HAMPSHIRE   97

NEW JERSEY   102

NEW YORK   115

PENNSYLVANIA   **219**

FOREWORD ·

American museums are important cultural resources. Their collections span a broad spectrum from world-famous masterpieces to works of art of regional significance. The scholar and specialist through long study and access to museum archives know the locations of the objects in which they have a particular professional interest, wherever they are scattered among our nation's museums. On the other hand, the art lover who visits a city may be unaware of the riches of the local museum or other nearby collections. This book, *Curators' Choice,* has been written to fill a long-felt need for a reference guide to the art collections of America. Such a vast undertaking wisely has been organized into regional sections.

You as a private collector or avid museumgoer undoubtedly know quite well the museum of your hometown. But, when you visit another city, will you know all of the museums that you may wish to visit and what their specialities are? The author, Babbette Brandt Fromme, having long worked in museums, recognized that the best way of summarizing a museum's collection is to entrust the task to the actual curators of the various institutions. Accordingly, she asked the staffs of the museums to make a curator's choice of the objects of art in their museums that typify the collections and that should be on a "Don't Miss" list.

We are all accustomed to the books that are museum guides, but here is a book that is a guide to museums.

Joseph Veach Noble
Director, Museum of the City of New York
Past President, American Association of Museums

PREFACE

Often, on entering a museum for the first time, I've found myself eagerly wondering: What are its strengths? Are my special interests represented? What should I definitely try to see? There is always so little time, and it is so easy to get tired and miss things you later regret. So many others feel this way too that I embarked upon this guide. Its aim: to furnish the museumgoer with a sampling of the collections so as to heighten his or her enjoyment of the actual time spent in the museum. I want to stress that this is only a representative sampling, the tip of the iceberg, so to speak, compiled with the interested but unprofessional viewer in mind.

The selections are not mine but have been made by the directors, the curators or other experts in each museum. The descriptions of the objects were either supplied by the museums or culled from books on the particular subject.

Where no gallery locations are given next to an object, it is because (a) the museum is small enough to make this unnecessary, (b) the item is in storage waiting to be rotated for exhibition or (c) it is out on loan.

Museums today are living entities and are constantly growing and changing. Therefore it is virtually impossible to keep totally abreast of each museum's facilities, hours and admissions. A phone call made just before your visit might spare you possible disappointment.

There is a great deal publicly available for our pleasure in the world of art. I hope this book makes it easier for you to find your way among the centuries of artistic treasures so generously represented in the museums in this country.

ACKNOWLEDGMENTS

One of the nicest dividends derived from collating the material in these books was the enthusiasm and generous support I enjoyed. Museum personnel throughout the country expressed their approval by offering the information I requested and taking time to check the finished copy.

During the lengthy time it took me to complete the project, my husband was always available for guidance. This involved long discussions on the manuscript as well as frequent interruptions of his own work with questions to which he unfailingly responded with good cheer. He endured many hours on dull roads to reach museums of real interest (to him) and assumed more than his share of household tasks in order to free my time.

The members of the Public Information Department at the Metropolitan Museum of Art made their expertise available to me and opened doors to other sources when needed, always expressing keen interest in my project. For this I am grateful to John Ross, Berenice Heller, Richard Pierce, Joan Ingalls and Joan Gould. My special thanks are offered to Jack Frizelle, the department's director, who encouraged me to undertake this job in the first place when its size and practical problems suggested that I scotch the effort.

It was a pleasure to work with Betty Brandt (no relation) who spent many hours in libraries, relentlessly tracking down dates and obscure facts, while maintaining a sense of humor.

I felt always able to call upon my good friend Norma Rayman when additional research help was required. Her company on a variety of junkets made the work a pleasure.

My own compliments and those of my publishers go to Gilda Charwat and Dorothy Edwards for typing this very complex manuscript almost entirely free of error. Always available and deeply committed to the work, they turned what could have been a nightmare into a joy.

Crown Publishers themselves deserve special mention; they were never discouraged by either the enormity of this task or its esoteric sections: Herb Michelman provided me with the opportunity to publish these books; Rosemary Baer, production editor, for example, seemed always more willing the more difficult the problems; finally, my editor, Brandt Aymar, who guided me through the complexities of this undertaking with great open-mindedness and without drama, "Thank you, Brandt."

CONNECTICUT

FARMINGTON

HILL-STEAD MUSEUM
671 Farmington Ave.
Farmington, CT 06032
Tel: (203)677–9064

Hill-Stead, overlooking the Farmington Valley, was built in 1901 for Mr. and Mrs. Alfred Atmore Pope and designed by Stanford White in a neo-Colonial style. The house was built not only as a home but to house Mr. Pope's collection of French Impressionist paintings and other art objects. It remains today virtually the same as it was when the Popes resided there.

SAMPLING THE COLLECTION

EDOUARD MANET
French, 1832–1883

The Guitar Player
ca. 1865
Oil on canvas

1st Floor,
Drawing
Room

The somber tonal quality exhibited here shows the influence Velásquez exerted over Manet, who achieved great impact with spare details.

The Absinthe Drinker
1859
Wash drawing

Manet's daring subject matter was frowned upon by French officialdom. He incorporated the realism of the past with the new Impressionist style.

La Pasada
ca. 1863
Oil on canvas

This painting was occasioned by the visit of a Spanish dance group to Paris and reawakened Manet's earlier interest in Velásquez and Goya.

HILAIRE GERMAIN EDGAR DEGAS
French, 1834–1917

The Tub
ca. 1885
Pastel over gouache

1st Floor,
Drawing
Room

Probably the finest work in the museum's collection. Although a contentious bachelor, unused to the homelike scenes he often painted, Degas conveyed the essence of 19th-century Parisian life with great feeling.

Dancers
ca. 1880
Oil on canvas

Degas found a wealth of material to paint at the ballet. Frequent placement of figures at odd angles produced a photographic effect and a more lifelike quality.

Jockeys
1886
Pastel on buff paper

Degas was the first artist to achieve any work of importance in pastels. This flexible mode of expression enabled him to attain splendid results in color, tone and line.

1st Floor, Drawing Room

CLAUDE MONET
French, 1840–1926

View of the Bay and Maritime Alps at Antibes
1888
Oil on canvas

Monet would have liked "a palette of diamonds and precious stones" but rather than experiment anew this painting is a reaffirmation of a style he had already mastered.

1st Floor, Ell Room

Haystacks
1889
Oil on canvas

Haystacks
1890
Oil on canvas

Two in Monet's series of haystack paintings, the first most likely painted on an autumn morning, the latter in late summer. Both results of Monet's passionate concern with the transience of light.

1st Floor, Dining Room

JAMES A. MCNEILL WHISTLER
American, 1834–1903

Symphony in Violet and Blue
ca. 1884
Oil on canvas

The manner in which Whistler placed his shapes, the reserved use of color and the measured harmony of his tones are all expressed in this work.

1st Floor, Dining Room

CHINESE
Sung Dynasty, A.D. 960–1279

6 Pieces Celadon
Porcelain

Although greatly admired throughout the world, this glaze has never been able to be copied, even in China.

1st Floor, Parlor Bedroom

CHIPPENDALE
English, 18th c.

Secretary

Chinese influence blends with the Rococo to produce the Chippendale style. This piece closely resembles a model in Chippendale's *Book of Designs.*

1st Floor, 2nd Library

JAMES A. MCNEILL WHISTLER
American, 1834–1903

The Blue Wave
1862
Oil on canvas

This example of Whistler's early work is painted in a naturalistic style before his canvases were influenced by the Orient.

1st Floor, Morning Room

CLAUDE MONET
French, 1840–1926

Boats Leaving the Harbor
ca. 1865
Oil on canvas

There is a hint in this work that several years later would give rise to a new movement in the art world when Monet would paint his "impression" of a sunrise.

Upstairs, Green Room

MARY CASSATT
American, 1845–1926

Mother and Two Children
1901
Oil on canvas

Mothers and children were frequent subjects for Cassatt's palette. She used color and light in the Impressionist manner, combined with the linear brushwork she had observed in the work of Degas.

Upstairs, Sitting Room

SUZUKI HARUNOBU
Japanese, 1725–1770

Prints
Woodblocks

KITAGAWA UTAMARO
Japanese, 1753–1806

KATSUSHIKA HOKUSAI
Japanese, 1760–1849

ANDO HIROSHIGE
Japanese, 1797–1858
Originally developed to answer the tourist need for an inexpensive souvenir, it was these prints that were to influence the Impressionists' canvases so deeply. It is interesting to be able to study both prints and paintings in the same museum.

FACILITIES

Guided Tours are available.

A *Sales Desk* carries postcards and a catalog booklet.

Hours: Wednesday, Thursday, Saturday, Sunday, 2 P.M.–5 P.M. *Closed:* Thanksgiving, Christmas.

Admission: Adults, $1.50; children under 12, 75¢.

HARTFORD

WADSWORTH ATHENEUM
600 Main St.
Hartford, CT 60103
Tel: (203)278–2670

Exterior view. Courtesy Wadsworth Atheneum, Hartford

Opened in 1844 in Daniel Wadsworth's Gothic Revival castle, the original collection numbered just 53 objects. An expansion program, completed in 1969, resulted in five connecting buildings that surround a sculpture court. The 30,000 items, valued at almost $100 million, comprise the permanent collection housed in 68 galleries. It ranges from ancient Egyptian artifacts to contemporary sculpture. The collection's greatest strength lies in its classical bronzes; Baroque paintings; 18th-century porcelain; American furniture; English and American silver; 19th-century French and American paintings and 20th-century art.

SAMPLING THE COLLECTION

Because of the size of the collection and gallery renovations not all of these works are on exhibit at any given time.

GREEK

Draped Warrior
late 6th C. B.C.
Bronze

The feet of this probably ornamental statuette are thought to be modern additions. Stylized drapery covers the harmoniously balanced figure.

16TH-CENTURY ART

ENGLISH

Tigerware Jug
1576
Stoneware and silver

English silversmiths often mounted tigerware with silver covers and bases, copying the clay bodies from continental models.

17TH-CENTURY ART

ENGLISH

Steeple Cup
Silver gilt

Steeple cups, whose covers resemble church spires, belong to the reign of James I. Employed in ceremonial functions, they were usually produced in sets of three, one being taller.

MICHELANGELO MERISI DA
CARAVAGGIO
Italian, ca. 1565–1609

The Ecstasy of Saint Francis
Oil on canvas

One of this country's four Caravaggios, it is also one of his few landscapes. It is notable for the realism of the saint's posture and the chiaroscuro which astounded his colleagues.

ORAZIO GENTILESCHI
Italian, ca. 1565–ca. 1647

*Judith and Maidservant with
the Head of Holofernes*
Oil on canvas

Influenced by Caravaggio, Gentileschi in turn influenced Northern European artists who lived in Rome. He often duplicated his themes and there is another version of this painting in the Vatican.

BERNARDO STROZZI
Italian, 1581–1644

St. Catherine of Alexandria
Oil on canvas

Strozzi's paintings were of religious or genre scenes. This work was probably painted in his maturity, in Venice, where he lightened his palette under the influence of Veronese.

FRANCISCO ZURBARAN
Spanish, 1598–1664

Saint Serapion
1628
Oil on canvas

Zurbarán depicted many saints often isolated against stark dark backgrounds and highlighted by sculptured forms of subdued pure color.

JUSEPE RIBERA
Spanish, 1591–1652

A Philosopher
1637
Oil on canvas

During this period Ribera adopted a lighter, more gentle style than his earlier one, which was marked by savage themes and dark colors.

JUAN VALDES – LEAL
Spanish, 1622–1690

Vanitas
1660
Oil on canvas

Valdés Leal's *Vanitas* themes are executed in gloomy emotional style with great technical skill and extravagant color.

AMERICAN
Plymouth, Massachusetts

Prince-Howes Press Cupboard
1660–1670
Oak, maple, yellow pine,
painted

The press cupboard was painted and carved, the most elegant furniture found in the Early American home. Used for storage and display, it conferred status upon its owner.

AMERICAN
Plymouth, Massachusetts

Samuel Fuller Cradle
1620–1650
Oak and pine

This unusually constructed cradle is a modified chest believed to have been made by John Alden or Kenelm Winslow. The spindled three-sided hood allowed the baby to be seen from all angles.

AMERICAN

Salisbury Communion Table
1650–1660
White oak

This table, of interest because of its square feet and carving on its frame, was likely viewed by the congregation as it stood somewhat raised on a dais before them.

SIR ANTHONY VAN DYCK
Flemish, 1599–1641

The Resurrection of Christ
Oil on canvas

Van Dyck was Rubens's best-known assistant. His religious paintings are more subdued than the paintings of his master and, though well accepted when executed, he is most famous for his portraits.

18TH-CENTURY ART

FRENCH
Mennecy

Bust of Louis XV
ca. 1755
White porcelain

This bust was inspired by a statue honoring the king. Porcelain from the Mennecy factory of this period is considered the loveliest of its kind ever manufactured.

FRENCH
Vincennes

Teaset
ca. 1752
Porcelain

Before being removed to Sèvres, Vincennes was the royal porcelain factory. All other factories were prohibited from making porcelain. This teaset is decorated by Viellard in the yellow glaze of Vincennes.

J. J. KAENDLER
German, Saxony, 1706–1775

Judgment of Paris
Meissen
Porcelain group

In 1731, Kaendler became the principal modeler for the Meissen porcelain factory. The vividly colored figurines he fashioned so deftly were often used to adorn lavish dining tables.

GERMAN
Saxony

Garniture de Cheminée
ca. 1725–1730
Meissen porcelain

Oriental porcelain was finally well copied in 1710 and at that time the first Meissen factory was established. This piece was created for the king.

J. P. REINICKE
German, Saxony
18th c.

Continent of Asia
Meissen porcelain group

In the mid-18th century porcelain groups were still in demand as table decorations. Symbolic subjects were depicted as well as those drawn from daily life.

HOCHST FACTORY
German, 1746–1796

Hercules with Skin of the
Nemean Lion
Höchst porcelain

The secret of porcelain production escaped from the Meissen factory with its workmen. The Höchst factory copied Meissen. A red-purple was the only color innovation.

WILLIAM LUKEN
British, 18th c.

George I Cup and Cover
ca. 1715
Silver gilt

In contrast to continental silver, the surfaces of 18th-century English silver were much plainer, silversmiths preferring to show the metal itself to advantage.

LOUIS ROUBILIAC
French/English, 1695–1762

Garniture
Porcelain

During the 18th century the Far East and the Continent provided design inspiration for English china. Although mainland Europe had learned the secret of hard porcelain, English soft porcelain was still being improved.

Wadsworth
Building

PHILIP HAMMERSLOUGH COLLECTION OF AMERICAN SILVER
LATE 17TH CENTURY–LATE 19TH CENTURY

The collection comprises between 500 and 600 designs of American silver produced by this country's outstanding silversmiths. Arranged in 13 cases by geographical area, there are examples from Maine, New York, Pennsylvania, Connecticut, Maryland, New Hampshire, Rhode Island, New Jersey and the Southern states.

ELIPHALET CHAPIN
American, 1741–1807

Chippendale-style Armchair
Mahogany and pine

Most Connecticut furniture was made of cherry. This is the only armchair by Chapin known to be of mahogany. The upholstery may be the original. There is also a high chest by Chapin.

19TH-CENTURY ART

PAUL CEZANNE
French, 1839–1906

Portrait of a Child
1883–1884
Oil on canvas

Cézanne was interested in the underlying geometric forms of his subject. He modeled in color using tones to project or recess the surface planes to achieve the solidity he sought.

EDOUARD MANET *The Beach at Berck*
French, 1832–1883 1873
Oil on canvas

In the 1870s Manet abandoned his early dark-toned works to adopt the gayer palette of the Impressionists. He painted outdoors, attempting to capture the radiance of sunlight on canvas.

CLAUDE MONET *Beach at Trouville*
French, 1840–1926 1872
Oil on canvas

Beach at Trouville was executed two years before the First Impressionist Exhibition held in Paris. It was among the first pictures in this style brought to America. Monet became the leading Impressionist.

JACQUES LOUIS DAVID *The Lictors Bringing*
French, 1748–1825 *Back to Brutus*
the Bodies of His Sons
1789
Oil on canvas

This painting was exhibited prior to the French Revolution, when patriotic themes were popular. Under the new regime David became dictator of the arts and continued to extol the government on canvas.

HENRI DE TOULOUSE-LAUTREC *Jane Avril Leaving the Moulin*
French, 1864–1901 *Rouge*
1892
Gouache on cardboard

Lautrec painted Jane Avril many times. His work almost always portrayed the depraved world of Montmartre, whose inhabitants he rendered in flat surfaces of bold color, often cropping the figures.

EUGENE DELACROIX *Turkish Women Bathing*
French, 1798–1863 1854
Oil on canvas

Delacroix claimed to be especially concerned with the effect of reflected light upon colors in this painting. He made studies for these figures previously in Morocco.

HILAIRE GERMAIN EDGAR DEGAS *Before Curtain Call*
French, 1834–1917 ca. 1892
Pastel

Degas concentrated on figures in action. Because of his failing eyesight he worked increasingly in pastels which enabled him to use color while preserving line.

THOMAS COLE *Mount Etna from Taormina*
American, 1801–1848 1843
Oil on canvas

Cole painted Mount Etna four times, this version executed in just five days. The major painter of the Hudson River School, his early romantic canvases became more sweeping, audacious and fanciful.

JAMES A. MCNEILL WHISTLER *The Coast of Brittany* or
American, 1834–1903 *(Alone with the Tide)*
1861
Oil on canvas

Whistler exhibited with the early Impressionists and was especially influenced by Japanese prints. He simplified forms almost to abstraction, attempting to create a mood that stressed the esthetic aspect of his paintings.

FREDERIC EDWIN CHURCH
American, 1826–1900

Hooker and Company Journeying Through the Wilderness from Plymouth to Hartford, in 1636
1846
Oil on canvas

Church, a landscapist influenced by Thomas Cole, sold his first full-scale landscape to the Atheneum for $130. He generally painted broad panoramas rendered in great detail demonstrating an interest in light.

THOMAS EAKINS
American, 1844–1916

Portrait of John McClure Hamilton
1895
Oil on canvas

After posing a nude male model before his class at the Pennsylvania Academy, Eakins was made to resign. He then turned to painting genre scenes and portraits of penetrating insight.

Morgan Building, Gallery 124

The Goodwin Parlor
1873

The "Goodwin Castle," an outstanding 19th-century Hartford home constructed in Gothic style, was torn down in 1939. *The Parlor,* taken from it, exhibits the museum's costume collection dating from the 1870s.

20TH-CENTURY ART

PABLO PICASSO
Spanish, 1881–1973

The Bather
1922
Oil on panel

During this period Picasso began to paint huge female nudes presaging his later investigation of Surrealism.

SALVADOR DALI
Spanish, b. 1904

Apparition of Face and Fruit Dish on a Beach
1938
Oil on canvas

Dali's Surrealist paintings are much influenced by Freud. He imposes distorted dreams and images on the real world, rendering them in rich color and precise detail. He calls this the paranoiac-critical method.

ROBERT RAUSCHENBERG
American, b. 1925

Retroactive I
1964
Oil on canvas

Rauschenberg is a Pop artist whose work is grounded in and retains elements of Abstract Expressionism. He combines topical subjects with a variety of objects uniting the whole with loose brush strokes.

JACKSON POLLOCK
American, 1912–1956

Number 9, 1949
Egg tempera on gesso panel

Pollock's Action Paintings were executed on unstretched canvas. Overall designs were dripped and spattered to the edge suggesting a continuation of the painting. The accidental element was controlled to advantage.

ANDREW WYETH
American, b. 1917

Northern Point
1950
Tempera on panel

Wyeth's realistic paintings portray in careful detail the people and landscapes of rural Pennsylvania and Maine. A sense of separation and sadness pervades his work.

FACILITIES

Gallery Tours are conducted on Saturday, Sunday, 2 P.M. **Meet in Main Lobby**

Take Ten at Twelve Noon and *Art Now* are brief talks that focus on a specific **Meet in** painting or object in the collection. Scheduled several times weekly. **Main Lobby**

Lectures are frequently given on art-related topics.

Temporary Exhibitions culled from the museum's collection or *Loan Exhibitions* from other institutions are regular features of the museum's program.

The *Atheneum Cinema* is downtown Hartford's only motion picture theater. It features new releases from abroad and classic American films.

The *Lions Gallery of the Senses* examines art through the imaginative use of **1st Floor,** the senses. Changing exhibitions introduce the visitor to the artistic process, **Avery** experiments in sound and other media or an exploration of the perceptions **Building** received through different senses. Workshops and demonstrations are often included. Careful installation, Braille labels and specially trained personnel make this exhibit accessible to the handicapped.

MATRIX is an informal and flexible approach to the exhibition of a broad **1st Floor,** sample of the work of contemporary artists offering primary experiences of **Avery** recent developments. A relatively small gallery provides five separate exhibition **Building** spaces on its four walls and floor. The work of each artist is displayed for a minimum of six weeks.

The *Auerbach Art Library* is open Tuesday–Friday, 11 A.M.–3 P.M. **1st Floor**

EAT Restaurant is a cheerful dining place with a small but interesting menu. **1st Floor** Open Tuesday–Friday, Sunday, 11:30 A.M.–2 P.M.; Thursday 5 P.M.–7 P.M. (except July, August).

Snack Bar open weekdays, 11:30 A.M.–2 P.M. **1st Floor**

The *Atheneum Shop* carries a full range of museum quality items. Open during **1st Floor** regular museum hours.

Hours: Tuesday, Wednesday, Friday, 11 A.M.–3 P.M.; Thursday, 11 A.M.–8 P.M. (July, August to 3 P.M.); Saturday, Sunday, 11 A.M.–5 P.M. *Closed:* Mondays, New Year's, July 4, Thanksgiving, Christmas.

Admission: Suggested voluntary contribution: adults, $2; 12–18 years, $1; free to children under 13, and to all on Thursdays after 3 P.M.

MIDDLETOWN

DAVISON ART CENTER, WESLEYAN UNIVERSITY
301 High St.
Middletown, CT 06457
Tel: (203)347–9411

The center was founded in 1952 and is quartered in Alsop House (1838–1840), a pre-Civil War mansion in the Italian Villa style. The Davison Art Center collection contains fine prints from the early 15th century to the present day and a growing photography collection. The works are not on permanent display, but the collection is available for scholarly and study purposes on weekdays by appointment. Exhibitions selected from the collection are presented several times each year in the gallery in addition to exhibitions organized from outside sources.

FACILITIES

Occasional *Lectures* on art are arranged and are open to the public.

Catalogs of Davison Art Center exhibitions are available; list upon request.

Hours: Tuesday–Friday, 12 P.M.–4 P.M.; Saturday, Sunday, 2 P.M.–5 P.M.
Closed: During academic recess periods and holidays.

Admission: Free.

NEW BRITAIN

NEW BRITAIN MUSEUM OF AMERICAN ART
56 Lexington St.
New Britain, CT 06052
Tel: (203)229–0257

In 1937, the museum moved to a former mansion bequeathed to it by Mrs. Grace Judd Landers. Since then it has enjoyed three additions while maintaining its homelike setting. The collection encompasses over 1,500 examples representing America's finest artists from the earliest limners to present-day painters and includes graphics and sculpture.

SAMPLING THE COLLECTION

Gallery B   JOHN SINGLETON COPLEY   *Portrait of Mrs. Lydia L.*
1738–1815   *Walter*
ca. 1762–1764
Oil

Copley, considered the most important Colonial painter, was largely self-trained. Working in England from 1774, his work became more polished but sacrificed the early forthrightness and vigor observed here.

Gallery C   ALBERT BIERSTADT   *Seal Rock*
1830–1902   1872
Oil

Bierstadt's strikingly lit paintings of the American wilderness found immediate favor with the public.

Gallery D   ANDREW WYETH   *The Revenant*
b. 1917   1949
Tempera

Wyeth was trained by his father, the illustrator N. C. Wyeth. He depicts mostly rural scenes although this is a self-portrait.

Winslow Homer, The Butterfly Girl. *Courtesy New Britain Museum of American Art, New Britain*

CHARLES BURCHFIELD   *Lavender and Old Lace*
1893–1967   1939–1947
     Watercolor

Raised amid the melancholy Midwestern landscape of dull towns and farms, Burchfield developed his own style of painting. His somewhat Surrealistic work captures the quality of these locales endowing them also with a certain poetry.

Gallery E   WINSLOW HOMER   *The Butterfly Girl*
     1836–1910   1878
     Oil

Homer, mostly uninfluenced by European art, spent his early days as an illustrator and painter of Civil War scenes. He was profoundly interested in nature, depicting it with great realism.

Gallery F   MAXFIELD PARRISH   *Dusk*
     1870–1966   1942
     Oil

Parrish, a painter and illustrator, was most widely accepted during the 1920s when his idealized representational prints were bought by the millions.

Philip Stanley   ROCKWELL KENT   *Toilers of the Sea*
Gallery   1882–1971   1907
     Oil

Kent was a painter, illustrator and printmaker as well as an author. His paintings are forceful and unaffected.

THOMAS HART BENTON   *Arts of Life in America*
1889–1975   1932
     Tempera with oil glaze or oil

Rejecting the modern art observed during his years in Paris, Benton devoted himself to painting life in America. These three murals have great vitality and humor in their mannered style.

Alix Stanley   AARON SHIKLER   *Girl in the Window*
Gallery   b. 1922   Pastel on canvas

The woman sitting on the ledge of a window dressed in a striped robe is believed to be the artist's wife.

Cooper   SOLON H. BORGLUM   *One in a Thousand*
Gallery   1868–1922   1901
     Bronze

Popular for his public sculptures, Borglum was also appreciated for his smaller works which often depicted Western subjects.

FACILITIES

Changing Exhibitions are regularly featured.

The *Sales Shop* offers postcards, catalogs of the collection and of exhibitions, tote bags and note cards.

Hours: Tuesday–Sunday, 1 P.M.–5 P.M.; Wednesday, 12 P.M.–5 P.M. Mornings by appointment for groups. *Closed:* Mondays, New Year's, Easter, Memorial Day, July 4, Sunday before Labor Day, Thanksgiving, Christmas.

Admission: Free.

NEW HAVEN

YALE CENTER FOR BRITISH ART
1080 Chapel St.
New Haven, CT 06520
Tel: (203)432–4594

Opened in 1977, the four-story center was the last achievement of architect Louis I. Kahn before his death. Along with Yale's large holdings of British letters and its strength in the teaching of British history and literature, it makes New Haven the most important place for the study of British culture outside of England. Natural light and basic fabrics create a dignified interior integrated by a double courtyard. The collection surveys the development of English art, life and thought from the Elizabethan period to the middle of the 19th century. There is an emphasis on works between the birth of Hogarth (1697) and the death of Turner (1851), considered by many to be the "golden age" of English art.

SAMPLING THE COLLECTION

GEORGE STUBBS 1724–1806	*A Lion Attacking a Horse* *A Lion Attacking a Stag* Oils	**2nd Floor, Library Court**

Stubbs, largely self-taught, was a great student of anatomy and was best known for his highly technical paintings of animals.

PETER PAUL RUBENS Flemish, 1577–1640	*Peace Embracing Plenty* 1632–1634 Oil	**4th Floor**

Rubens is the outstanding painter of Baroque art. He was commissioned by Charles I to paint the ceiling of the Banqueting House in Whitehall.

WILLIAM HOGARTH 1697–1764	*The Beggar's Opera* 1729 Oil	**4th Floor**

Hogarth began his career as a portraitist. He was especially successful with group portraits or conversation pieces. Determined to reform society through his satirical illustrations, he painted moral subjects.

ARTHUR DEVIS 1712–1787	*Mr. and Mrs. Hill* 1748–1750 Oil	**4th Floor**

Devis painted mostly small portraits and conversation pieces (group portraits of individuals) using upper-middle-class subjects. His figures are usually portrayed in parklike settings.

JOSHUA REYNOLDS 1723–1792	*Miss Sarah Campbell* 1777–1778 Oil	**4th Floor**

Reynolds, an academic, constantly alluded to antiquity and the Old Masters. He did much to raise the status of English painters from that of skilled craftsmen to artists.

JOSEPH WRIGHT OF DERBY 1734–1797	*The Blacksmith's Shop* 1771 Oil	**4th Floor**

Exterior view. Courtesy Yale Center for British Art, New Haven

Wright established himself in Derby and remained there for most of his life. He specialized in lighting effects, such as moonlit landscapes and candlelit interiors.

4th Floor   JOSEPH MALLORD WILLIAM
TURNER   *Dort or Dordrecht*
1775–1851   1818
                                 Oil

Turner painted atmospheric landscapes. Attracted to the brilliant Italian sunlight in his travels, he played with the varying effects of light on his landscapes.

4th Floor   JOHN CONSTABLE   *Hadleigh Castle*
1776–1837   Oil

Constable chose views of where he lived as subjects of most of his landscapes. He avoided the classical 17th-century landscape style of his day, creating his own art from the English countryside.

4th Floor   HENRY WALLIS   *The Death of Chatterton*
1830–1916   1856–1858
                                 Oil

Wallis was one of the Pre-Raphaelite Brotherhood, depicting scenes and events as they took place regardless of how undecorative the result. This work was painted in the very attic where Chatterton's death had occurred.

FACILITIES

A *Reference Library* contains volumes on British art history and topography. It is noncirculating.

A *Photographic Archive* contains reproductions of British art from the 15th through the 20th centuries, computer-indexed by subject.

Temporary Exhibitions drawn from the center's collection or *Loan Exhibitions* including works from other institutions are regular features of the center's program.

A *Sales Desk* offers books on British art, exhibition catalogs, postcards, slides and photographs of the collections.

The *Lecture Hall* is the location for center-sponsored *Lectures, Films, Symposia* **1st Floor** and other special events.

A *Study Room* is provided where prints, drawings and rare books may be **2nd Floor** researched.

Hours: Tuesday–Saturday, 10 A.M.–5 P.M.; Sunday, 2 P.M.–5 P.M. *Closed:* Mondays, New Year's, July 4, Thanksgiving, Christmas.

Admission: Free.

YALE UNIVERSITY ART GALLERY
1111 Chapel St.
New Haven, CT 06520
Tel: (203)436–0574

The Yale University Art Gallery is the oldest university art museum in the Western Hemisphere and is continually expanding. It was founded in 1832 and represents virtually all national schools and important periods in the history of art. Two connecting architectural units comprise the present gallery. One, built in 1928, is based on the design of a Gothic palace in Viterbo, Italy. The other, completed in 1953, was designed by Louis I. Kahn. The new gallery was the first building in modern style to be erected on the university campus.

Exterior view. Courtesy Yale University Art Gallery, New Haven

SAMPLING THE COLLECTION

Basement   *ANCIENT ART*

ASSYRIAN   *Four Reliefs of Divinities and*
                                 Attendant Figures
                                 9th c. B.C.
Sumerian influence is visible in these reliefs which were completed during the
height of Assyrian power.

THE BERLIN PAINTER   *Amphora (depicting Athena*
Greek   *and Hermes)*
                                 Red-figure clay
                                 ca. 480 B.C.
The red-figured painting style permitted the artist greater freedom of expression.
Details of landscape are omitted, the human figure being of more importance
in Greek art.

ROMAN   *Mithraeum*
                                 3rd c. A.D.
Graeco-Roman and Oriental styles are traced from this frescoed mithraeum
(underground room) found at Dura-Europos, a Roman outpost in the Syrian
desert. Here can be seen the early origins of medieval art.

3rd Floor   *AMERICAN ART*

JOHN SMIBERT   *Dean George Berkeley and*
1688–1751   *His Entourage*
                                 1729
                                 Oil on canvas
Painted in Smibert's early Baroque style, this was the first group portrait in the
history of American painting.

BENJAMIN WEST   *Agrippina Landing at Brundisium*
1738–1820   *with the Ashes of Germanicus*
                                 1768
                                 Oil on canvas
West traveled to Italy, was influenced by Classical subjects and then spent most
of his life working in England.

JOHN SINGLETON COPLEY   *Portrait of Isaac Smith*
1738–1815   1769
                                 Oil on canvas
Copley was influenced by John Smibert and his Old Masters copies of European
paintings. He soon became the greatest of the Colonial portraitists.

JOHN TRUMBULL   *The Declaration of Independence*
1756–1843   1786–1797
                                 Oil on canvas
Trumbull painted mostly historical works and portraits. He too was influenced
by John Smibert's Old Masters copies.

JEREMIAH DUMMER   *Candlesticks*
1645–1718   1680–1690
                                 Silver
Dummer was one of the men who developed the silver trade from its earliest
days in America. Engraving was the only form of decoration used by American
silversmiths at that time.

SIMEON SOUMAIN   *Sugar Bowl*
1685–1750   Silver
Soumain was born in London but worked mostly in New York.

MASSACHUSETTS   *Chest of Drawers*
Boston   17th c.
It was during this period that the chest of drawers came into popular use.

RHODE ISLAND   *Desk and Bookcase*
Newport   1785
The interior drawers of this desk use the block form developed to the highest degree in Boston and Newport at this time.

MASSACHUSETTS   *Chest on Chest*
Dorchester and Boston
Most American design is simpler than that of the English of this period but Boston craftsmen treated their pieces with more delicacy than did those in New York.

EUROPEAN PAINTINGS   **2nd and 3rd Floors**

GENTILE DA FABRIANO   *Madonna and Child*
Italian, 1370–1427   1424–1425
                               Egg tempera on panel
Gentile painted in the Florentine manner prior to Masaccio. Vivid colors, gilt relief decoration and formal composition mark his work.

ANTONIO POLLAIUOLO   *Hercules and Deianira*
Italian, ca. 1431–1489   late 15th c.
                               Egg tempera and oil(?)
                               Now on canvas
Pollaiuolo was a sculptor, goldsmith and engraver as well as a painter. His intensive study of anatomy enabled him to achieve great realism in his work.

FRANS HALS   *Portraits of Heer and Mevrouw*
Dutch, ca. 1581–1666   *Bodolphe*
                               1643
                               Oil on canvas
Hals is best known for his lively portraits which reproduce his sitters' transient expression. The informality of his paintings and the cursory definition of linear brushwork anticipate Impressionism.

VINCENT VAN GOGH   *The Night Café*
Dutch, 1853–1890   1888
                               Oil on canvas
At this point in his career van Gogh had rejected much of Impressionism and developed his own energetic and bold style.

MARCEL DUCHAMP   *Tu'm*
French, 1887–1968   1918
                               Oil on canvas with long
                               brush and safety pins attached
Painted at the request of a friend to fit a long narrow space, *Tu'm* was an expression of Duchamp's important ideas and preoccupations up to that time.

ORIENTAL ART   **4th Floor**

CHINESE   *Pole Top*
Shang Dynasty, ca. 1523–1028 B.C.   Bronze

The Shang bronzes were probably cast by a piece-mold method. These people's skill in bronze work was the most highly developed of the preindustrial age.

CHINESE
Ch'ing Dynasty,
K'ang Hsi Reign, 1662–1722

Plum Blossom Jar
Porcelain

Quadrilateral Vase
Porcelain

The Chinese called these porcelains wares with "raised enamel" decorations or sometimes "foreign enamel." Nearly all examples of this reign have the mark of the reign on the base.

FACILITIES

Gallery Talks are held weekly from mid-September to mid-May, Tuesday, 2 P.M., Thursday, 1 P.M. and 6 P.M.

Art à la Carte is held October–April, Wednesday, 12:20 P.M. Brief lectures on a single work of art by scholars. You are invited to bring your own lunch.

Films, Lectures and *Concerts* are offered on Sundays, October–April, 3 P.M. Free of charge.

Temporary Exhibitions culled from the art gallery's collection or *Loan Exhibitions* from other institutions are regular features of the art gallery's program.

The *Sales Desk* carries postcards, art books, prints and a selection of jewelry and gifts.

Hours: Tuesday–Saturday, 10 A.M.–5 P.M.; Thursday evenings, 6 P.M.–9 P.M. mid-September–mid-May; Sundays, 2 P.M.–5 P.M. *Closed:* Mondays, New Year's, July 4, Thanksgiving, Christmas.

Admission: Free.

NEW LONDON

LYMAN ALLYN MUSEUM
100 Mohegan Ave.
New London, CT 06320
Tel: (203)443–2545

The museum, a Greek Revival building of granite, consists of nine permanent galleries plus four for changing exhibitions. It has been expanded three times since its opening in 1932. The permanent collections encompass objects from world civilizations covering a time range of 5,000 years, and include paintings, sculpture, drawings, prints, decorative arts and costumes.

SAMPLING THE COLLECTION

Basement Corridor

AMERICAN

Dollhouse with Period Contents
ca. 1850

Although the house was built in 1962, the contents are 19th century. They were collected over forty years and include not only toys and toy furniture but apprentice pieces and salesmen's samples as well.

THOMAS COLE
American, 1801–1848

Mount Etna from Taormina, Sicily
1844
Oil on canvas

1st Floor, Palmer Gallery

The foreground of this canvas pictures the ephemeral achievements of man against enduring Mount Etna. An earlier and larger rendition is in the Wadsworth Atheneum in Hartford, Connecticut.

EGYPTO-ROMAN

Head of a Boy
1st C. A.D.
Black basalt

2nd Floor, Miles Gallery

This portrait head, typical of the Augustan age, does not make use of the usual Roman realism in portrait sculpture. Egyptian influence is seen in the use of basalt, a difficult material to carve.

SCHOOL OF TILMAN RIEMENSCHNEIDER
German, 1468–1531

St. George and the Dragon
Oak or linden

2nd Floor, Powers Gallery

This figure was most likely part of an altarpiece. Although Italianate taste was rapidly replacing Gothic at this time, the incisive line and acute edges show Riemenschneider's lingering attachment to the Gothic.

CHINESE
T'ang Dynasty, A.D. 618–906

Figure of an Actress
Glazed earthenware

2nd Floor, Stamm Gallery

This mortuary statue was one of a pair of actresses. Most of the coloring, still

Thomas Cole, Mount Etna from Taormina, Sicily. *Courtesy Lyman Allyn Museum, New London*

visible, makes it easy to envision what the clothing looked like. Long sleeves denoted an accomplished dancer.

FACILITIES

Tours are available for groups by appointment.

Changing Exhibitions of the work of a variety of artists is a regular museum feature.

The *Museum Shop* stocks only one-of-a-kind small antiques and collectibles located by the staff at auctions, other shops and travels abroad.

Auditorium in Basement   *Lectures, Concerts, Movies and Other Activities* are offered at various times throughout the year. Call for more specific information.

1st Floor   *Art History Reference Library* is opened weekdays during museum hours.

Hours: Tuesday–Saturday, 1 P.M.–5 P.M.; Sunday 2 P.M.–5 P.M. *Closed:* Mondays, New Year's, Thanksgiving, Christmas.

Admission: Free, but donations are appreciated.

NORWICH

THE SLATER MEMORIAL MUSEUM AND CONVERSE ART GALLERY
Norwich Academy
108 Crescent St.
Norwich, CT 06360
Tel: (203)887–2505

Originally built to house Greek, Roman and Renaissance casts, this museum has broadened its spheres to include 17th- through 20th-century American art and furniture, American Indian artifacts, Oriental, African and Egyptian art, a gun collection and textiles.

SAMPLING THE COLLECTION

THOMAS DOUGHTY   *Landscape Painting*
American, 1793–1856   19th c.
Doughty was one of the founders of the Hudson River School of painting. These artists painted scenes of the unspoiled Hudson River Valley.

Bowl of Chief Uncas
This hand-carved bowl was a possession of Uncas, Chief of the Mohegan Indians.

MICHELANGELO BUONARROTI   *Moses*
Italian, 1475–1564   Plaster
This is a life-size reproduction of the original which is in the church of San Pietro in Vincoli in Rome.

AMOS DOOLITTLE   *Early Woodcuts*
American, 1754–1832
Doolittle was one of the earliest American engravers. These woodcuts depict the War of Independence.

Exterior view. Courtesy Slater Memorial Museum and Converse Art Gallery, Norwich

FACILITIES

Sales Desk sells postcards only.

Hours: *September–May:* Weekdays, 9 A.M.–4 P.M.; Saturday–Sunday, 1 P.M.–4 P.M. *June–August:* Tuesday–Sunday, 1 P.M.–4 P.M. *Closed:* Mondays, holidays.

Admission: Free.

RIDGEFIELD

ALDRICH MUSEUM OF CONTEMPORARY ART
258 Main St.
Ridgefield, CT 06877
Tel: (203)438–4519

Housed in a post-Revolutionary mansion erected in 1783 by two lieutenants in the Revolutionary War, the museum stands on a street lined with 18th- and 19th-century houses. It was subsequently used as a grocery and hardware store, a meeting place, a home and a church before opening in 1964 as a museum of contemporary art. The 3½-acre lawn is the setting for monumental nonobjective sculptures. Three floors contain galleries devoted to innovative contemporary painting and sculpture by celebrated and emerging artists. Nearly 250 works of the 1960s and '70s have been assembled.

SAMPLING THE COLLECTION

The permanent collection is not on view at all times; selections from it are generally presented in the winter exhibition. The sculpture in the garden is permanently installed.

Sculpture Garden

EDUARDO PAOLOZZI
Scotch/Italian, b. 1924

Lhaxu
1967
Stainless steel

Paolozzi constructed sculpture of mechanical parts suggesting human forms. He has severely simplified these while retaining some mechanical feeling.

Sculpture Garden

ANTHONY PADOVANO
American, b. 1933

Citadel
1964
Painted steel

Padovano's metal constructions often look like sections of complicated machines, even though his subjects are largely imaginary. He has said he knows what he wants to accomplish only when it emerges.

Sculpture Garden

DEWAIN VALENTINE
American, b. 1936

Summer Domino
1967
Fiberglass

Valentine creates elegant and simple technological sculptures emphasizing physical mass. Disks and wedges constructed of polyester resin or fiberglass are thinner at the edges varying the intensity of the color.

Sculpture Garden

DAVID VON SCHLEGEL
American, b. 1920

Untitled
1967
Stainless steel and aluminum

Von Schlegel's large minimal sculptures are based on engineering theories and are often influenced by the aircraft industry.

Inside the Museum, Rotated for Exhibition

JAMES ROSENQUIST
American, 1933

Waco, Texas
1966
Oil on canvas

Rosenquist, a Pop artist concerned with images of modern life, uses his early occupation as a billboard painter to advantage in his large canvases of photolike enlargements, spliced and blended into an editorial statement.

FACILITIES

Gallery Tours are available on Saturday afternoons.

Lectures by artists and collectors are offered.

Panel Discussions with artists represented in current exhibitions are sponsored.

Films, coordinated with current exhibitions, feature experimental narrative work, videotapes, interviews and monographs of artists and specific art movements. Background material and a discussion period are included at each showing. Call for program information.

DeWain Valentine, Summer Domino. *In the Sculpture Garden of the Aldrich Museum of Contemporary Art, Ridgefield*

Hours: Wednesday, Saturday, Sunday, 1–5 P.M. Groups at other times by appointment.

Admission: Adults $1; students and senior citizens, 50¢.

STORRS

WILLIAM BENTON MUSEUM OF ART
University of Connecticut
Storrs, CT 06268
Tel: (203)486–4520

This university museum was opened in 1966. The original collection has grown from some 200 works to include over 2,500 objects housed in three galleries.

The permanent collection is exhibited on a rotating basis; therefore not all of the following items may be on view. However, they are available for study by special arrangement.

SAMPLING THE COLLECTION

GEORGE BELLOWS
American, 1882–1925

Criehaven
1917
Oil

Bellows was a painter of the Ashcan School. Although this landscape is different from his cityscapes and sporting events, the vigorous brushwork and succinct style of the objects makes it believably his work.

MARY CASSATT
American, 1845–1926

Helene de Septeuil
ca. 1890
Pastel

Cassatt frequently painted mothers and children. She was much influenced by Degas and lived and exhibited in Paris with the Impressionists.

JAN DE BRAY
Dutch, ca. 1626–1697

Portrait of Jan Vos
1679
Oil

De Bray painted portraits, biblical and historical canvases most of which can still be seen in his native Haarlem. His portraits and group portraits are considered his most notable work.

WILLEM C. DUYSTER
Dutch, 1599–1635

Soldiers and Hostages
ca. 1630
Oil

Duyster was known for his portraits and interior scenes. He was especially skilled in painting fabrics.

EASTMAN JOHNSON
American, 1824–1906

Portrait of Horatio Bridge
ca. 1856–1860
Oil

Johnson made his reputation first in Europe. He is known both for his portraits and Dutch-influenced genre scenes.

MAURICE PRENDERGAST
American, 1859–1924

Lighthouse at St. Malo
1909
Oil

Prendergast was a Post-Impressionist landscape painter whose use of vivid colors was combined into mosaiclike results. His work began to be recognized only shortly before his death.

SCHOOL OF GUIDO RENI
Italian, 1575–1642

St. Sebastian
1630s(?)
Oil

Reni's paintings were grounded in Classicism. He enjoyed the highest reputation until it was tarnished by Ruskin in the 19th century. Only now is his work regaining popularity.

BENJAMIN WEST
American, 1738–1820

Venus Admonishing Cupid
before 1783
Oil

Venus Comforting Europa
1772
Oil

West favored Classical subjects. He was the first to paint his sitters in modern dress and was widely imitated.

THE LANDAUER COLLECTION OF KÄTHE KOLLWITZ PRINTS AND DRAWINGS

Käthe Kollwitz (German, 1867–1945) was a graphic artist greatly influenced by Goya and Daumier. Her works depict the oppression suffered by mankind.

FACILITIES

Gallery Talks, Films, Lectures and *Concerts* are given in conjunction with the several exhibitions that are held each year.

Changing Exhibitions are regularly featured.

The *Museum Shop* offers postcards, art reproductions, original artifacts and museum-related jewelry ranging in price from 50¢ to $200.

Hours: Monday–Saturday, 10 A.M.–4:30 P.M.; Sundays, holidays, 1 P.M.–5 P.M. *Summer hours:* Presently closed June 1–September 1. *Closed:* Between exhibitions and on national holidays.

Admission: Free.

MAINE

BRUNSWICK

BOWDOIN COLLEGE MUSEUM OF ART
Walker Art Bldg.
Brunswick, ME 04011
Tel: (207)725–8731

The Walker Art Building, designed by McKim, Mead and White, dedicated in 1894, houses a collection begun in 1811 by the bequest of James Bowdoin III. Included are Colonial and Federal portraits; Old Masters prints and drawings; the Warren Collection of Classical Antiquities; the Winslow Homer Collection and Memorabilia; the Molinari Collection of Medals and Plaquettes; important works by 19th- and 20th-century artists.

SAMPLING THE COLLECTION

Bowdoin Gallery
GILBERT STUART
American, 1755–1828
Thomas Jefferson
1805–1807
Oil on canvas
Stuart was the leading Federal portraitist. He was only interested in painting faces that were noted for their show of character, although he idealized his subjects in the manner of Joshua Reynolds.

Bowdoin Gallery
JOHN SINGLETON COPLEY
American, 1738–1815
Thomas Flucker
probably 1770–1771
Oil on canvas
Copley's realistic portraits of prominent Americans were carefully constructed and executed with sincerity and insight. Although well accepted in Colonial America, he moved to England prior to the Revolution, spending the rest of his life there where his art, reputation and health all suffered.

Bowdoin Gallery
THOMAS DENNIS
American, ca. 1638–1706
Armchair (Wainscot)
Oak
The 17th-century furniture in America reflected medieval English yeoman tastes. Forms were massive and rectilinear. Red oak was the most popular wood.

Halford Gallery
ROMAN
Portrait Head of the Emperor Antoninus Pius
ca. A.D. 138–150
Marble
Roman sculpture was grounded in reality. Exact likenesses were demanded by the sitter. Typically, the sculpture recalls the men who ruled the ancient world.

Boyd Gallery
ATT. TO JAN FYT
Flemish, 1611–1661
Still Life, Birds
Oil on canvas
Known for his animal and still-life paintings, Fyt was a prolific artist who employed others to execute the figures in his paintings.

MARTIN JOHNSON HEADE
American, 1819–1904

Newburyport Marshes
ca. 1865–1870
Oil on canvas

**Walker
Gallery**

Heade began his career as a portraitist and genre painter. After settling in New York City, he met some of the leading landscapists and turned to painting seascapes and salt marshes in various lights.

PIETER BRUEGHEL, THE ELDER
Flemish, ca. 1525–1569

View of Waltersburg
ca. 1554
Sepia drawing

**Becker
Gallery
(Not on View
at All Times)**

Brueghel, known for humorous, satyrical scenes of peasant life, traveled in Italy in 1552 and 1553. Returning to Antwerp through France, he drew the landscape and later used this material in paintings and engravings.

WINSLOW HOMER
American, 1836–1910

The End of the Hunt
1892
Watercolor

**Homer
Gallery**

Homer was first an illustrator for *Harper's Weekly* magazine, gaining recognition for his Civil War scenes. Afterward he portrayed country life, leaving us the best recordings of the times. His last years were spent on the Maine coast, painting seascapes.

FACILITIES

Changing Exhibitions are regularly featured, and are the work of a variety of artists.

The *Sales Shop* has stained glass, jewelry, pewter and books among its most popular wares for sale. Prices range from $5 to $50.

A program of *Classic Films* is offered.

**Kress
Auditorium**

Hours: *After Labor Day to June 30:* Tuesday–Friday, 10 A.M.–4 P.M.; Saturday, 10 A.M.–5 P.M.; Sunday, 2 P.M.–5P.M. *July 1–Labor Day:* Tuesday–Saturday, 10 A.M.–5 P.M. and 7 P.M.–8:30 P.M. additionally. *Closed:* Mondays, state holidays.

Admission: Free.

OGUNQUIT

BARN GALLERY
**Cor. of Shore Rd. and Bourne Lane
Ogunquit, ME 03907
Tel: (207)646–5370**

The Barn Gallery can be visited from mid-June until mid-September. It offers changing exhibitions of paintings, sculpture and graphics by members of the professional Ogunquit Art Association, and special shows presented in the Dunaway Room.

FACILITIES

Concerts of both classical and modern music are offered.

Lectures, some by internationally known individuals, are scheduled.

Films are shown on art and avant-garde subjects.

Demonstrations of various crafts are held from time to time.

Upstairs A *Collector's Gallery* where unframed and unmatted works from the changing exhibitions are for sale.

Hours: *Mid-June to mid-September:* Daily, 10 A.M.–5 P.M.; Sunday, 2 P.M.–5 P.M. Open evenings in July and August, 8 P.M.–10 P.M.

Admission: Free. $1 fee for programs.

MUSEUM OF ART OF OGUNQUIT
Shore Rd.
Ogunquit, ME 03907
Tel: (207)646–8827

The museum, opened in 1952, sits on the rocky shore, once a favorite painting place for some of the very artists represented inside. Large glass windows provide a lovely view of the ocean immediately upon entering, while the carefully controlled grounds provide a natural background of trees and shrubs. The collection is devoted to contemporary American art from 1910 to present. Yearly exhibitions are presented during the summer months.

SAMPLING THE COLLECTION

ALEXANDER BROOK   *Passing Through Richmond*
American, b. 1898   1958
                                  Oil

Brook lives and works in Sag Harbor, New York. His paintings hang in many museums and he is the recipient of many awards.

JOHN B. FLANNAGAN   *Morning*
American, 1895–1942   ca. 1938
                                  Stone

Flannagan's roughly textured small-scale pieces were usually carved of fieldstone which he considered appropriate to the natural themes he depicted, usually of birth and growth.

MARSDEN HARTLEY   *Mountains, New Mexico*
American, 1877–1943   1919
                                  Oil

After investigating Cubism and German Expressionism, Hartley returned to representational landscapes. Before settling in Maine he painted darkly outlined, highly colored landscapes of the Southwest.

YASUO KUNIYOSHI   *Still Life with Candy Lady*
Japanese/American, 1893–1953   1929
                                  Oil

Kuniyoshi's early, whimsical paintings combined still lifes or landscapes with figures in quiet backgrounds.

JACK LEVINE   *The Bride*
American, b. 1915   1964
                                Oil
Levine is a figurative painter whose satyrical social commentaries on contemporary life are handled with great technical skill in both medium and subject
matter.

FACILITIES

Hours: *July–Labor Day:* Monday–Saturday, 10:30 A.M.–5 P.M.; Sunday, 1:30
         P.M.–5 P.M.
Admission: Free.

ORONO

UNIVERSITY OF MAINE AT ORONO ART COLLECTION
Carnegie Hall,
Orono, ME 04469
Tel: (207)581–7165

Since its inception over thirty years ago, the collection has grown to more than
4,000 items, making the Orono/Bangor campus a nucleus in the state for
contemporary art in all mediums and styles, with emphasis on work by artists
who live or work in Maine. The collection is distributed throughout the campus
buildings, in public areas, making it accessible to all.

SAMPLING THE COLLECTION

ADOLPHE WILLIAM BOUGUEREAU   *The Young Musician*   **Fogler**
French, 1825–1905   ca. 1900   **Library**
                             Oil
Bouguereau was very popular in the France of his day. As director of the
Académie Julian, he fought experimentation in art, even Impressionism.

BERNARD BUFFET   *Fleurs 3/220*   **Fogler**
French, b. 1928   ca. 1962   **Library**
                             Color lithograph
Buffet, an Expressionist painter, won critical recognition in the 1950s depicting
the misery of modern man and the violence of the angry postwar youth.

CLARK FITZ-GERALD   *Girl's Head*   **Fogler**
American, b. 1917   1968   **Library**
                             Wood
Fitz-Gerald's sculptures are usually large abstracts accomplished in metal or
wood or in combination of the two.

BEVERLY HALLAM   *Tidewater*   **Fogler**
American, b. 1922   1962   **Library**
                             Mica-talc and acrylic on
                             Belgian linen

Hallam is a Maine resident and is considered a pioneer in the use of polyvinyl acetate.

Oakes Room,
Fogler
Library

ANDREW WYETH
American, b. 1917

On Bar Island
ca. 1947
Watercolor

Wyeth studied with his father, N. C. Wyeth, the painter and illustrator. The settings of his highly detailed and realistic scenes are usually Maine or Pennsylvania.

Special
Collections,
Fogler
Library

MARSDEN HARTLEY
American, 1877–1943

Sketch of Mt. Katahdin
1940
Black crayon drawing

Hartley's style, with its cold harsh color, demonstrates his early interest in Expressionism and Cubism. Despite his travels abroad his major interest remained in the dramatic austerity of New England.

Damn
Yankee Room,
Memorial
Union
Building

WALDO PEIRCE
American, 1884–1970

Great Head
1949
Oil

After traveling to Europe and North Africa, Peirce returned to Maine in the 1930s to develop his own painting style.

Memorial
Room,
Memorial
Union
Building

WINSLOW HOMER
American, 1836–1910

Eight Bells
1887
Etching

Homer made his reputation in the 1860s and 1870s with his scenes of country life, but his fame rests mainly on his New England landscapes and seascapes done in later life.

Lobby,
Carnegie
Hall

WILLIAM ZORACH
American, 1887–1966

Awakening
1942
Bronze relief

Zorach's early paintings showed the influence of Fauvism and Cubism. His sculpture was more influenced by primitive and Egyptian art.

FACILITIES

Temporary Exhibitions, culled from the museum's collection or the work of area artists, are regularly featured.

Hours: Check respective buildings.

Admission: Free.

PORTLAND

PORTLAND MUSEUM OF ART
111 High St.
P.O. Box 4018
Portland, ME 04101
Tel: (207)775–6148

The museum, founded in 1882, presently includes the McLellan-Sweat House which was built by Major Hugh McLellan in 1800 and is designated a Registered

National Historic Landmark. In 1908 a gallery wing was added to contain a growing collection of American and European art from 1800: Early American and Federal decorative arts, 19th-century American painting, and contemporary art, Japanese prints, 19th-century glass and furniture. Plans are underway for a major new building designed by I. M. Pei & Partners to house the State of Maine Collection, including 17 paintings by Winslow Homer, and the Hamilton Easter Field Art Foundation Collection. Of special interest in the house are a flying staircase and double-story entrance hall, two Palladian windows, the original fence, roof, and portico balustrades with urn finials, a pre-1882 Scotch ingrain rug, silver and furniture of the Federal period.

SAMPLING THE COLLECTION

BENJAMIN PAUL AKERS   *The Dead Pearl Diver*
American, 1825–1861   1858
                          Marble

This life-sized Neoclassic sculpture was executed in Rome by the Maine artist, Akers. It was praised by Nathaniel Hawthorne in *The Marble Faun.*

CONTEMPORARY PRINTS AND DRAWINGS

Roy Lichtenstein, Claes Oldenburg, Andy Warhol, Alexander Calder, Robert Motherwell, James Brooks, Cy Twombly, Lee Krasner, are a few of the artists represented in a small but estimable collection.

19TH- AND 20TH-CENTURY PAINTINGS

Charles Codman, Harrison Bird Brown, Charles F. Kimball, Asher B. Durand, James A. McNeill Whistler and Childe Hassam are among the American artists

Benjamin Paul Akers, The Dead Pearl Diver. *Courtesy Portland Museum of Art, Portland*

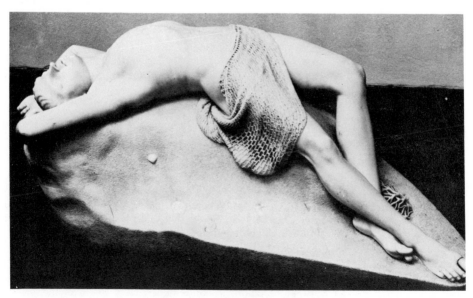

on exhibition. Also included are works by Marsden Hartley, Yasuo Kuniyoshi, Stuart Davis, Niles Spencer, Robert Laurent, Winslow Homer, Gaston Lachaise and William Zorach. Pierre Auguste Renoir, Jean-Baptiste Camille Corot and Jean Arp are among the European artists represented.

FACILITIES

Gallery Talks and *Lectures* are presented by the staff or visiting authorities. *Changing Exhibitions* are regularly featured.

The *Gift Shop* sells postcards, note cards, jewelry and art books priced from 30¢ to $20.

Hours: Tuesday–Saturday, 10 A.M.–5 P.M.; Sunday, 2 P.M.–5 P.M. *Closed:* Mondays, holidays.

Admission: Galleries, free. McLellan-Sweat House: Adults, $1; children, 50¢

WATERVILLE

COLBY COLLEGE MUSEUM OF ART
Mayflower Hill
Waterville, ME 04901
Tel: (207)873–1131

Founded in 1955 with a group of loaned Winslow Homers, the museum has been quartered since 1973 in a building suited to exhibit its greatly enlarged collection. Dramatically changing levels accommodate movable walls displaying the art to its best advantage. Although the collection contains some European paintings, it is predominantly composed of 18th–20th-century American art. It is particularly notable for its primitive American paintings and drawings; 19th-century American painting and folk sculpture; 19th-century American academic painting and 25 John Marin watercolors, oils and prints.

SAMPLING THE COLLECTION

The following paintings are hung on a rotating basis and, therefore, may not always be on view.

JOHN SINGLETON COPLEY   *Mrs. Metcalf Bowler*
American, 1738–1815   Oil on canvas
Until 1774, when Copley settled in England, he painted portraits of prominent citizens. Carefully rendered straightforward likenesses earned him the reputation of greatest portraitist of Colonial times.

GILBERT STUART   *Lady Judith Maxwell*
American, 1755–1828   Oil on canvas
Early in his career Stuart painted in England under Benjamin West. Becoming extremely successful on his own, he overextended his pocketbook and was forced to flee to escape debtors' prison.

GEORGE INNESS   *The Valley on a Gloomy Day*
American, 1825–1894   Oil on canvas
Inness's meticulously detailed, grand, early landscapes were later replaced by looser more personal renditions in atmospheric silvery tones reminiscent of Corot.

WINSLOW HOMER
American, 1836–1910
The Trapper
Oil on canvas

Homer's paintings often pitted man against nature in powerful firmly constructed renditions. Like the French Impressionists he was concerned with light but his work was independent of them.

MARY CASSATT
American, 1845–1926
Meditation
Oil on canvas

Cassatt exhibited with the Impressionists in France. Upon her return to this country, she helped to familiarize American collectors with their work. She herself painted mainly domestic scenes, mothers and children.

WILLIAM MERRITT CHASE
American, 1849–1916
Prospect Park, Brooklyn
Oil on canvas

Chase was a teacher as well as a painter. His early dark-colored style became more Impressionistic, less flamboyant but similar to Sargent.

JOHN MARIN
American, 1870–1953
Opera House, Stonington
Watercolor with painted frame

Marin is known for his watercolors, many of them executed on the Maine coast. Although his work was rendered in varying degrees of Abstraction, it always reveals some element of Cubism.

John Marin, Opera House, Stonington. *Courtesy Colby College Art Museum, Waterville*

ANDREW WYETH   *Edge of the Field*
American, b. 1917   Watercolor
Rural Pennsylvania and Maine provide Wyeth with his subject matter. The paintings of these familiar environs are carefully drawn and are pervaded by a sense of loneliness and melancholy.

NEIL WELLIVER   *Duck Trap*
American, b. 1929   Oil on canvas
Welliver usually paints large detailed landscapes of Maine, doing either drawings or small paintings on locale or, sometimes, relying on memory.

FACILITIES

Changing Exhibitions are regularly featured.

The *Sales Desk* specializes in books and postcards related to the collection.

Hours: Monday–Saturday, 10 A.M.–12 P.M.; 1 P.M.–4:30 P.M.; Sunday, 2 P.M.–4:30 P.M.   *Closed:* New Year's, Easter, Memorial Day, July 4, Labor Day, Thanksgiving, Christmas.

Admission: Free.

MASSACHUSETTS

AMHERST

MEAD ART GALLERY
Amherst College
Amherst, MA 01002
Tel: (413)542-2335

The gallery houses a permanent collection of painting, sculpture, graphic work and minor arts of all periods and places. It is noted for its fine American painting and furniture, as well as a vast collection of etchings and prints. In addition to the exhibitions in the Main Gallery, smaller galleries contain the Bassett Gallery of American Art and the Collins Print Room. The Nineveh Room houses Assyrian reliefs and the Rotherwas Room displays paneling and furniture from a 17th-century English manor.

SAMPLING THE COLLECTION

All items are frequently rotated, making it impossible to specify locations.

DOMENICO PULIGO   *Madonna and Child with the*
Italian, 1475–1527   *Infant St. John*
                              Oil on panel
Active in Tuscany during the Renaissance, Puligo painted gentle Madonnas and altarpieces in the Classical style of his time.

GIROLAMO DA SANTA CROCE   *Madonna and Child with*
Italian, fl. 1503–1556   *St. Ambrose*
                              Oil on panel
Girolamo was one of a group who painted in the Venetian Renaissance style. His paintings are characterized by the use of soft color and an interest in the effect of light and color.

PETER PAUL RUBENS   *Charity, with Three Children*
Flemish, 1577–1640   Oil on panel
Rubens, known as a master of warm and natural color, was much influenced by the Italian Renaissance. He was devoted to Catholicism. After returning from a trip to Italy, most of his commissions were for religious works.

FRANCO-ITALIAN   *Herakles Epitrapezius*
                              17th c.
                              Gilt bronze
By the end of the 17th century large groups of foreigners, especially Frenchmen, studied sculpture in Italy, the center of Baroque sculpture, which was characterized by movement and emotional expressiveness.

JOSEPH BLACKBURN   *Sir Jeffrey Amherst*
British, fl. 1752–1778   ca. 1760
                              Oil on canvas
A popular portraitist in Portsmouth, New Hampshire and Boston, Blackburn helped to train Copley.

CHARLES WILLSON PEALE   *Portrait of James Peale*
American, 1741–1827   1789
     Oil on canvas
Best known for his portraits, Peale was self-taught, although he later studied with Copley and West. His work was able but uneven perhaps because of his many other interests.

ASHER BROWN DURAND   *In the Woods*
American, 1796–1886   Oil on canvas
Durand, a prominent member of the Hudson River School, is considered a founder of American landscape painting. He was influential in turning young artists from moralistic interpretations to realistic ones.

THOMAS COLE   *Present*
American, 1801–1848   1838
     Oil on canvas

     Past
     1838
     Oil on canvas
Cole, a very successful Romantic landscapist, was a leader of the Hudson River School. After a trip to Europe, he became interested in painting allegorical works in series.

HENRY MOORE   *Stringed Figure*
British, b. 1898   1938
     Gold patinated bronze
Moore, influenced by primitive sculpture, has fashioned some of his works directly from stone, wood or bronze. Others were modeled and cast. His pieces are mainly concerned with human forms.

BARBARA HEPWORTH   *Trezion III, Project for Wood*
British, 1903–1975   *and Strings*
     1959
     Oil, gesso and pencil on board
Hepworth always carved directly from wood or stone. She was interested in relationships and tensions between forms in space.

FAIRFIELD PORTER   *Boathouses and Lobster Pots*
American, 1907–1975   1968–1972
     Oil on canvas
Porter's landscapes, still lifes, interiors and portraits are carefully composed. He developed his own style uninfluenced by current movements in art.

FACILITIES

Changing Exhibitions are regularly featured.

Lectures and *Films* are offered.

The *Sales Desk* features catalogs and the always popular set of postcards of examples from the collections for $1 sets or 10¢ each.

Hours: *School year:* Monday–Friday, 10 A.M.–5 P.M.; Saturday–Sunday, 1 P.M.– 5 P.M. *June–July:* 1 P.M.–4 P.M.. *Closed:* August, New Year's, Christmas.

Admission: Free.

ANDOVER

ADDISON GALLERY OF AMERICAN ART
Phillips Academy
Andover, MA 01810
Tel: (617)475-7515

Founded in 1931, the gallery serves as a museum and art center for Phillips Academy, a secondary school, and the community at large. The entire collection is devoted to American art, ranging from Colonial to contemporary times. Included are paintings, sculpture, drawings, prints and photographs, as well as examples of model ships from the era of sail through that of the steam engine. The holdings of the museum are recognized as a distinguished specialized collection: Allston, Copley, Morse, Stuart, West and others represent the Colonial period. Of special importance among the many paintings of the 19th century are examples by Cole, Doughty, Eakins, Homer, Inness, LeFarge, Ryder, Twachtman and Whistler. The early part of the present century is shown in the work of Bellows, Davies, Demuth, Hassam, Hopper, Luks, Marin, Prendergast and Sloan. Contemporary artists are represented by works of Calder, Lippold Moholy-Nagy, Hofmann, O'Keeffe, Pollack, Shahn, Wyeth and Deborah Remington; photographs by Walker Evans, Paul Strand, Carleton Watkins, William Jackson and others are in the collection.

SAMPLING THE COLLECTION

JOHN SINGLETON COPLEY
1738–1815

Mary Elizabeth Martin
1771
Oil on canvas

Copley, Colonial America's most celebrated portraitist, painted his most successful portraits before settling in England in 1774. With meticulous execution, he conveyed great realism.

WINSLOW HOMER
1836–1910

Eight Bells
1886
Oil on canvas

In common with the early French Impressionists, Homer experimented with light and color. He was attracted by the sea and settled in Maine, pitting man against nature in somber, dramatic seascapes.

ANDREW WYETH
b.1917

Mother Archie's Church
1945
Tempera on panel

Wyeth's realistic landscapes and genre subjects are carefully detailed, emphasize earth tones and project a certain melancholy.

GEORGIA O'KEEFFE
b. 1887

Wave, Night
1928
Oil on canvas

A photographic quality underlies O'Keeffe's paintings of natural themes. Form is distinguished by a subtle shifting of color areas with scant attention paid to ordinary uses of light and shadow.

Winslow Homer, Eight Bells. *Courtesy Addison Gallery of American Art, Andover*

PETER ABATE   *Wandering*
b. 1915   1947
                                     Bronze
Abate's somewhat attenuated nude male figure is perhaps a statement on
today's alienated society.

FACILITIES

Changing Exhibitions of contemporary art are regularly featured.

Concerts by faculty and students are presented.

Hours: Tuesday–Saturday, 10 A.M.–5 P.M.; Sunday, 2:30 P.M.–5 P.M.. *Closed:*
         Mondays, New Year's, July 4, Memorial Day, Labor Day, Thanksgiv-
         ing, Christmas. (Also weekends if the holidays fall on weekends.)

Admission: Free.

BOSTON

BOSTON ATHENAEUM
10½ Beacon St.
Boston, MA 02108
Tel: (617)227-0270

The Boston Athenaeum, founded in 1807, is a National Historic Landmark owned and supported by shareholders. Having outgrown its original quarters, the present building was erected in 1847 to house an art gallery as well as the library. In 1876, when the Museum of Fine Arts was constructed in Boston, the Athenaeum lent it most of its art collection, laying the foundation for the museum's collection. At that time, the building at 10½ Beacon Street was converted mainly into a library. Two floors were added in 1913–1914, enlarging it to its present size. Still retaining its 19th-century flavor, it is an unusually pleasant place, reminiscent of more serene times, in which to browse or study. Five lofty reading rooms contain alcoves furnished with tables looking out on mostly intimate views, a quiet oasis in a bustling city. Special collections from the reading material include Confederate States imprints; books from the libraries of George Washington and Henry Knox; tracts from the libraries of the Adams family, the King's Chapel Collection (1698); Gypsy literature; 19th-century tracts; and early United States documents. The strength of the art collection still under its roof consists of 19th-century American sculpture, including a bust by Jean Antoine Houdon (1741–1828) of George Washington that once graced the home of Thomas Jefferson; European and American paintings of the 18th and 19th centuries, which include portraits of some of the early United States Presidents and portraits by John Singleton Copley (1738–1815), Gilbert Stuart (1755–1828), Thomas Sully (1783–1872) and John Singer Sargent (1856–1925). There is also a print collection, mostly of 19th-century lithographs of Boston and New England towns.

FACILITIES

Tours of the building are offered Tuesdays and Thursdays, 3:30 P.M. Call in advance.

The *Sales Desk*'s most popular items are reproductions of Boston views and publications relating to the collection. Prices range from $5 to $15.

Hours: Monday–Friday, 9 A.M.–5:30 P.M.; *October–May,* Saturday, 9 A.M.–4 P.M.. *Closed:* Sunday, Saturday in summer, all Massachusetts holidays.

Admission: Free.

CHILDREN'S MUSEUM
Museum Wharf
300 Congress St.
Boston, MA 02210
Tel: (617)426-6500

The museum, founded in 1913, moved in 1979 to new red brick quarters it shares with the Museum of Transportation. It can be recognized easily by the

40-foot-high Hood Milk Bottle. A park in front of Museum Wharf is peopled by jugglers and street musicians and a play area has been developed for young children. From here one can survey downtown Boston, the bustling harbor containing the ship that hosted the Boston Tea Party, and Logan Airport. The second and third floors of the building are devoted to the museum and the fifth and sixth floors to the Museum of Transportation, which may be reached by a giant glass elevator on the outside of the building. The fourth floor is for shared functions; the ground floor is reserved for retail shops.

SAMPLING THE COLLECTION

The "Hands-on" exhibits are primarily designed for preschool children through early teens.

The Giant's Desktop
A telephone, postcard, ruler, paper clips and assorted junk, all twelve times normal size, have been re-created on *The Giant's Desktop.*

The Giant's Desktop. *Courtesy Children's Museum, Boston*

City Slice
This X-ray view of a city street and mansard cottage illustrates how buildings are constructed, how toilets and utility services work and how growing things survive beneath the backyard soil.

The Grandparent's House
Here, in a three-story house, children are encouraged to use grandfather's tools at his cellar workbench, play games in the first floor parlor, churn butter in the

kitchen and try on old clothes in the attic. From the first floor they can walk out onto the street and climb down a telephone company manhole.

Adult Work Settings

Across the street from *The Grandparent's House* a neighborhood convenience store, garage and health center invite children to try out the tools of these adult trades.

How Movies Move

Zoetrope machines allow children to make their own movies.

JAPANESE   *Artisan's House*

Kyoto

This two-story Japanese house and artisan's shop have been contributed by Boston's sister city.

FACILITIES

Four *Study Modules* provide additional data through the use of graphics, films, books, display materials and activities.

The *Sit Around* is a small amphitheater presenting puppeteers, magic shows and sing-alongs.

The *Museum Restaurants* include McDonald's; the Hood Milk Bottle, serving salads and frozen yogurt; and Trawlers, a seafood restaurant and a snack bar.

The *Recycle Shop* has barrels of industrial scrap materials—foam, fabric, lenses, scrap wood, etc.—for use in craft projects. $3 per bag.

The *Museum Shop* carries quality toys, books and educational materials. Prices range from 5¢ to $8.

Special Events are held during school vacations and Friday evenings at 7:30 P.M. Call for schedule (617)426–8855.

Hours: *July–Labor Day:* Daily, 10 A.M.–6 P.M.; Friday until 9 P.M. *Rest of year:* Tuesday–Sunday, 10 A.M.–5 P.M.; Friday until 9 P.M.. *Closed:* Mondays, except Boston school vacations and holidays; New Year's; Labor Day; Thanksgiving; Christmas.

Admission: Adults, $3; children 3–15, and senior citizens, $2; children under 3 free. Maximum per family $12. Family Night (Friday, 6 P.M.–9 P.M.), $1 per person.

INSTITUTE OF CONTEMPORARY ART
955 Boylston St.
Boston, MA 02115
Tel: (617)266–5151

The ICA is housed in a renovated 19th-century police station in Boston's Back Bay area. Although the inside has been totally remodeled, the outside remains untouched. The institute does not have a permanent collection, but presents a changing schedule of contemporary art exhibits. Presenting bold new examples of 20th-century art by artists of national and international reputation, exhibitions deal with a wide range of art forms and media including painting, sculpture, video, performance and crafts. The ICA also sponsors performing arts events including music, dance, theater, film and poetry.

FACILITIES

The *Hermitage Restaurant* serves Russian cuisine and is open for lunch and dinner.

The *Museum Store* sells exhibit catalogs, posters, cards, calendars, contemporary crafts and jewelry with prices ranging from 10¢ to several hundred dollars.

Hours: Tuesday–Saturday, 10 A.M.–5 P.M.; Wednesday, 10 A.M.–9 P.M., Sunday, 12 P.M.–5 P.M.; *Closed:* Mondays, national holidays.

Admission: Adults, $1.25; students, children, senior citizens, 75¢.

ISABELLA STEWART GARDNER MUSEUM
280 The Fenway
Boston, MA 02115
Tel: (617)566–1401

Fenway Court, incorporated as a museum in 1900, is the achievement of Isabella Stewart Gardner, whose purpose was to create an atmosphere for the enjoyment of flowers, music and art. The collection of paintings, sculpture, tapestries, stained glass, furniture and other objects of art is exhibited in a building erected in the style of a 15th-century Venetian palace. The central court offers a display of flowers.

SAMPLING THE COLLECTION

Gothic Room JOHN SINGER SARGENT   *Portrait of Mrs. Gardner*
American, 1856–1925   1888
Oil on canvas
Sargent, an extremely popular society portraitist, was a close friend of Mrs. Gardner. During the winter of 1902–1903 he used the Gothic Room on the third floor as his studio.

Spanish Cloister Opposite the Public Entrance   *El Jaleo*
1882
Oil on canvas
The Moorish arch and lighting from below reinforce the idea of the stage on which Sargent had seen flamenco dancers.

Chinese Loggia CHINESE   *Votive Stele*
Buddhist   543
Stone
This sculpture was advanced in style for its period. The central figure, Sakyamuni, extends his right hand in the gesture of fearlessness, with his left that of charity.

Center Court ROMAN   *Mosaic Floor*
2nd c.
Small stones set in concrete
This floor of small stones set in concrete is from a Roman villa. It is decorated with birds and scrolls surrounding the head of Medusa.

West Cloister ROMAN   *Sarcophagus*
3rd c.
Marble

Courtyard. *Courtesy Isabella Stewart Gardner Museum, Boston*

Reveling figures adorn this coffin which still reflects Classical elements in its details.

Room of **Early Italian** **Paintings,** **Top of** **Stairs**	SIMONE MARTINI Italian, Sienese, ca. 1284–1344	*The Madonna and Child with* *Four Saints* Tempera on panel

Simone filled this five-part altarpiece with the symbolism and color developed in the Byzantine Church.

	FRA ANGELICO Italian, ca. 1400–1455	*The Death and Assumption of* *the Virgin* ca. 1430 Gold and tempera on wood

In this painting we have a foretaste of Italian Renaissance ideals as developed in Florence. The faces have a more individual character and the space is more apparent.

Room of **Early Italian** **Paintings**	FRANCESCO PESELLINO Italian, 1422–1457	*The Triumphs* (illustrates the poem written by Petrarch) ca. 1448 2 panels, tempera on chestnut wood

These two panels were part of a wedding chest. They represent the allegorical figures of Love, Chastity, Death, Fame, Time and Eternity.

Room of **Early Italian** **Paintings**	PIERO DELLA FRANCESCA Italian, ca. 1420–1492	*Hercules* Fresco

This fragment, originally a full-length figure, done by the artist to decorate a villa, probably his home, shows interest in the human form and in classical mythology fostered by the Italian Renaissance.

Raphael **Room**	RAPHAEL (RAFFAELO SANZIO) Italian, 1483–1520	*Count Tommaso Inghirami* ca. 1513 Oil on nutwood

The sitter held many important positions and was a gifted preacher and scholar. Raphael has diminished his physical shortcomings by rotating his enormous bulk and allowing the wandering eye to look upward.

Raphael **Room**		*Pietà* Oil on wood panel

This was part of a large altarpiece done in the artist's youth. Along with Michelangelo and da Vinci, Raphael was one of the giant talents of the High Renaissance.

	SANDRO BOTTICELLI Italian, Florentine, ca. 1444–1510	*The Story of Lucretia* after 1500 Tempera(?) and oil on hard wood panel

Botticelli repudiated naturalism. His paintings were linear and lyrical. In three scenes this painting tells the legend of the event which led to the founding of the Roman republic, ca. 510 B.C.

Long **Gallery**		*The Madonna of the Eucharist* ca. 1475 Tempera (possibly with some oil in the shadows) on nut(?) wood

This is an unusually sculptural rendition for Botticelli. It concentrates on symbolism, setting him apart from Filippo Lippi, his probable master. The corn and grapes symbolize the Eucharist, the Child, the Redeemer.

PAOLO UCCELLO   *The Young Lady of Fashion*   **Long**
Italian, 1397–1475   mid-15th c.   **Gallery**
Oil(?) on wood
This characteristic 15th-century portrait emphasizes color and the tense outline of the figure.

BARTOLOME BERMEJO   *Saint Engracia*   **Tapestry**
Spanish, fl. 1474–1498   ca. 1477   **Room**
Gold and oil on pine wood
Bermejo was one of the first Spanish painters to work in oils. This central panel from a large altarpiece was dedicated to the Spanish martyr killed in the 4th century.

BELGIAN   *Ten Tapestries*   **Tapestry**
Brussels   ca. 1550   **Room**
Wool and silk on linen warp
The tapestries with Latin inscription represent scenes from the life of Abraham, the others the life of Cyrus the Great. The border of fruits and birds is typical of the 16th century.

PETER PAUL RUBENS   *Thomas Howard, Earl of Arundel*   **Dutch**
Flemish, 1577–1640   Oil on canvas   **Room,**
Rubens was an accomplished diplomat as well as a master painter. His paint- **Opposite the**
ings linked the Italian Renaissance with 17th- and 18th-century European art. **Court**

JAN VERMEER   *The Concert*   **Dutch**
Dutch, 1632–1675   Oil on canvas   **Room**
Less than 40 works survive by Vermeer. His use of light to define form and space is unequaled.

REMBRANDT HARMENSZ VAN RIJN   *Self-Portrait*   **Dutch**
Dutch, 1606–1669   ca. 1629   **Room**
Oil on oak
Rembrandt absorbed the traditions of European art, evolving a style and method of his own. He was a master at portraying the emotions through attitudes and expressions.

Double Portrait
1633
Oil on canvas
Rembrandt executed this painting in the fashionable style of portraits then being done in Amsterdam.

The Storm on the Sea of Galilee
1633
Oil on canvas
Christ is seen in the stern of the boat and Rembrandt himself looks out at the viewer. During his first years in Amsterdam, Rembrandt painted a number of religious works.

The Obelisk
1638
Oil on oak
In this painting, Rembrandt's figures seem overwhelmed by the ominous surroundings.

TITIAN (TIZIANO VECELLIO)   *The Rape of Europa*   **Titian**
Italian, Venetian, ca. 1490–1576   ca. 1560   **Room**
Oil on canvas

Painted for Philip II of Spain, this is one of the most important Italian paintings in America. Titian's work is sensual rather than intellectual, reflecting his intense appreciation of natural and human passions.

Titian   BENVENUTO CELLINI   *Portrait Bust*
Room   Italian, Florentine, 1500–1571   Bronze
               The sitter is Bindo Altoviti, a Florentine banker and patron of the arts. This is one of two surviving portrait busts by the Mannerist sculptor and goldsmith.

Gothic   GIOTTO DI BONDONE   *The Presentation of the*
Room   Italian, ca. 1266–1337   *Infant Jesus in the Temple*
                                                    Gold and tempera on wood
               Giotto's gift for narrative is expressed in this small panel. Naturalistic solid figures using simple gestures changed the course of European painting, preparing the ground for the painters of the next century.

FACILITIES

Accoustiguide Tour units available during open hours.

Music programs are offered free on Tuesday, 8 P.M.; Thursday and Sunday, 4 P.M. No music in July and August.

A *Café* located next to the *Sales Desk* serves lunch and afternoon tea in pleasant surroundings.

For *Information* on concerts and hours call (617)734–1359.

Hours: *September–June:* Tuesday, 1 P.M.–9:30 P.M.; Wednesday–Sunday, 1 P.M.–5:30 P.M.. *July–August:* Tuesday–Sunday, 1 P.M.–5:30 P.M. *Closed:* Mondays, all national holidays.

Admission: There is no required admission fee. Visitors are asked to make a contribution at the door—$1 is suggested.

MUSEUM OF FINE ARTS, BOSTON
465 Huntington Ave.
Boston, MA 02115
Tel: (617)267–9300

The museum is located on thirteen acres of land and contains nearly four acres of gallery space. It caters to over half a million visitors each year and its nine curatorial departments are responsible for a comprehensive and outstanding collection. Founded in 1870, the museum has been at its present site since 1909. It is still expanding. Its latest addition, the Foster Gallery, opened in 1975, exhibits contemporary art.

SAMPLING THE COLLECTION

1st Floor,   *AMERICAN DECORATIVE ARTS AND SCULPTURE*
Zone C
                  The museum's collections of American decorative arts and sculpture range from the Colonial period up through the present time, with major emphasis on pre-Civil War New England.

                  JOHN COGSWELL   *Chest-on-Chest*
                  Boston, Massachusetts, 1738–1818   1782
                                                     Mahogany

Exterior view with Cyrus Dallin's Appeal to the Great Spirit. *Courtesy Museum of Fine Arts, Boston*

This chest-on-chest, united in form and ornament, is regarded as the most important piece of Boston furniture in the Chippendale style. It is signed and dated by its maker.

THOMAS SEYMOUR
Boston, Massachusetts, 1771–1843

Commode
1809
Mahogany and satinwood

This semicircular commode was inspired by George Hepplewhite's *The Cabinet Maker and Upholsterer's Guide,* as were many pieces of American and European furniture.

JOHN CONEY
Boston, Massachusetts, 1655–1722

Sugar Box
ca. 1680–1690
Silver

This is one of the most ornately decorated pieces of Early American silver. Because sugar and sweetmeats were so precious in Colonial times, they were kept in elaborate boxes.

ATT. TO JOHN PEASE, JR.
Connecticut, 1654–1734

Chest
ca. 1700–1714
Oak and pine

Pease, very probably, made this chest for his daughter when she married. The designs are carved in complex flat relief.

PAUL REVERE   *The Liberty Bowl*
Boston, Massachusetts 1735–1818   1768
                                     Silver
This bowl commemorates the Sons of Liberty with their names engraved around its rim. It is the most historic piece of American silver extant.

THOMAS CRAWFORD   *Hebe and Ganymede*
1813–1857   1842
                                     Marble
Inspired by a Greek myth, Crawford made a plaster model which was the prototype for this marble one.

ASIATIC ART

The museum's Asiatic collections are extensive, varied and prestigious. They are divided into three principal units. The Far Eastern includes China, Japan and Korea. That of Islam encompasses the Middle East to North Africa, eastward to India and into Southeast Asia. The Indian unit extends as far north as Nepal and Tibet and south through Sri Lanka, Java, Burma, Thailand and Cambodia. Commencing with items from the 3rd millennium B.C., the collections terminate with contemporary woodblock prints from Japan.

JAPANESE   *Dai-Itoku Myō-ō*
Heian Period, 794–1185   11th c.
                                     Ink, colors and kirigane on
                                     silk
Strong outlines contrast with delicate details in this vividly colored, energetic Buddhist painting thought to be one of the finest to leave Japan, although its origins remain a mystery.

EASTERN JAVANESE   *Bhairava or Mahākāla*
                                     14th c.
                                     Andesite
This was probably a portrait sculpture of a deceased person of royal blood whose features were combined with those of the god with whom his spirit was believed to have blended.

CHINESE   *Mongolian Youth*
Warring-States Period,   ca. early 4th c. B.C.
ca. 480–222 B.C.   Bronze with two birds in jade
This early sculpture is interesting because of its non-Chinese appearance. The braided hair and the left-folded dress agree with Chinese accounts of the nomads who dwelt in the northern steppes.

CHINESE   *Bodhisattva, from the White*
Northern Wei Dynasty,   *Horse Monastery, Lo Yang*
ca. A.D. 386-535   ca. A.D. 530
                                     Limestone
The workmanship of the back suggests that this is a very early Buddhist free-standing figure from China. It is one of the biggest ever to be taken from there.

INDIAN   *Yaksī Torso*
Sanchi   1st c. B.C.
                                     Sandstone
This tree-dryad from an entrance gate of a Buddhist stūpa, a commemorative monument, exhibits the artist's skill in fashioning a three-dimensional figure that extols the voluptuous beauty of this fertility symbol.

CAMBODIAN
Khmer Empire

Celestial Dancer
late 12th–early 13th c.
Bronze

This casting was most likely a part of a lamp or standard. Some of the important monuments of Khmer architecture had rows of celestial dancers done in stone relief.

IRANIAN

Battle of Alexander and the Dragon
14th c.
Leaf from a Shah-Nameh

The free interpretation of this epic history of the Iranian people exemplifies the height of Persian painting during this period. One can see the influence of Byzantine and Chinese styles.

DEPARTMENT OF CLASSICAL ART

Because it is almost entirely free of ordinary objects and because of its esthetic excellence, the museum's collection of Classical art is considered to be exceptional. It includes all phases of Greek, Roman and Etruscan art but is especially noteworthy for its objects of the 6th, 5th and 4th centuries B.C.

GREEK

Earring
mid-4th c. B.C.
Gold

This earring was probably dedicated to a goddess. Although found in a tomb, it was possibly designed to hang from the ear of a cult statue.

CRETAN

Snake Goddess
ca. 1600–1500 B.C.
Gold and ivory

One of the few sculptures in the round to survive from Minoan days, this mother goddess was most likely from the palace treasury at Knossos, where she protected the royal household.

FOUND IN ROME

Three-Sided Relief
ca. 470–460 B.C.
Marble

This sculpture, and the Ludovisi Throne in Rome, were probably the decoration on two wings framing the steps of a grand altar of Aphrodite.

GREEK

Head of Aphrodite
late 4th c. B.C.
Marble

The *Aphrodite,* named for its donor, is known as the Bartlett Head. Approximating the work of Praxiteles, it is regarded as one of the loveliest surviving pieces of Greek sculpture.

GREEK

Head of Homer
late Hellenistic or Graeco-Roman
Marble

Since Homer lived long before Greek art explored portraiture, this sculpture is the artist's concept of what Homer ought to have been. The head was perhaps part of a seated statue.

ETRUSCAN

Portrait of a Roman
late 1st c. B.C.
Terracotta

This bust of a man found in a villa northwest of Naples is so lifelike that it was possibly made with the aid of a mask.

EGYPTIAN AND ANCIENT NEAR EASTERN ART

The museum has outstanding collections covering all periods of Egyptian art from the Middle, New Kingdom and the Late periods. It is particularly strong in examples from the Old Kingdom and Kushite art from the Sudan. A small but superior collection of sculpture, bronzes and other objects from Mesopotamia, the Syrian Coast, Anatolia and Persia are also under the jurisdiction of this department.

PROBABLY FROM MEMPHIS   *Relief of the Cup-Bearer*
Reign of Amenhotep III,   *Tja-Wy*
Dynasty XVIII, 1410–1372   (Detail) Limestone
The household musicians are entertaining as Tja-Wy and his parents are served a bowl of food or drink.

2nd Floor,   GIZA   *"Reserve Head"* of a *Princess*
Gallery 16   Reign of Cheops, Dynasty IV,   White limestone
                  2656–2633 B.C.
Heads with African features were put into tombs as substitutes for mummies should they be destroyed. These realistic sculptures of their owners are the finest in Egyptian history.

2nd Floor,   GIZA   *Triad*
Gallery 16   Dynasty IV, 2599–2571 B.C.   (Detail) slate schist
These triads of Mycerinus were carved by the best court sculptors. In the temple, the triads represented gifts offered from the provinces or nomes. This king and nome are linked with Hathor, goddess of fertility.

EUROPEAN DECORATIVE ARTS

This department's special strength lies in its medieval holdings. It also has an extensive collection of English silver from the 15th into the 19th century and an excellent collection of French decorative arts of the 18th century. The Mason Collection of Musical Instruments is under the jurisdiction of this department and offers a program of performance and instruction in ancient musical instruments.

In Storage   CLAUDE-NICHOLAS LEDOUX   *Wall Panels*
                 French, 1756–1806   ca. 1770–1772
                                                  Eight carved oak panels painted
                                                  in watercolors and a gilt on gesso
These *boiseries* are outstanding examples of the Louis XVI style. Brought from a salon of the Hotel Montmorency, Paris, in the 1850s, they depict Classical figures in an elegantly elongated style.

1st Floor,   MADE BY WILLIAM WILLIAMSON;
Zone C,   ENGRAVED BY DANIEL POMAREDE   *Racing Trophy*
Gallery 20   Irish   1751
                                                  Silver, engraved
The beauty and importance of this punch bowl made in Dublin derives from its size and handsome shape and from the engraving that explains its origin. The horse race commemorated here halfway encircles the bowl.

2nd Floor,   FRENCH   *Virgin and Child*
Zone C,   Ile-de-France   early 13th c.
Gallery 4   Polychromed and gilded oak
The highly developed drapery style of this statue with its undulating, deep-cut folds is characteristic of Early Gothic cathedral sculpture of northern France.

DONATELLO	*Madonna of the Clouds*	**2nd Floor,**
Italian, Florentine 1386–1466	ca. 1425–1428	**Zone C,**
	Marble in extremely low relief	**Gallery 17**

This masterpiece is one of the few accepted works by Donatello in the United States. The sculptor created a believable illusion of space around the Madonna by using very low relief and inscribed forms.

PAUL GAUGUIN	*Soyez Amoureuses Vous*	**2nd Floor,**
French, 1848–1903	*Serez Heureuses*	**Zone D**
	ca. 1889	
	Carved, polished and polychromed	
	lindenwood	

Carved in Pont-Aven, Brittany, after Gauguin's return from Martinique, anticipating his later Tahitian style, this relief combines images of passion and suffering with rich variations of surface texture, form and applied color.

DEPARTMENT OF CONTEMPORARY ART

The relatively new Department of Contemporary Art was founded in 1971. Its major concern is with paintings and sculpture from 1945 on when Abstract painting regained its popularity along with the ascendancy of the New York School.

MORRIS LOUIS	*Alioth*
American, 1912–1962	1962
	Acrylic on canvas

The museum has nine paintings by Louis, the largest selection in any public institution. *Alioth* is one of "stripes" of contrasting bleeding color.

Delta Gamma
Acrylic on canvas

Delta Gamma is a painting from Louis's "unfurled" cycle. He believed these to be his best work in that he attained new expressive power in his arrangement of color.

Beth Tet
1958
Acrylic on canvas

This is one of the grandest works from Louis's "veil series." He has applied color into color on this unprimed canvas by staining layer upon layer with one transparent hue on top of another.

JACKSON POLLOCK	*Number 10*
American, 1912–1956	1949
	Oil on canvas

Painted at the zenith of Pollock's career, this painting illustrates his classical drip period. The network of black pigment, aluminum paint and daubs of color lend the work clarity and variety.

DEPARTMENT OF PAINTINGS

With its continuing growth, the painting collection has become one of the most important in the world, ranging from the 11th to the early 20th century. Only six other museums have a French collection of the same caliber. It includes 36 canvases by Monet, the largest number in any museum outside of France. The Colonial and early Federal portraits and the 18th- and 19th-century American paintings are also outstanding.

ROGIER VAN DER WEYDEN
Flemish, ca. 1399–1464

Saint Luke Painting the Virgin
ca. 1436
Oil on panel

It is now agreed that this painting was the prototype for three other versions in major European museums. Although influenced by Jan Van Eyck, van der Weyden brought more refinement to his work.

IL ROSSO FLORENTINO
Italian, 1494–1540

The Dead Christ with Angels
ca. 1524–1527
Oil on panel

This Mannerist work contradicts the principles of Renaissance painting with bright colors, jarring tonal contrasts and tension achieved by the containment of huge forms in a small area.

REMBRANDT HARMENSZ VAN RIJN
Dutch, 1606–1669

The Artist in His Studio
Oil on panel

Rembrandt portrays himself with stunning frankness in self-portraits painted over the 40 years of his career.

EL GRECO (DOMENICOS
THEOTOCOPOULOS)
Spanish, 1541–1614

Fray Felix Hortensio Paravicino
ca. 1609
Oil on canvas

In this forceful and expressive work, El Greco deceives us with the contemporary simplicity of his broad style.

JOSEPH MALLORD WILLIAM
TURNER
British, 1775–1851

The Slave Ship
1840
Oil on canvas

Although this painting is based on history, it is more concerned with portraying nature. Turner's interest in atmosphere, light and arrangement of color greatly influenced the Impressionists.

HILAIRE GERMAIN EDGAR DEGAS
French, 1834–1917

Carriage at the Races
ca. 1872
Oil on canvas

This painting of a friend of Degas's and his family in a carriage is small in size. However, the way in which Degas handled the composition and atmosphere make the dimensions seem more ample.

JOHN SINGLETON COPLEY
American, 1738–1815

Watson and the Shark
1778
Oil on canvas

This is a copy of the original that hangs in the National Gallery in Washington, D.C. Both canvases were painted by Copley. This work, painted while he was living in England, succeeded in promoting realism in narrative painting.

FITZ HUGH LANE
American, 1804–1865

New York Harbor
1850
Oil on canvas

Lane gained his reputation for harbor scenes painted vividly and with great credibility.

JOHN SINGER SARGENT
American, 1856–1925

Daughters of Edward D. Boit
1882
Oil on canvas

Sargent's portraits were generally reflections of Boston's upper-class society. The influence of Velázquez can be seen in this portrayal of the four daughters of his friend.

DEPARTMENT OF PRINTS AND DRAWINGS

This department is responsible for half a million prints, drawings, watercolors, illustrated books and photographs of European and American origin which date from the 15th century to the present. The department's exhibitions are changed on a regular basis using its six galleries and offering one special exhibition with a catalog. Material not on view in the galleries may be seen in the Print Study Room, Tuesday through Friday between 1 P.M. and 4:30 P.M. by appointment.

REMBRANDT HARMENSZ VAN RIJN   *Christ Presented to the People*
Dutch, 1606–1669   1655
                                                                   Drypoint

Rembrandt was considered one of the outstanding printmakers of all time. As he matured, there was a deepening of human values in his etchings as well as in his paintings.

ALBRECHT DURER   *Joachim and Anna Meeting*
German, 1471–1528   *at the Golden Gate*
                                                            1504
                                                            Woodcut, from *The Life of*
                                                            the Virgin

Dürer completely changed the craft of the woodcut, spreading his fame throughout Europe. He was responsible for bringing the Renaissance movement from Italy to the north.

TEXTILE DEPARTMENT

The broad range of the museum's textile collection extends from the pharaonic days in Egypt to the present. Due to the fragility of the articles, most of them are kept in storage. However, they are rotated in changing exhibitions in the two textile galleries on Floor 1.

FACILITIES

Walks through the Museum to familiarize visitors with its contents are conducted by volunteers. Walks last approximately one hour. Groups meet in the Huntington Avenue lobby; call the members' room for times.

Frequent *Lectures, Gallery Talks* and *Slide Talks* are given in connection with current exhibitions and the permanent collections. Guest speakers from all over the world often lecture on the arts.

Films, silent, classic, foreign and avant-garde, are featured. For information call ext. 395.

Concerts are held in the galleries, using the ancient instruments from the museum's collection of Musical Instruments. For information call the Musical Instruments Collection.

The *Children's Room* is open Wednesday–Friday, 3:15 P.M.–4:30 P.M.; Saturday, 10:30 A.M.–11:30 A.M. Free, unregistered art workshops for children in grades 1–6. Meet at Fenway entrance. For information call ext. 311.

The *Library* has an extensive research library which is open to the public.

The *Museum Shop* offers jewelry; reproductions from the museum's collections; silver and pewter items; needlepoint patterns and an abundance of other wares. Prices range from 20¢ for cards to a reproduction of a Paul Revere teaset costing over $400.

For the *Handicapped,* wheelchairs are available at the staff entance off the parking lot. Parking is reserved for handicapped visitors at this door.

The *Gallery Dining Room and Snack Bar* overlook the Sculpture Court and offer full bar service as well as food. The *Dining Room* is open Tuesday–Friday, 11:30 A.M.–2:30 P.M.; Sunday, 12 P.M.–3 P.M.; Tuesday evening, 5 P.M.–7:30 P.M. The *Snack Bar* is open Tuesday–Sunday, 10 A.M.–4 P.M.

Afternoon Tea is served weekday afternoons except holidays, October–May, 2:30 P.M.–4 P.M.

For a *Recorded Listing* of weekly events and schedule changes, dial A-N-S-W-E-R-S (267–9377).

The *Museum of Fine Arts* at Faneuil Hall in downtown Boston offers changing exhibitions of top quality. It occupies the top floor of the reconstructed South Market Building in this historic site. The original building, in Greek Revival style, was erected in the 1820s.

Hours: Wednesday–Sunday, 10 A.M.–5 P.M.; Tuesday, 10 A.M.–9 P.M. *Closed:* Mondays, New Year's, July 4, Labor Day, Thanksgiving, December 24–25.

Admission: $2. Tuesday evenings (5 P.M.–9 P.M.) free. Sunday $1.50, free to anyone under 16 and to members. Senior citizens free on Fridays. Children under 14 must be accompanied by an adult.

BROCKTON

BROCKTON ART CENTER, FULLER MEMORIAL
Oak St. on Upper Porter's Pond
Brockton, MA 02401
Tel: (617)588-6000

The center, founded in 1969, is adjacent to the 750-acre D. W. Field Park. The permanent collection features 19th-and 20th-century American art and Early American Sandwich Glass. Contemporary sculpture is exhibited in the courtyard.

SAMPLING THE COLLECTION

MAXFIELD PARRISH   *Winter Dusk*
American, 1870–1966   1943
                                     Oil on artists' board
Parrish retired as an illustrator to paint landscapes. His mixture of fantasy and realism had great popular appeal.

CHAUNCEY RYDER   *Over There*
American, ca. 1863–1949   1919
                                     Oil on canvas
This painting depicts a crowd scene on the northern coast of France.

JOHN J. ENNEKING   *Evening Sunset*
American, 1841–1916   1894
                                     Oil on panel
After studying figure and landscape painting in Paris, Enneking became a landscapist.

THOMAS EAKINS
American, 1844–1916

The Portrait of Walter
Copeland Bryant
1903
Oil on canvas

Eakins was a realist who painted portraits and genre scenes. Since he was interested in anatomy, he posed a nude male model in his class, incurring censure from a prudish public. In later years he mostly painted portraits depicted with great insight.

FACILITIES

Guided Tours are available at group rates.

Lectures, Theater, Concerts, Films and *Dance Programs* are scheduled frequently.

Changing Exhibitions are regularly featured.

The *Saturday Stagecoach* provides monthly theatrical performances for young people.

The *Gift Shop* carries museum reproduction jewelry and sculpture, books and handcrafted items.

The *Art Sales* and *Rental Gallery* has a wide selection of original paintings and graphics which may be borrowed or purchased.

Hours: Tuesday, Wednesday, Friday, Saturday, 1 P.M.–5 P.M. Sunday, 1 P.M.–6 P.M.; Thursday, 1 P.M.–10 P.M. *Closed:* Mondays, New Year's, July 4, Thanksgiving, Christmas.

Admission: Adults, $1; students and senior citizens, 50¢. Children under 16 free. Free to all, Thursdays, 1 P.M.–7 P.M.

CAMBRIDGE

BUSCH-REISINGER MUSEUM, HARVARD UNIVERSITY
29 Kirkland St.
Cor. of Divinity Ave.
Cambridge, MA 02138
Tel: (617)495-2338

Founded in 1901 by Kuno Francke, a Harvard professor of German, the collection of the museum was initially composed of reproductions. Its present Rococo building houses Romanesque, Gothic and Renaissance areas appropriate to the art displayed, plus a sculpture garden and small pool. By 1930, original works from Central and Northern Europe were being assembled and the museum continues to build a notable collection in this field. Its special strength is in late medieval, Renaissance and Baroque sculpture; 16th-century painting; 18th-century porcelains and particularly 20th-century sculpture and painting.

SAMPLING THE COLLECTION

MAX BECKMANN
German, 1884–1950

The Actors, 1942
Triptych
Oil on canvas

Renaissance
Hall

Max Beckmann, Self-Portrait in Tuxedo, 1927. *Courtesy Busch-Reisinger Museum, Cambridge*

Beckmann was closely identified with Expressionism, which he turned to after his experiences in World War I. This is one of his important triptychs displaying the brutal realism of his work of this period.

Self-Portrait in Tuxedo, 1927
Oil on canvas

An example of the many self-portraits that were prominently featured in the artist's work.

ERICH HECKEL	*Convalescence of a Woman*	**Renaissance**
German, 1883–1970	1913	**Hall**
	Oil on canvas	

Heckel was an Expressionist painter who sought to depict emotions not objectively but through the use of strong color, irregular shapes and dynamic design. Done early in his career, this painting is typical of his lonely, agonizing women.

ERNST LUDWIG KIRCHNER	*Self-Portrait with Cat*	**Renaissance**
German, 1880–1938	1913	**Hall**
	Triptych, oil on canvas	

An Expressionist painter, Kirchner was influenced by van Gogh, Munch and also primitive art. Painted in Berlin during his early, intense period, this is a fine example of Expressionist art.

LYONEL FEININGER	*Bird Cloud*	**Renaissance**
American, 1871–1956	1926	**Hall**
	Oil on canvas	

This was painted during the period Feininger was a member of the "Blue Four," a group of Expressionists based in Germany whose work evolved into total Abstraction.

FACILITIES

Changing Exhibitions are regularly featured.

There is a *Germanic Garden Court* in which to relax.

Sales Desk offers postcards, 10¢–25¢; catalogs, 5¢–$6.

Hours: Monday–Saturday, 9 A.M.–4:45 P.M. *Closed:* Sundays; holidays; during July and August—Saturdays, Sundays.

Admission: Free.

FOGG ART MUSEUM
Harvard University
32 Quincy St.
Cambridge, MA 02138
Tel: (617)495-2378

The museum, founded in 1891, was opened in 1895. It has been established since 1927 in its present Georgian-style quarters adjoining the northeast corner of Harvard Yard. It contains the most important works of art owned by Harvard University, displayed in galleries surrounding a naturally illuminated central court. There are approximately ten times more university-owned paintings hanging in the libraries, common rooms, and professors' studies. The museum serves as a laboratory for the university's Fine Arts Department. These works illustrate the whole evolution of art, Eastern and Western, from ancient to modern times. Particularly distinguished are the collections of prints, drawings,

Exterior view. Courtesy Fogg Art Museum, Cambridge

Romanesque sculpture, Italian primitives, French 19th-century painting, Chinese jades, bronzes, ceramics and sculpture and Japanese prints, *surimono* and calligraphy.

SAMPLING THE COLLECTION

FRENCH
12th c.

Romanesque Capitals from Moutier-St. Jean
ca. 1125–1130
1922.16–27

The Moutier Master was possibly a colleague of Gislebertus who produced some of the finest French Romanesque capitals. Romanesque sculpture is usually carved in relief and placed in architectural settings.

CHINESE
Shang Dynasty, ca. 1523–1028 B.C.

Ritual Vessel of the type "fang-i" with "t'ao-t'ieh mask"
12th–11th c. B.C.
Bronze

Shang ceremonial bronzes had strong forms embellished by traditional designs implying real or fanciful animals and birds. The most common figure was the mythological "t'ao-t'ieh," whose significance is not entirely understood.

CHINESE
Eastern Chou period,
ca. 770–256 B.C.

Disk (pi)
ca. 4th c. B.C.
Jade (nephrite)

In ancient China, the "pi" signified heaven and was used in ritual ceremonies paying homage to heaven. During this period, artisans attained unparalleled achievements in jade work.

CHINESE
Shansi Province, T'ien-lung-shan,
Northern Wei period, ca. 386–535

*Asparas (Heavenly Nymphs) from
Ceiling of Cave II*
early 6th c.
Limestone

So alive and varied were the subjects discovered in the 29 Buddhist caves at T'ien-lung-shan, that these must rank among the finest of Chinese sculptures.

CHINESE
Kansu Province, Tun-Huang,
T'ang Dynasty, A.D. 618–906

Head of a Bodhisattva
ca. 8th c.
Polychrome wall painting

Tun-Huang was an important hub on the "Silk Road" to China. The vivid coloring of the deity's robe is still visible in this fragment of a wall painting strongly influenced by India and Central Asia.

CHINESE
Yüan Dynasty, 1260–1368

*Large Plate with Persian
Inscription*
mid-14th c.
Porcelain with underglaze
decoration

China was dominated by the Mongols during the Yüan period who introduced virility and invention in their designs. Ceramic decorations were more often painted than inlaid or incised. The technique of painting porcelain with designs in underglaze cobalt was invented in the Yüan dynasty.

SIMONE MARTINI
Italian, Sienese, ca. 1284–1344

Christ on the Cross
ca. 1320
Tempera and gold on wood
Purchase, Hervey E. Wetzel,
Bequest
1919.51

Simone was the foremost Sienese painter of his time, much influenced by French Gothic art. His linear style was accomplished with great delicacy.

FRA ANGELICO
Italian, Florentine, ca. 1400–1455

Crucifixion
ca. 1446
Tempera and gold on wood with
gabled top and engaged frame
Purchase, Hervey E. Wetzel,
Bequest
1921.34

Probably once the center of a portable tabernacle, the *Crucifixion* is extreme in its simplicity and religiosity. The idealized proportions and illusion of a three-dimensionality are intensified by pale hues.

FRA DIAMANTE
Italian, Florentine, ca. 1430–1498

*Saint Jerome in the Desert with
Saint John and Saint Ansanus*
Tempera on panel
Gift, Edward W. Forbes
1963.111

Fra Diamante was a student and follower of Fra Filippo Lippi and his work is often indistinguishable from that of his master. This panel is noteworthy for its size and quality.

PAUL CEZANNE
French, 1839–1906

Nature Morte à la Commode
ca. 1885
Oil on canvas
1951.46

Painted during his greatest period, Cézanne, one of the most important innovators in modern art, displayed the underlying geometric forms of his subject matter while still capturing the natural light of Impressionism.

CLAUDE MONET   *Gare Saint-Lazare, Paris*
French, 1840–1926   1877
                                    Oil on canvas
                                    1951.53

Monet often chose outdoor subjects to paint in series in varying seasons or times attempting to capture the transient light on his canvas.

VINCENT VAN GOGH   *Self-Portrait*
Dutch, 1853–1890   1888
                                    Oil on canvas
                                    1951.65

This portrait was painted a year before van Gogh was admitted to an insane asylum. Both in color and line he exercised great control but intimations of madness are also visible.

FACILITIES

Guided Tours may be arranged. Call (617)495-2397.

Lectures and *Seminars* by visiting scholars and museum staff may be attended by the public. Call (617)495-4544 for reservations.

Changing Exhibitions are regularly featured.

Concerts are held in the courtyard on Sundays, 4 P.M. Call (617)495-2387 for reservations.

The *Sales Desk* carries postcards, 10¢–35¢; folding cards, 35¢; posters, $1–$5; catalogs, $1–$35.

Hours: Monday–Friday, 9 A.M.–5 P.M.; Saturday, 10 A.M.–5 P.M.; Sunday, 1 P.M.–
        4 P.M.   *Closed:* Weekends between July and September; national
        holidays.

Admission: Free.

MASSACHUSETTS INSTITUTE OF TECHNOLOGY COMMITTEE ON THE VISUAL ARTS
Room 7-145, MIT
77 Massachusetts Ave.
Cambridge, MA 02139
Tel: (617)253-4400

Hayden Gallery
Hayden Memorial Library Bldg.
160 Memorial Dr.
Cambridge, MA 02139
Tel: (617)253-4680

The MIT Committee on the Visual Arts organizes an active program in contemporary visual arts that includes exhibitions in Hayden Gallery and Hayden Corridor Gallery, the MIT permanent collection of fine art, and nonacademic educational activities including lectures, symposia, artist-in-residencies and film series. More than 800 works of art contained in the permanent collection are sited throughout the institute's public spaces and offices. Gallery talks and tours of the collection can be arranged. The focus of the collection is on contemporary art in all mediums with emphasis on large-scale sculpture.

SAMPLING THE COLLECTION

ALEXANDER CALDER
American, 1898–1976

The Big Sail
1966
Painted steel

**McDermott
Court**

One of Calder's major stabiles and also one of his tallest, measuring forty feet in height. A seven-foot model, near the main entrance on Massachusetts Avenue, shows only slight changes were made in the final piece.

Alexander Calder The Big Sail. *Massachusetts Institute of Technology Permanent Collection. Courtesy of MIT Committee on the Visual Arts, Boston*

| Killian Court | HENRY MOORE British, 1898 | *Three Piece Reclining Figure, Draped* 1976 Bronze |

Plaza, Surrounded by Building 66, Landau Building, East Campus Alumni Houses

Moore's later work is executed in bronze generally. His favorite theme, the reclining figure, often is divided into three parts allowing the viewer to walk through it, as in this piece.

| | LOUISE NEVELSON American, b. 1900 | *Transparent Horizon* 1975 Painted steel |

This very large piece is a departure from Nevelson's boxlike constructions. It is one of the many outdoor sculptures she created while investigating materials other than wood, mainly steel.

Westgate Complex (Near Hyatt-Regency Hotel)

| | TONY SMITH American, b. 1912 | *For Marjorie* 1961 Painted steel |

Smith is a Minimalist sculptor whose large, austere works suggest his background in architecture. This monumental sculpture, painted fire-engine red, serves as a ceremonial arch at one end of the campus.

Building E52, Sloan Building, 1st Floor Lobby and Building 13, Bush Building, 1st Floor Lobby

| | LARRY BELL American, b. 1939 | *The Iceberg and Its Shadow* 1976 Inconel and silicon dioxide on plate glass |

Bell's monumental sculpture consists of 56 modular sections constructed of sheets of plate glass. They can be arranged in almost limitless configurations and are often assembled in smaller numbers in several locations simultaneously.

FACILITIES

The *Hayden Gallery* and *Hayden Corridor Gallery* offer an active *Exhibition Program* for contemporary art. Catalogs and brochures are published frequently.

Lectures may be attended. Call for availability.

A *Catalog* of the collection should be used in conjunction with the *Walking Tour* in order to best appreciate the art work.

Hours: The gallery is open 7 days a week, 10 A.M.–4 P.M.; Wednesday evenings, 6 P.M.–9 P.M. *Closed:* Holidays. The outdoor sculpture may be seen at any hour.

Admission: Free.

FITCHBURG

FITCHBURG ART MUSEUM
Merriam Parkway
Fitchburg, MA 01420
Tel: (617)345-4207

Opened in 1928, the museum has grown over the years to provide educational programs and social events as well as changing exhibitions and a permanent collection. The collection contains Fine and Decorative Arts, including furniture, Old Masters, antique silver, tapestries and contemporary paintings.

SAMPLING THE COLLECTION

JOSEPH WRIGHT OF DERBY
British, 1734–1797

Portrait of Sarah Clayton
ca. 1770
Oil on canvas

Wright established himself in Derby and remained there for most of his life. He specialized in lighting effects, particularly those created by moonlight or candlelight.

WILLIAM HARNETT
Irish/American, 1848–1892

Still Life with Bottle of Olives
1877
Oil on canvas

Harnett was a trompe-1'oeil painter of still lifes who chose simple subjects and reproduced them with great accuracy. His realistic renditions of printed matter often looked pasted, anticipating the advent of collage.

EDWARD HOPPER
American, 1882–1967

Two Lights, Maine
Watercolor

Spurning other influences, Hopper developed his own style of painting. His oils and watercolors were spare, tranquil and desolate, evoking feelings of loneliness and anonymity.

JOAN MIRO
Spanish, b. 1893

Trace sur le Parois
Color lithograph

Miró, an Abstract Surrealist, paints with great humor. He uses a brilliant palette to create his fanciful works.

FACILITIES

Gallery Talks on exhibitions can be arranged by any interested group.

Temporary Exhibitions culled from the museum's collection or *Loan Exhibitions* from other institutions are regular features of the museum's programs.

Poetry in the Galleries features poetry readings by distinguished poets.

The *Museum Shop* features inexpensive items.

Hours: Tuesday–Saturday, 9 A.M.–5 P.M.; Sunday, 2 P.M.–5 P.M. *Closed:* Mondays, New Year's, Thanksgiving, Christmas.

Admission: Free.

LINCOLN

DE CORDOVA MUSEUM
Sandy Pond Rd.
Lincoln, MA 01773
Tel: (617)259–8355

The museum opened in 1938 in a castlelike structure located in a beautifully landscaped 33-acre sculpture park. It is dedicated to the collection and exhibition of contemporary art although its 800 pieces include every style from

Exterior view. Courtesy De Cordova Museum, Lincoln

traditional landscapes and marine scenes to Op Art, Pop Art, Super-Realism, neon sculpture and contemporary crafts. Its major concentration is on the work of New England artists, those of major reputations and particularly those who are yet unknown.

SAMPLING THE COLLECTION

The works listed below are shown on a rotating basis and therefore may not be on view at this time.

FRANZ KLINE   *Figure*
American, 1910–1962   1956
                                               Oil on canvas
After viewing fragments of his own representational paintings Kline turned to

Abstraction. His large canvases give equal exposure to the architecturally constructed blacks and whites in which he composes broad-brushed calligraphic-like paintings.

LEONARD BASKIN
American, b. 1922

Tobias and the Angel
1952
Lithograph

Baskin's creations are generally concerned with death or man's moral decadence. His Expressionist works, influenced by European sculptured tombs, combine yesterday's art with today's beliefs.

BARRY LEWIS
American, b. 1939

Thank You Dr. Watson
1971
Serigraph

Lewis translates man's recent knowledge of the universe into artistic interpretations which are in his own words "structured, linear and rational."

MARTHA JANE BRADFORD
American, b. 1946

Notre Dame from Le Pont de Archevêché
1976
Serigraph

Bradford's color produces a feeling of atmosphere that touches the emotions. Selective realism maintains a balance between the quiet of the foreground and the activity of the partly obscured background.

FACILITIES

Changing Exhibitions of the works of regional artists are presented.

The *Amphitheater* is a woodsy setting for the *Concerts, Dance* and *Theatrical Programs* offered during the summer months.

The *Sales Desk* carries catalogs of past and present exhibitions.

Hours: Tuesday–Friday, 10 A.M.–5 P.M.; Saturday, 12 P.M.–5 P.M.; Sunday, 1:30 P.M.–5 P.M.; Wednesday evening, 5 P.M.;–9:30 P.M. *Closed:* Mondays.

Admission: Adults $1.50; children (under 21), 50¢

MILTON

MUSEUM OF THE AMERICAN CHINA TRADE
215 Adams St.
Milton, MA 02186
Tel: (617)696–1815

The museum was established in 1965 and reorganized in 1971 to illustrate the importance of early American trade with East Asia in this country's maritime and industrial growth. The collections are housed in two buildings, the 1833 Captain Robert Bennett Forbes House, a modified Greek Revival mansion declared a National Historic Landmark, and the 1800 Dr. Amos Holbrook House, a Federal mansion. The Chinese Export Art is especially strong in examples of ceramics, pewter, silver and furniture as well as in photographic and documentary material. A portrait of Houqua (1769–1843), the leading Chinese merchant to deal with the American China Traders, hangs in the ca. 1850 Chinese parlor. Over 3,000 examples of Chinese export porcelain range from 1600 to 1900 and include plates from services of George Washington, Paul Revere and Thomas Jefferson. There are 750 examples on permanent view in the Ceramic Study Gallery.

SAMPLING THE COLLECTION

**China
Trade
Gallery**

CHINESE
Ch'ing Dynasty, 1644–1912

Pair of Teapots
ca. 1730
Silver with gilt highlights

These finely wrought teapots were made by Cantonese artisans for the British market. The finials and applied and chased decoration have been fire gilded.

**Chinese
Parlor**

CHINESE
Ch'ing Dynasty, 1644–1912

Punch bowl
ca. 1800
Porcelain

This punch bowl decorated at Canton was made for the Scottish market.

**Furniture
Gallery**

CHINESE
Ch'ing Dynasty, 1644–1912

Tea Table
ca. 1770
Enamel on copper with inset panels
in rose palette decor

An enameled tray serves as the top of this lacquered table which was made for the European market.

Chinese Export Punchbowl. *Courtesy Museum of the American China Trade, Milton*

FACILITIES

Special Lectures on the China Trade and related topics are presented.

The *Archive* contains documents, original and microfilmed, of information pertaining to the American China Trade.

The *Museum Shop* stocks articles from the People's Republic of China similar to those available in the early China Trade. There are nests of lacquer trays and boxes; Canton enamel; export porcelain; and special needlepoint designs, wallpapers and fabrics based on museum treasures. Prices range from $1 to $125.

Hours: Tuesday–Saturday, 1 P.M.–4 P.M. Group tours by appointment in mornings. *Closed:* Sundays; Mondays, holidays.

Admission: Adults, $3; students with I.D., $1.50.

NORTHAMPTON

SMITH COLLEGE MUSEUM OF ART
Tyron Hall
Elm St. at Bedford Terrace
Northampton, MA 01063
Tel: (413)584–2700, ext. 2236

The collection was founded in 1879 and has outgrown three homes. It has been housed since 1973 in a three-story structure, part of a large Fine Arts center. The building is approached from the inner campus by a sculpture courtyard whose mirrored glass windows seem to double its size and from which one may glimpse the main gallery. Fabric-covered wooden walls, movable partitions, natural lighting and easily accessible storage space create an atmosphere where staff, students and visitors can use the collection to greatest advantage. The collection embraces Classical, medieval, Renaissance and 19th- and 20th-century art, but its most comprehensive holdings are in its 19th-century paintings.

SAMPLING THE COLLECTION

EGYPTIAN
New Kingdom, Dynasty XX,
1200–1085 B.C.

Jackal-Headed God Anubis
ca. 1100 B.C.
Black granite

Anubis, the Egyptian god of the dead, was portrayed with the body of a man and the head of a jackal or dog.

DIRK BOUTS
Dutch, 1420–1475

Portrait of a Young Man
ca. 1462
Silverpoint on a white paper

Bouts was a particularly adept landscapist. Although his figures were stilted and unfeeling, he was an accomplished portraitist.

MATHIAS GRUNEWALD
German, ca. 1466–1528

Study of Drapery
ca. 1512
Black chalk on tan paper

Grünewald was aware of Renaissance techniques but his work was mainly influenced by Gothic ideas. There are very few of his drawings extant.

JOHN SINGLETON COPLEY
American, 1738–1815

The Honorable John Erving
ca. 1772
Oil on canvas

Copley was the most prominent portraitist in Colonial America. Before taking up residence in England, he painted many penetrating, meticulously executed portraits of New England personages.

JEAN-BAPTISTE CAMILLE COROT
French, 1796–1875

Jumièges
ca. 1830
Oil on canvas

In 1825, Corot traveled to Italy, where he evolved a style dependent on tonal relationships instead of line or color. His naturalism was replaced by a hazy silver-green treatment emulated by later painters.

GUSTAVE COURBET
French, 1819–1877

Preparation of the Dead Girl
(formerly known as *Preparation of the Bride)*
1850–1855
Oil on canvas (unfinished)

M. Nodler, the Elder, at Trouville
1865
Oil on canvas

Courbet was a dedicated Realist who endowed his paintings with forceful naturalism. His reactions to academic art and to French politics in particular resulted in his exile to Switzerland.

HILAIRE GERMAIN EDGAR DEGAS
French, 1834–1917

Portrait of René de Gas
ca. 1855
Oil on canvas

Jephthah's Daughter
ca. 1861–1864
Oil on canvas (unfinished)

Influenced by Ingres, Degas's early family portraits and paintings were in the academic tradition. They were acutely insightful and showed evidence of fine draftsmanship.

CLAUDE MONET
French, 1840–1926

The Seine at Bougival
1869
Oil on canvas

Field of Poppies
1890
Oil on canvas

The Seine at Bougival was painted at the outset of Monet's career before the term *Impressionism* had been coined. *Field of Poppies* was completed when he was famous and about to embark on his great series paintings.

PAUL CEZANNE
French, 1839–1906

La Route Tournante à la Roche-Guyon
ca. 1885
Oil on canvas (unfinished)

From this period on Cézanne brought a solidity to Impressionism which was expressed in the underlying geometric forms of his canvases. This development greatly influenced Cubism and modern art.

Gustave Courbet, The Preparation of the Dead Girl. *Courtesy Smith College Museum of Art, Northampton*

HENRI FANTIN-LATOUR
French, 1836–1904

Portrait of Mr. Becker
1886
Oil on canvas

Although Fantin-Latour is today most appreciated for his floral pieces, his sober portraits of unadorned realism are also notable. Although friend of the Impressionists, he never adopted their style.

EDWIN ROMANZO ELMER
American, 1850–1923

Mourning Picture
1890
Oil on canvas

Elmer, a primitive, self-taught artist, was also a jack of many trades, inventing several practical machines. Portraits of dead children were popular subjects among 19th-century painters.

EDOUARD VUILLARD
French, 1868–1940

The Suitor (also called *The Workshop;* formerly called *Interior at L'Étang-la-ville*)
1893
Oil on millboard panel

Vuillard painted simple, intimate subjects. His early works were decorative and boldly patterned in flat colors. He believed that a painting should not be a separate entity but should complement its setting.

CHILDE HASSAM   *Union Square in Spring*
American, 1859–1935   1896
                              Oil on canvas

Hassam painted gaily colored Impressionistic pictures of New York City and the countryside. He also painted rural New England landscapes.

THOMAS EAKINS   *Mrs. Edith Mahon*
American, 1844–1916   1904
                              Oil on canvas

Eakins, a Realist, rendered paintings in careful anatomical detail with great integrity. Forced from the Pennsylvania Academy after posing a nude male model before his class, he continued to paint family and friends.

ERNST LUDWIG KIRCHNER   *Dodo and Her Brother*
German, 1880–1938   1908–1920
                              Oil on canvas

Kirchner was a founder of *Die Brücke,* the German equivalent of the French Fauves movement. His canvases, rendered in shrill color with intensely distorted forms, always maintained a sense of the German Gothic.

AUGUSTE RODIN   *Walking Man*
French, 1840–1917   1911
                              Bronze

Rodin's sensitively modeled sculptures impart a real feeling of movement. He was much esteemed during his lifetime. *Walking Man* and *Torso* culminated in the sculpture, *John the Baptist.*

JUAN GRIS   *Glasses and Newspaper*
Spanish, 1887–1927   1913–1914
                              Oil, watercolor and crayon
                              on paper

Gris embraced Cubism after Braque and Picasso, bringing tangible elements to its architectonic shapes. He later incorporated collage and color in his work, becoming an early proponent of Synthetic Cubism.

PIERRE BONNARD   *Norman Landscape*
French, 1867–1947   1920 (completed later)
                              Oil on canvas

Bonnard's early decorative paintings of intimate interiors were restrained in color and influenced by Japanese prints. He replaced this style with an Impressionistic one and, still later, combined features from both styles.

CHARLES SHEELER   *Rolling Power*
American, 1883–1965   1939
                              Oil on canvas

Sheeler portrayed precise close-up scenes of industrial subjects which became less factual with time.

FRANK STELLA   *Damascus Gate (Variation III)*
American, b. 1936   1969
                              Oil on canvas

Stella's geometrically shaped and strongly colored canvases have become three-dimensional, suggesting a fine line between painting and sculpture.

FACILITIES

Tours of the collection are offered.

Changing Exhibitions are regularly featured.

Storage Areas of paintings, decorative arts and prints not on view are available for study to visitors by appointment with the registrar.

The *Museum Documentary Files* may be used by scholars.

The *Sales Desk* carries exhibition catalogs and posters and postcards.

Hours: *September–May:* Tuesday–Saturday, 11 A.M.–4:30 P.M.; Sunday, 2 P.M.–4:30 P.M. *June:* weekdays by appointment. *July–August:* Tuesday–Saturday, 1 P.M.–4 P.M. *Closed:* Mondays, New Year's, July 4, Labor Day, Thanksgiving, Christmas.

Admission: Free.

PITTSFIELD

BERKSHIRE MUSEUM
39 South St.
Pittsfield, MA 01201
Tel: (413)442–6373

The museum, founded in 1903, is a lively institution of art, science and history. Its permanent collection contains art from Egyptian to modern times including Old Masters, American art, Far Eastern art and American and English silver. There are additional galleries devoted to Minerals, Biology, Animals, Birds and Man, plus a historical room displaying local memorabilia.

SAMPLING THE COLLECTION

Most of the works, except those noted, are shown on a rotating basis.

ATT. TO AMMI PHILLIPS   *Mrs. Goodrich and Child*
American, 1788–1865   Oil on canvas
Phillips was an itinerant painter of folk portraits, executing over 1,000 canvases in his lifetime. When compared to existing daguerreotypes, it is apparent that he achieved good likenesses.

GEORGE H. DURRIE   *Winter Scene*
American, 1820–1863   1860
                                          Oil
Durrie was a landscapist. His depictions of wintertime in New England became famous when they were reproduced in prints by Currier and Ives.

FRANCIS PICABIA   *Force Comique*
French, 1878–1953   Transparent watercolor
Beginning as an Impressionist, Picabia's work later espoused Cubist, Dadaist and Surrealist teachings. His abstract circumscribed forms are arranged to evoke a specific subject.

ALEXANDER CALDER
American, 1898–1976

Arc and the Quadrant
1932
Wire and red ball

This motor-driven mobile evolved from the wire sculptures Calder constructed after exposure to the Parisian circus. These led him, in turn, to the creation of his famous wind mobiles.

**American
Portrait
Gallery**

CHARLES WILLSON PEALE
American, 1741–1827

Portrait of General David Forman
Oil on canvas

Peale was a competent portraitist who painted many Revolutionary War heroes. He was an energetic man as passionately interested in the natural sciences as in the arts.

**Old Masters
Gallery**

JUAN PONS
Spanish, act. 1476–1492

Adoration of the Magi
1477
Oil, transferred from wood
to canvas

Pons painted in Valencia and was known to have done several altars there.

**Old Masters
Gallery**

JOACHIM PATINIR
Flemish, ca. 1485–1524

The Flight into Egypt
Oil

Patinir painted landscapes. His favorite theme was *The Flight into Egypt.* His narratives were set against fanciful scenery in which blues predominate. He often employed others to paint the figures.

Joachim Patinir, The Flight into Egypt. *Courtesy Berkshire Museum, Pittsfield*

ANTHONY VAN DYCK   *Duke of Richmond*   **Old Masters**
Flemish, 1599–1641   after 1632   **Gallery**
                               Oil on canvas
After working in Italy, Van Dyck, once Rubens's principal assistant, became
painter to the English court under Charles I. His elegant portraits influenced
English style in the 17th century.

FACILITIES

Lectures, some accompanied by films, are offered in the winter program.

Changing Exhibitions are regularly featured.

Musicales are held from time to time.

Films from all countries are screened continuously during the summer.

The *Corner Shop's* most popular items are museum reproductions of jewelry
and artifacts. Children enjoy minerals and models of prehistoric animals. Prices
range from 5¢ to $200.

Hours: Tuesday–Saturday, 10 A.M.–5 P.M.; Sunday, 2 P.M.–5 P.M. *Closed:* Mon-
          days except July–August, New Year's Day, July 4, Thanksgiving,
          Christmas.

Admission: Free. Adults are invited to make a contribution.

ROXBURY

MUSEUM, NATIONAL CENTER OF
AFRO-AMERICAN ARTISTS
300 Walnut Ave.
Roxbury, MA 02119
Tel: (617)442–8820

The museum is allied with the Boston Museum of Fine Arts which assisted in
its establishment and continues to help in its development. The collection
consists of over 172 African objects and 234 Afro-American paintings, prints
and photographs.

SAMPLING THE COLLECTION

AFRICAN   *Drum*
Ghana, Ashanti Tribe   Wood and animal skin
Ashanti society forbids depiction of the human form so there are no masks or
statues. Their decorations are sometimes representational and sometimes convey proverbial teaching.

EDWARD MITCHELL BANNISTER   *Untitled Landscape*
Afro-American, 1828–1901   ca. 1885
                               Watercolor
Bannister was a painter who lived and worked in Boston and Providence. His
Barbizon-like landscapes made him an important figure among the artists who
established a visual culture in Providence in the latter part of the 19th century.

WEST AFRICAN   *Pot*
Cameroon, Tikar Tribe   Brass
The lost wax technique was employed in the making of this vessel. The pot must

Drum. *Courtesy of National Center of Afro-American Artists, Boston*

be an old one because the Tikar no longer work in brass. Elaborately decorated with human, bird and reptilian motifs, its stopper is a buffalo's head.

FACILITIES

The museum features *Changing Exhibitions,* both historical and contemporary, of Afro-American as well as African and West Indian art.

A *Slide Library* is available for use on the premises or for short-term, local loans.

The *Sales Shop* offers prints and jewelry ranging in price from $3 to $75.

Hours: Tuesday–Friday, 10 A.M.–5 P.M.; Saturday, Sunday, 12 P.M.–4 P.M.
Closed: Mondays, holidays.

Admission: Adults, $1.25; children over 12, 75¢.

SOUTH HADLEY

MOUNT HOLYOKE COLLEGE ART MUSEUM
South Hadley, Ma 01075
Tel: (413)538-2245

The museum is quartered in the Art Building, a brick and concrete structure with classic modern lines erected in 1971. The permanent collection consists of Egyptian, Greek, Roman, medieval and Asian art and European and American prints, drawings, paintings and sculpture.

SAMPLING THE COLLECTION

GREEK   *Statuette of an Athlete*   **Ancient**
                                           ca. 475 B.C.   **Gallery**
                                           Bronze
This heroic athlete captures, on a small scale, something of the grandeur of ancient Greek sculpture. The youth was probably pouring a libation from a vessel in his right hand.

WEN CHENG-MING   *Scroll Painting*   **Oriental**
Chinese, 1470–1559   **Gallery**
Wen was the consummate gentleman, a scholar, poet, calligrapher, painter and a man of discriminating taste. His expertise with the paintbrush enabled him to paint in a variety of styles.

WANG HUI   *Scroll Painting*   **Oriental**
Chinese, 1632–1717   **Gallery**
Wang borrowed from many Old Masters and really had no individual style. He produced a large body of distinguished work.

DUCCIO DI BUONINSEGNA   Panel from *Maesta*   **Medieval**
Italian, Sienese, ca. 1255–1319   early 14th c.   **Gallery**
                                           Tempera
Although his paintings depended largely on Byzantine traditions, Duccio's work shows intimations of the Gothic style. His powerful narrations were infused with his own brand of humanism.

Exterior view. Courtesy Mount Holyoke College Art Museum, South Hadley

Main   ALBERT BIERSTADT   *Hetch-Hetchy Canyon*
Gallery   American, 1830–1902   ca. 1876
                                                          Oil on canvas
Bierstadt's paintings of the American Western wilderness enjoyed great popularity in his lifetime. He elaborated the sketches he made on a Western trip into enormous canvases.

Main   GEORGE INNESS   *Conway Meadows*
Gallery   American, 1825–1894   1876
                                                          Oil on canvas
Inness was a landscapist who painted in the Romantic tradition. His grand early scenes were followed by works of hazy silver tones in a mystical vein.

FACILITIES

Group Tours given by trained guides may be arranged by contacting the museum.

Changing Exhibitions are regularly featured.

Postcards and note cards of objects in the collection as well as *catalogs* from past and present exhibitions are for sale.

Hours: *September–May:* Monday–Friday, 11 A.M.–5 P.M. Saturday–Sunday, 1 P.M.–5 P.M. *June–August:* Monday–Friday, 1 P.M.–4 P.M. *Closed:* Major holidays.

Admission: Free.

SPRINGFIELD

GEORGE WALTER VINCENT SMITH ART MUSEUM
222 State St.
Springfield, MA 01103
Tel: (413)733-4214

The Italian Renaissance building was opened to the public in 1895. It is constructed of buff-colored Pompeian brick with terracotta ornamentation. A frieze, high across the front, is modeled after that of the library of the Ducal Palace in Venice. The two-story museum, consisting of nine large galleries and two smaller ones, contains a large terrazzo-tiled entrance hall featuring a wide oak-paneled staircase. The collection houses 17th- and 18th-century Japanese gold lacquer writing boxes and accoutrements; cloisonné pieces from the 15th to the 19th century; Near Eastern carpets; European furniture and paintings from the 16th to the 19th century; Chinese and Japanese ceramics including Imari ware, Satsuma brocadeware and *sang-de-boeuf* porcelain; 19th-century American paintings; objects of jade, ivory, lacquer, crystal and amethystine quartz; plaster casts of ancient and Renaissance sculpture; and Japanese armor.

SAMPLING THE COLLECTION

MIOCHIN NOBUIYE Japanese, 16th c.	*Helmet* Iron, shakudo, leather, lacquer	**1st Floor,** **Japanese** **Armor Room**

At times in Japan decorative rather than practical armor was demanded. Commencing in the mid-12th century the Miochin family became the court armormakers for six centuries. Their product was thin and light but very tough.

FREDERIC EDWIN CHURCH American, 1826–1900	*Scene in the Catskills* 1851 Oil	**2nd Floor,** **19th-c.** **American**

Church is among the second generation of landscape painters from the Hudson **Painting** River School. He carefully depicted the grandeur of nature, paying particular **Gallery** attention to light and atmosphere.

NAMIKAWA SOSUKE Japanese, 1847–1910	*Tray Portraying 2 Doves* Basse-taille enamel	**2nd Floor** **Landing,**

Sosuke founded a school of enameling in Tokyo which developed a new **Top of Main** method of making cloisonné enamel. The metal partitions (cloisons) were con- **Staircase** cealed, enhancing the pictorial quality of the design.

FACILITIES

Changing Exhibitions are regularly featured.

A *Sales Desk* carries catalogs of some of the collection and of special exhibitions from $2 to $10.

Hours: Tuesday–Sunday, 12 P.M.–5 P.M. *Closed:* Mondays, national holidays.
Admission: Free.

MUSEUM OF FINE ARTS
49 Chestnut St.
Springfield, MA 01103
Tel: (413)733–5857

The museum, founded in 1933, is located in a quadrangle shared by the George Walter Vincent Smith Art Museum, the Connecticut Valley Historical Museum, the Science Museum and the City Library. In eighteen intimate galleries around a central court are displayed European and American painting and sculpture from the 14th century to the present and Chinese bronzes and ceramics. Japanese prints, Italian chiaroscuro prints and early 20th-century American prints are highlights of the graphics collection that can be seen in periodic changing exhibitions.

SAMPLING THE COLLECTION

17th-c.
Dutch
Gallery

JAN JOSEPHSZ VAN GOYEN
Dutch, 1596–1656

River View with Leyden
in the Background
1651
Oil on wood panel

Van Goyen was one of Holland's finest landscapists. His mature works of simple tonal compositions are predominantly light green and yellow-brown in color.

Venetian
and French
18th-c.
Gallery

GIOVANNI BATTISTA TIEPOLO
Italian, 1696–1770

Madonna and Child
1759
Oil on canvas

Tiepolo was the foremost 18th-century Rococo painter. His decorative and theatrical style was much in demand and his work graced many churches and palaces.

Venetian
and French
18th-c.
Gallery

JEAN-BAPTISTE-SIMEON CHARDIN
French, 1699–1779

Still Life (Rafraîchissements)
1764
Oil on canvas

Chardin was a genre and still-life painter of familiar homely subject matter depicted in solid color and constructed in a forthright manner. Possibly the finest painting in the collection.

Central
Court

ERASTUS SALISBURY FIELD
American, 1805–1900

Historical Monument of the
American Republic
ca. 1876
Oil on canvas

Field, a primitive painter, executed this picture in commemoration of the 100th anniversary of American independence. It took two years to complete and represents his own peculiar vision of the American dream.

WILLIAM MICHAEL HARNETT   *Emblems of Peace*   **Central**
Irish/American, 1848–1892   1890   **Court**
Oil on canvas
Harnett painted boldly composed trompe-l'oeil still lifes of ordinary objects.
These precisely naturalistic pictures often included printed matter forecasting
the later use of collage.

William M. Harnett, Emblem of Peace. *Courtesy Museum of Fine Arts, Springfield*

GEORGIA O'KEEFFE   *New Mexican Landscape*   **Lower**
American, b. 1887   1930   **Corridor**
Oil on canvas   **South**
O'Keeffe has long been attracted to the Southwest, where she paints natural
subjects in a semiabstract style.

CLAUDE MONET   *Haystack*   **Upper**
French, 1840–1926   1893   **Corridor**
Oil on canvas   **North**
One of a series of haystack paintings Monet painted in his mature years at
Giverny. He painted these in different seasons and different hours, seeking to
capture the evanescent light on canvas.

FACILITIES

A program of *Tours, Lectures, Gallery Talks, Films* and *Concerts* is offered. Call for further information.

Changing Exhibitions are regularly featured.

The *Sales Shop* has a selection of cookbooks, postcards, note paper, catalogs, jewelry and handcrafted items from $1 to $75.

Hours: Tuesday–Sunday, 12 P.M.–5 P.M. *Closed:* Mondays, national holidays.

Admission: Free.

STOCKBRIDGE

CHESTERWOOD
Off Rte. 183, Glendale, MA
Follow signs from west end
of Main St.
Stockbridge, MA 01262
Tel: (413)298-3579

Exterior view. Courtesy Chesterwood, Stockbridge

Chesterwood was "heaven" to Daniel Chester French, the American sculptor who built his studio and summer retreat in the Berkshire Hills of Massachusetts. French engaged his friend, architect Henry Bacon, to design the studio in 1898 and the Colonial Revival residence in 1900–1901. The two men later collaborated on the Lincoln Memorial in Washington, D.C. French modeled the famous statue of Lincoln. Among the architectural innovations in the studio design were a pair of 23-foot-high doors and a modeling table on railroad tracks that enabled French to roll his monumental sculptures outdoors to see their effect in natural light.

SAMPLING THE COLLECTION

DANIEL CHESTER FRENCH   *Seated Lincoln*   **Studio**
American, 1850–1931   1916
      Plaster cast
The original sculpture, made of Georgian white marble, graces the front of the Lincoln Memorial in Washington, D.C. French's first attempt at this commission was only 10 feet high and he soon realized that it would be dwarfed in the massive hall. The present statue is nearly double in size. Both versions in plaster are on view.

      The Minute Man   **Barn**
      1889–1890
      Bronze study reduction,
Erected at North Bridge for the centennial of the Battle of Concord, French, although unknown at the time, succeeded in creating one of the most famous American statues.

FACILITIES

Guided Tours

The *Barn Sculpture Gallery* has been remodeled into an exhibition gallery where sketches and working models of some of French's works are displayed.

The *Residence* is open for viewing.

Please Touch Area

Nature Trail

Picnic Area

A *Sales Shop* sells books on historic preservation, sculpture, art and New England. There are also reproductions. Prices range from 10¢ to $50.

Hours: *June–Labor Day:* Daily and holidays, 10 A.M.–5 P.M. Weekends through Columbus Day.

Admission: Adults, $1; children, 25¢. Group rate available.

WALTHAM

ROSE ART MUSEUM, BRANDEIS UNIVERSITY
415 South St.
Waltham, MA 02145
Tel: (617)647-2402

Exterior view. Courtesy Rose Art Museum, Waltham

Opened in 1961, the museum, a boxlike structure of glass and stone, was enlarged in 1974, making more exhibition and storage space available. The collection is composed of 19th- and 20th-century American and European paintings and sculpture, modern painting being well represented with Post-Impressionist, School of Paris, Cubist and early 20th-century American works. It is particularly rich in Abstract Expressionism, Pop Art, Color Field painting and recent examples of figurative painting. There are also ceramics featuring French faïence fine, English cream-colored ware and canary yellow ware; Oceanic Art and Tibetan Buddhist Art.

SAMPLING THE COLLECTION

The following paintings are on periodic display. They may be seen by appointment at any time.

JASPER JOHNS   *Drawer*
American, b. 1930   1957
                                     Encaustic and assemblage on canvas
By painting ordinary images in an unusual manner, Johns jars our perception into new ways of seeing them.

WILLEM DE KOONING   *Untitled*
American, b. 1904   1961
                                     Oil on canvas

De Kooning, an Abstract Expressionist, is particularly known for his series of brightly colored *Woman* pictures. In the late 1950s he returned to the abstraction of broadly brushed architectural compositions.

ROBERT MOTHERWELL   *Elegy to the Spanish Republic,*
American, b. 1915   *No. 58*
     1957–1961
     Oil on canvas
Motherwell, an Abstract Expressionist, painted nearly 150 variations on this theme expressing his concern over the Spanish revolution. Black and white paintings are composed of ovals set between broad strips.

WILLIAM BECKMAN   *Double Nude*
American, b. 1941   1978
     Oil on canvas
Beckman's realistic canvases are meticulously rendered. He most frequently paints scenes of upper New York State.

GREGORY GILLESPIE   *Self-Portrait*
American, b. 1936   1976–1977
     Oil on masonite
Gillespie often paints his studio surroundings using trompe-l'oeil effects that lend mystery to ordinary objects. His self-portraits are intensely subjective.

WILLIAM BAILEY   *Manfroni Still Life*
American, b. 1930   1978
     Oil on canvas
Bailey paints simple objects on bare surfaces set against plain backgrounds, the whole bathed in even golden light. His subtly colored, detached and precise work appears tranquil and serene.

FRENCH   *Tureen*
     ca. 1815–1833
     Faïence fine
Faïence fine is a high-fired earthenware produced during the Napoleonic era in an attempt to imitate the fine porcelain of China.

ENGLISH   *Chocolate Pot*
     ca. 1810
     Earthenware with canary
     yellow ground
High-fired earthenware produced by the English was opaque and porous. Chocolate was introduced in England in the mid-17th century, at first a drink only the wealthy could afford.

AUSTRALIAN   *Ancestor Figure*   **Schwartz**
Arnhem Land   Wood, traces of red, black   **Hall**
     and white pigment
Mythical-religious traditions revolve around supernatural figures, ancestors and heroes who created an unchanging natural world. Unbroken tradition has resulted in an art whose designs have remained the same.

MELANESIAN   *Trophy Head*   **Schwartz**
Solomon Islands   predates Westernization   **Hall**
     Human skull, wood, clay, fiber,
     mother-of-pearl
These people believed that spiritual and bodily health were derived from the power inside heads captured by their hunters. Heads were modeled over the skulls, painted black and decorated with shells.

TIBETAN BUDDHIST ART

Approximately 200 items include examples of tankas (painted scrolls) from all the major art-producing areas of Tibet. A diamond scepter and bell, central to Tibetan Buddhist ceremonies, are among the ritual objects. This collection is not always on view.

FACILITIES

Changing Exhibitions are regularly featured.

Gallery Talks and *Lectures* by the staff or visiting authorities are frequently offered.

The *Sales Desk* carries exhibition catalogs, $1 to $10.

Hours: Tuesday–Sunday, 1 P.M.–5 P.M. *Closed:* Major holidays.

Admission: Free.

WELLESLEY

WELLESLEY COLLEGE MUSEUM, JEWETT ARTS CENTER
Wellesley, MA 02181
Tel: (617)235–0320

Jewett Arts Center is the first major commission ever received by the architect Paul Rudolph (b. 1918). The museum, founded in 1883, is flanked by two wings housing music, art and theater functions. Made of pink brick and concrete, Rudolph's nascent style with organic curving slabs and forms of concrete are barely visible in the piers that support and piece the building. The collection's special strengths are in antique art, Baroque painting, early 20th-century European art and 19th-century and Renaissance sculpture.

SAMPLING THE COLLECTION

Since exhibitions are constantly being changed the following selections may not always be on view.

PAUL CEZANNE   *Portrait Romantique*
French, 1839–1906   1868–1870
                                      Oil on canvas

Cézanne painted this early work in Romantic style still influenced by academic painters. Nevertheless it exhibits some of the solidity and forthrightness of his later work.

FERNAND LEGER   *Mother and Child*
French, 1881–1955   1921
                                      Oil on canvas

Léger, a member of the second generation of Cubist painters, achieved this lively picture through his manipulation of formal elements rather than human, psychological components.

Fernand Léger, Mother and Child. *Courtesy Wellesley College Museum, Wellesley*

KENNETH NOLAND   *Celestalert*
American, b. 1924   1964
                                  Acrylic on canvas
This large striking painting represents Noland as a Hard Edge painter and demonstrates notions which steered the art of the 1960s.

Marble   POLYCLITUS   Roman copy of *Athlete* or
Sculpture   Greek, act. 450–420 B.C.   *Discophoros*
Court   3rd quarter of 1st C. B.C.
                                                  Marble
Polyclitus believed in an arithmetical system of sculpture. Each part of the figure had specific dimensions complete in itself but subordinate to the whole. This is one of the finest copies in America.

FACILITIES

Changing Exhibitions are regularly featured.

Guided Tours, Lectures and *Gallery Talks* are frequently offered.

Concerts by the Music Department are performed in the gallery and sculpture court.

A *Sales Desk* carries postcards, 10¢–20¢, and exhibition catalogs, $2–$20.

Hours: Monday–Saturday, 10 A.M.–5 P.M.; Sunday, 2 P.M.–5 P.M. *Closed:* Summers.

Admission: Free.

WILLIAMSTOWN

STERLING AND FRANCINE CLARK ART INSTITUTE
South St.
Williamstown, MA 01267
Tel: (413)458–8109

Williamstown, with its educational and cultural advantages and natural beauty, was the Clarks' choice for an institute to house their collections. The Classical white building, opened in 1955, is located in a pastoral setting off a quiet street. The galleries, designed on a domestic scale, suggest a private residence. A red granite addition serves as the main entrance offering more gallery space and facilities. The collections include paintings, sculpture, prints, drawings, silver, furniture and china.

SAMPLING THE COLLECTION

The locations are not noted as they change frequently.

PIERO DELLA FRANCESCA   *Virgin and Child Enthroned*
Italian, ca. 1420–1492   *with Four Angels*
                                   Tempera/oil on panel
Piero is a major Quattrocento painter. His mathematical arrangement of space and delicate coloring lend his work a certain tranquillity.

JEAN-HONORE FRAGONARD
French, 1732–1806

Portrait of a Man (The Warrior)
late 1760s
Oil on canvas

One of a Fantasy Portraits series Fragonard painted, it is remarkable for its bravura and spontaneity of brushwork. Like his others, it was probably done in a short period of time.

PIERRE AUGUSTE RENOIR
French, 1841–1919

Sleeping Girl with a Cat
1880
Oil on canvas

More than 30 Renoir canvases, painted over 35 years, are usually on display. Primarily a figure painter, Renoir is known as an Impressionist. His work evolved from the spontaneous transmission of visual images on canvas to a studied application of color by which he interpreted nature.

WINSLOW HOMER
American, 1836–1910

Bridle Path, White Mountains
1867
Oil on canvas

Homer's love of the outdoors persisted throughout his life. He was largely self-taught and little influenced by other artists. He painted our best records of the country life of his time.

Winslow Homer, The Bridle Path, White Mountains. *Courtesy Sterling and Francine Clark Art Institute, Williamstown*

CLAUDE MONET
French, 1840–1926

Rouen Cathedral, the Façade in Sunlight
1894
Oil on canvas

One of the famous series on Rouen Cathedral, this painting is a bold mix of many colors, all of which combine in our eye to give the impression of the façade of the cathedral.

PAUL DE LAMERIE   *Cup and Cover*
British, 1688–1751   1742
                                   Silver
De Lamerie's two-handled cup is characteristic of the high Rococo with exuberant decoration covering the entire piece.

ALBRECHT DURER   *Knight, Death and the Devil*
German, 1471–1528   Engraving
Dürer is considered an equal of the Italian Renaissance masters. His copperplate engravings are thought to be his greatest works. He was one of the first to use drypoint engraving, to experiment with etching and to introduce portraits and landscapes to engraving. This is one of his three master prints.

PETER PAUL RUBENS   *Portrait of Thomas Howard,*
Flemish, 1577–1640   *Earl of Arundel*
                                   Brush and brown and black ink
                                   (oil?), brown and gray wash,
                                   heightened with white, with
                                   touches of red
The Earl of Arundel, in this drawing for a painting now at the Gardner Museum in Boston, is clad in armor looking out at us in this vivid interpretation of character.

MARY CASSATT   *Woman with Baby*
American, 1845–1926   Pastel on paper
Having been advised and influenced by Degas, most of Cassatt's work is in the Impressionist style. She specialized in mothers and children.

HILAIRE GERMAIN EDGAR DEGAS   *The Entrance of the*
French, 1834–1917   *Masked Dancers*
                                   Pastel on paper
Degas radicalized the use of pastels. The primary colors here, red, yellow and blue, are used to great advantage.

JEAN-BAPTISTE CAMILLE COROT   *The Castel Sant'Angelo, Rome*
French, 1796–1875   Oil on canvas
Corot was one of the outstanding landscapists of the 19th century. This painting was made after Corot had visited Italy several times.

ADOLPHE WILLIAM BOUGUEREAU   *Nymphs and Satyr*
French, 1825–1905   1873
                                   Oil on canvas
Bouguereau, a prominent teacher, critic and painter, did large paintings of myths and allegories. Presiding over the annual Salon of the Institute of Paris, he rejected any experimental work, especially that of the Impressionists.

JOSEPH MALLORD WILLIAM
TURNER   *Rockets and Blue Lights*
British, 1775–1851   *(close at hand) to Warn*
                                   Steamboats of Shoal Water
                                   1840
                                   Oil on canvas
Turner, possibly the greatest English painter to date, began his career as a topographical draftsman. He turned from recording details to interpreting nature's moods.

THOMAS GAINSBOROUGH
British, 1727–1788

Miss Linley and Her Brother
ca. 1768
Oil on canvas

Gainsborough, renowned for his portraits, preferred to paint landscapes. His only serious rival in portraiture was Joshua Reynolds but Gainsborough's less formal and more imaginative treatment of his subjects was often preferred.

FACILITIES

Gallery Talks are scheduled during the summer months at 3 P.M.

Guided Tours for groups of adults or schoolchildren can be arranged with adequate advance notice.

A *Recorded Tour* of the institute is available for 75¢ for one person, $1.25 for two.

The *Sales Desk* has art reproductions, puzzles, postcards and museum jewelry ranging in price from 50¢ to $10.

A *Library* of art reference books may be used on the premises.

Hours: Tuesday–Sunday, 10 A.M.–5 P.M. *Closed:* Mondays, New Year's, Thanksgiving, Christmas.

Admission: Free.

WILLIAMS COLLEGE MUSEUM OF ART
Main St.
Williamstown, MA 01267
Tel: (413)597–2429

The museum was founded in 1926. Located in Lawrence Hall, originally erected in 1846, its second-floor Ionic rotunda is an outstanding example of 19th-century American architecture. The museum boasts an extensive collection of paintings, sculpture, prints and drawings, decorative arts and furniture. The collection is especially strong in Spanish and Italian Baroque paintings; Asian art; French and Italian medieval and early Renaissance painting and sculpture; and American painting. Additionally, there are examples of African sculpture and works of art from pre-Columbian Mexico, Southeast Asia and ancient Greece and Rome.

SAMPLING THE COLLECTION

From time to time the objects listed below are rotated for exhibition and, therefore, may not always be on view at the listed location.

RHENISH (RECENTLY ATTRIBUTED TO THE RIMINI MASTER)

St. John the Evangelist
ca. 1415–1420
Alabaster

Blashfield Room

Realism in Renaissance sculpture freed the statue from the domination of architecture and enlivened it. Rhenish works have exaggerated expressions endowing them with a mystical quality. The angular figures place turbulent draperies in display.

**Blashfield
Room**

GIOVANNI DA MILANO
Italian, 1346–1396

St. Anthony Abbott
ca. 1350
Tempera on panel

The solemn dignity and massive weight of Giotto and the Early Renaissance is evident in this work although Giovanni often attempted naturalistic effects.

**West
Wing**

JUSEPE RIBERA
Spanish, 1591–1652

The Executioner
ca. 1650
Oil on canvas

Ribera studied in Italy and settled in Naples. Influenced by Caravaggio's realism, he completed many successful commissions while also executing paintings for the Spanish court.

**East
Wing**

JUAN VAN DER HAMEN Y LEON
Flemish/Spanish, 1596–1631

Still Life
ca. 1626
Oil on canvas

Juan was a prolific painter of delicate, carefully rendered still lifes. The greatest artists in Spain were attracted to this type of painting and he was probably influential in its development.

**Asian
Gallery**

INDIAN
Chandella Dynasty, ca. 831–13th c.

Rearing Sardula
10th–11th c.
Pink sandstone

Known chiefly for their reservoirs and other utilitarian works, the Chandellas also constructed many beautiful shrines and temples. Ornamental friezes feature well-modeled figures in elegant, elaborate compositions.

**Asian
Gallery**

CAMBODIAN
Khmer Style

Uma (Female Diety)
10th c.
Red sandstone

Cambodian sculpture of this period is very much related to its architecture. Stylized, severe figures were incorporated into the design of huge pyramids and temples.

Rotunda

JOHN SINGLETON COPLEY
American, 1738–1815

Reverend Samuel Cooper
1769
Oil on canvas

Copley was the leading Colonial portraitist. Until he took up permanent residence in England, he painted many prominent Colonists with great technical ability and realism.

Rotunda

THOMAS GAINSBOROUGH
British, 1727–1788

Portrait of Robert Butcher, Esq.
ca. 1770
Oil on canvas

Gainsborough, known for his portraits of the English gentry, was influenced by the portraiture of Van Dyck. Executed while he resided in Bath, a fashionable spa, this work was among his many lucrative commissions.

Rotunda

ASSYRIAN

Ashur-Nasir-Pal
9th c. B.C.
Stone relief

Assyrian stone reliefs intended for decoration were mostly secular and narrative and served to glorify the Assyrian monarchs. War and the chase were common subjects, executed quite realistically, even though proportion and perspective were of little concern.

**Cluett
Room**

EDWARD HOPPER
American, 1882–1967

Morning in the City
ca. 1935
Oil on canvas

This scene of American urban realism evokes the poetry and loneliness of the city at its best. Hopper's harshly lit canvas seems suspended in time.

THOMAS EAKINS	*Portrait of John Neil Fort*	**Cluett**
American, 1844–1916	1898	**Room**
	Oil on canvas	

Having been rejected by both painters and the public, Eakins turned to portraiture. His strongly realistic canvases were finally acclaimed with the advent of the Ashcan School and their devotion to Realism.

GRANT WOOD	*Death on the Ridge Road*	**Cluett**
American, 1892–1942	1935	**Room**
	Oil on masonite	

A leader among the Regionalists, Wood's paintings were often satirically tinged, as in his most famous work, *American Gothic. Death on the Ridge Road* is a very eerie, very unusual Wood.

FACILITIES

Lectures, Gallery Talks and *Concerts* are given from time to time.

Temporary Exhibitions culled from the museum's collection or *Loan Exhibitions* from other institutions are regular features of the museum's program.

The *Sales Desk* carries exhibition catalogs priced at about $1.

Hours: Monday–Friday, 9 A.M.–5 P.M.; Saturday, Sunday, 1 P.M.–5 P.M. *Summer Hours:* Daily, 1 P.M.–5 P.M. *Closed:* Legal and college holidays.

Admission: Free.

WORCESTER

WORCESTER ART MUSEUM
55 Salisbury St.
Worcester, MA 01608
Tel: (617)799–4406

The museum opened in 1898 and has had four additions. The latest, in 1970, the Higgins Wing, houses the professional museum school and studio areas for educational programs. The collections trace the development of man as seen through 50 centuries of his art, with emphasis on painting and sculpture.

SAMPLING THE COLLECTION

ANCIENT ART   **1st Floor**

EGYPTIAN	*A Nobleman Hunting on the Nile*
Old Kingdom, Dynasty VI,	ca. 2400 B.C.
2420–2258 B.C.	Limestone relief

Tomb sculpture predominates in ancient Egyptian art. The Egyptians believed that depicting a deed would guarantee its repetition after death. No effort was made at realistic portrayal.

Interior Gallery. *Courtesy Worchester Art Museum, Worchester*

EGYPTIAN
Old Kingdom, Dynasty V,
2565–2420 B.C.

The Royal Descendant,
Hetepheres
ca. 2440 B.C.
Limestone

Hetepheres was married to Re-Wer, a prominent official of the court. This sensitively fashioned figure from Re-Wer's tomb at Giza was the left-hand statue in a group portraying Re-Wer, his children and father.

CYPRIAN

Colossal Head from a
Votive Statue
slightly after 500 B.C.

Greek, Assyrian and Egyptian influences are apparent in this larger-than-life-sized head. It was most likely part of a votive statue erected in a sanctuary by a man hoping to receive a god's blessing.

ANTIOCHIAN
Daphne

Hunting Scenes
ca. A.D. 500
Mosaic

This mosaic, one of the biggest and most significant extant, was excavated from a summer resort in Daphne. It blends Hellenistic traditions with those of Persia and the Near East.

ROMAN   *Bust of a Roman Lady*
Antonine   ca. A.D. 165–183
                                      Bronze
This fine bronze Roman portrait, thought to have been found in Anatolia, is one of the very few extant.

FAR EASTERN ART   **1st Floor**

INDIAN   *Vishnu*
Bengal   12th c.
                                      Stone
In Hindu theology Vishnu is the preserver of the universe. This bejeweled sculpture is surrounded by symbolic references and is the epitome of a religious doctrine.

CHINESE   *Head of Kwan Yin*
Sung Dynasty, A.D. 960–1279   Wood
This deity of mercy displays Buddha-like qualities. His third eye, lump on the head, and long earlobes all affirm his nobility and supernatural insight.

MEDIEVAL ART   **1st Floor**

FRENCH   *Chapter House of the Priory
                                      of St. John at Le Bas Nueil*
                                      1160–1175
                                      Limestone
Originally located in Poitiers, this Romanesque chamber was once in the Benedictine Priory of St. John, active from the 11th century until the French Revolution. With small changes it survives in its original state.

RENAISSANCE ART   **2nd Floor**

PIERO DI COSIMO   *The Discovery of Honey
Italian, Florentine, 1462–1521   by Bacchus*
                                      Wood panel
This Ovid-inspired allegory is treated by Piero in terms of the civilizing effect of the event. The panel is one of two from the residence of Giovanni Vespucci in Florence.

FLEMISH   *The Last Judgment*
(probably Brussels)   ca. 1500
                                      Wood tapestry
Tapestries were protection against the cold, damp, stone walls of churches and castles. Over 100 figures are in this huge composition influenced by medieval mystery plays and paintings of artists like Rogier van der Weyden.

FRENCH   *Episode from the Legend of the
Rouen   Seven Sleepers of Ephesus*
                                      1210–1220
                                      Leaded stained glass
This glass and three others, in private collections, remain from the original Seven Sleepers Windows made for the nave of the cathedral at Rouen. It was rebuilt about the year 1200 when the Gothic style began to replace the Romanesque in France.

EUROPEAN PAINTING   **2nd Floor**

BERNARDO STROZZI   *The Calling of St. Matthew*
Italian, 1581–1644   Oil on canvas

Influenced by Tuscan Mannerism and later by Baroque works, this canvas bears great similarities to Caravaggio's Baroque altarpiece on the same subject.

EL GRECO (DOMENICOS
THEOTOCOPOULOS)
Spanish, ca. 1541–1614

The Repentant Magdalen
1577–1580
Oil on canvas

El Greco arrived at his distinctive style once he settled in Toledo, home of the Spanish Inquisition, in 1572. *The Repentant Magdalen* was a favorite subject of his with its allusions to spiritual and sensual powers.

QUENTIN MASSYS
Flemish, ca. 1466–1530

*The Rest on the Flight
into Egypt*
1509–1513
Wood panel

This panel, one of eight, formed a large altarpiece depicting *The Seven Sorrows of the Virgin.* The detailed landscape background with figures was radical for the time. Massys is especially recognized for it.

THOMAS GAINSBOROUGH
British, 1727–1788

A Grand Landscape
probably early 1760s
Oil on canvas

Gainsborough arrived at the style of this canvas through Flemish Baroque landscape painting. It is a complicated and whirling work within a square layout.

JEAN BAPTISTE PATER
French, 1695–1736

The Dance
Oil on canvas

This work of Pater's is most likely quite a late example of his Fête Galante themes adopted by his master, Watteau. These scenes depict romantic clusters of graceful court members set in dreamy landscapes.

SCHOOL OF FONTAINEBLEAU
French, ca. 1530–1560

Woman at Her Toilette
Wood panel

This boudoir painting, portraying the subject in such a personal pose, originated at the School of Fontainebleau and is almost unique to it.

PIETER SAENREDAM
Dutch, 1597–1665

*Interior of the Choir of
St. Bavo's Church at Haarlem*
1660
Oil on panel

The church stands today much the same as in Saenredam's time. He was the first Dutch artist to concentrate on church interiors and architectural scenes. His technique was exacting.

2nd Floor *IMPRESSIONIST AND POST-IMPRESSIONIST PAINTINGS*

PAUL GAUGUIN
French, 1848–1903

The Brooding Woman
1891
Oil on canvas

Painted during his early days in Tahiti, Gauguin combines symbolism, inspired by native art, with intense, unnatural color expressed in simplified form.

PAUL CEZANNE
French, 1839–1906

Study for "The Card Players"
1890–1892
Oil on canvas

The larger work, for which this is a study, is in the Metropolitan Museum. Experimenting with color, Cézanne created a complicated system of color planes with his terse brush strokes.

PRE-COLUMBIAN
3rd Floor

MEXICAN
Campeche, Mayan Culture,
Late Classic Period, ca. 600–900

Carved Column
ca. A.D. 850
Limestone

This deeply carved column, one of a pair, portrays a spear carrier, most likely a priest-king. It once flanked a temple door. The ornate animal headdress is characteristic of Mayan sculpture.

AMERICAN PAINTING AND SCULPTURE
3rd Floor

GILBERT STUART
1755–1828

Mrs. Perez Morton
ca. 1802
Oil on canvas

Stuart was known primarily as a portraitist, his work first gaining fame in London. He worked rapidly, bringing to the canvas a spontaneity and radiance evident in this unfinished sketch.

Gilbert Stuart, Mrs. Perez Morton. *Courtesy Worcester Art Museum, Worcester*

JOHN SINGLETON COPLEY
1738–1815

John Bours
ca. 1761
Oil on canvas

Copley, considered the outstanding portraitist of the pre-Revolutionary era, worked in Boston. In 1774, he retreated to London to paint free from the tumult of the Revolution. His subjects were depicted with great integrity.

AMERICAN

*Mrs. Elizabeth Freake
and Baby Mary*

Mr. John Freake
ca. 1674
Oil on canvas

The Freake paintings, although the sitters appear two-dimensional, show great care to detail. The artist seems to have had no formal training yet he has painted two exceptional 17th-century portraits.

THOMAS SMITH
Act. ca. 1680

Self-Portrait
Oil on canvas

The earliest work in New England to which an artist's name is attributable lacks parallel construction. Smith was a mariner who probably participated in the naval battle depicted in this painting.

FACILITIES

Changing Exhibitions are regularly featured.

Concerts are held on selected Sundays at 3 P.M.

Films, classical, foreign and for children are offered.

The *Art Reference Library* is for student and public use.

Slide Library is open Tuesday–Friday, 10 A.M.–1 P.M.; 2 P.M.–5 P.M.

The *Café Pomodoro* serves luncheon during the summer in the courtyard; *Across the Street* serves luncheon year-round.

The *Museum Shop* is bountifully stocked with gift items. Its attractive selections are sensibly priced. The most popular item is the museum's *Cookbook* with illustrations from the collection and 463 recipes for $9.95. Open Tuesday–Saturday, 10 A.M.–5 P.M.; Sunday, 2 P.M.–5 P.M.

Salisbury Street Lobby

General Tours are offered every Sunday except concert Sundays at 3 P.M. from September through May.

Other Tours and *Public Events* are posted at the main entrance.

Guided Tours of the collection and special exhibitions for groups may be arranged in advance through the Division of Education.

Hours: Tuesday–Saturday, 10 A.M.–5 P.M.; Sunday, 2 P.M.–5 P.M. *Closed:* Mondays, July 4, Thanksgiving, Christmas, New Year's.

Admission: Adults, $1.50; children under 14, adults over 65, $1. Children under 5, free. Wednesday free to all.

NEW HAMPSHIRE

CORNISH

SAINT-GAUDENS NATIONAL HISTORIC SITE
2 mi. north of Cornish
Windsor covered bridge on
N.Y. Rte 12A
Cornish, NH 03746
Tel: (603)675–2055

This historic site consists of the home, gardens and studios of Saint-Gaudens.
Original works and replicas of some of his most famous sculptures are on view.

SAMPLING THE COLLECTION

AUGUSTUS SAINT-GAUDENS   *Sculptures*
American, 1848–1907   Bronze
Saint-Gaudens was a 19th-century Realist sculptor. He was also a teacher.
Additionally he was active in raising funds to further the artists' cause both at
home and abroad. Among his best-known works are the *Diana,* which once

Little Studio. *Courtesy U.S. Department of Interior*

graced the tower of Madison Square Garden in New York City; the equestrian statue of General William T. Sherman; the bas-relief portrait of Samuel Ward, as well as the Standing and Seated Lincoln monuments. Altogether Saint-Gaudens created close to 150 sculptures.

FACILITIES

Sales Desk carries pamphlets and books mostly pertaining to Saint-Gaudens and his times are for sale from 30¢ up. There are also color postcards at 10¢ and souvenir medallions from $20 to $25.

Little Studio   *Concerts* are held on summer Sundays from mid-June to mid-August.

Hours: Last weekend in May through October. Buildings open, 8:30 A.M. – 5 P.M. daily. Grounds, 8 A.M. – dark.

Admission: 50¢ per person; children under 16, free. Golden Age and Golden Eagle passports are honored.

HANOVER

DARTMOUTH COLLEGE MUSEUM AND GALLERIES
Hopkins Center, Wilson Hall
Carpenter Gallery
Hanover, NH 03755
Tel: (603)646–2808

The collections are located in three buildings on the campus; Hopkins Center houses several galleries and a sculpture court, overlooking a lovely New England green; Carpenter Hall contains the permanent collection and temporary exhibitions; Wilson Hall exhibits the anthropological collections. Additionally, many works are distributed in other buildings and on the campus grounds.

SAMPLING THE COLLECTION

In Storage in Hopkins Center When Not on Display   PABLO PICASSO
Spanish, 1881–1973

Guitar on a Table
1912–1913
Oil, sand and charcoal on canvas

This work was executed in Picasso's Synthetic Cubist style which combines plastic mediums in space, color and linear movement.

On Wheeler Lawn   BEVERLY PEPPER
American, b. 1924

Thel
1975–1977
Steel, earth grass

Pepper, a painter and sculptress, is known for her monumental landworks using natural environments contained in metal or concrete.

Ground Floor, Baker Library   JOSE CLEMENTE OROZCO
Mexican, 1883–1949

Quetzalcoatl and the Aspirations of Mankind
1932–1934
Fresco murals

Orozco's work is suffused with symbolism. During this point in his career, it acquired an Expressionistic strength still fundamentally three-dimensional and figurative in its form.

MARK DI SUVERO	*X-Delta*	On **Dartmouth**
American, b. 1933	1970	**Green, in**
	Steel, wood, foam rubber	**Front of**

Di Suvero's sculptures usually consist of found and industrial objects. He is **Sanborn** interested in the formal rather than the romantic results of his assemblages. **House**

THOMAS EAKINS   *Portrait of John Joseph Borie*   **Carpenter**
American, 1844–1916   1896–1898   **Art Gallery**
                         Oil on canvas

Chiefly a portrait painter, Eakins's realistic canvases were bathed in light that mellowed as his art matured.

ASSYRIAN   *Mural Relief from the Palace*   **Carpenter**
                        of Ashurnazirpal II, King   **Art Gallery**
                        Ashurnazirpal II with Deities
                        9th c. B.C.
                        Stone

These murals, part of the palace walls, were executed in low relief. The people are conventionalized in formal style.

FACILITIES

Gallery Talks may be attended.

Changing Exhibitions are regularly featured.   **Hopkins**

A *Snack Bar* serves sandwiches and beverages.   **Center**

The *Sales Shop's* most popular items are Peruvian carvings, $5–$12; wrought- **Wilson Hall** iron pictures, $3; arrowheads, $1–$5; and Indian books, $1.

Hours: *Hopkins Center:* Wednesdays, 10 A.M. – 4 P.M.; Tuesday–Saturday evenings, 7 P.M. – 10 P.M.. Saturdays, Sundays, holidays, 12 P.M. – 4 P.M.

          Carpenter Hall: Daily, 11 A.M. – 4 P.M.; Saturdays, Sundays, holidays, 12 P.M. – 4 P.M.

          Wilson Hall: Weekdays, 9 A.M. – 5 P.M.; Saturdays, Sundays, holidays, 12 P.M. – 4 P.M..

Admission: Free.

MANCHESTER

CURRIER GALLERY OF ART
192 Orange St.
Manchester, NH 03104
Tel: (603)669–6144

The Renaissance-style gallery of limestone and marble with its handsome central court stands in the pleasantly landscaped gardens of the former home of Moody and Hannah Currier. Opened to the public in 1929, its contents are distinguished by quality rather than size. European art spans the 14th to the 20th century; American furniture emphasizes New Hampshire, ranging from vigorous Dunlap country pieces to the Federal furniture of Portsmouth; choice collections of New England silver, pewter and 19th-century American glass are also on view.

SAMPLING THE COLLECTION

CLAUDE MONET   *The Seine at Bougival*
French, 1840–1926   ca. 1870
                                               Oil on canvas
Monet, at this time, was painting in the style of his early maturity, using pure
flat color, on the threshold of the development of Impressionism.

JAN GOSSAERT (CALLED MABUSE)   *Self-Portrait*
Flemish, ca. 1478–1533   ca. 1515
                                  Oil on panel
Mabuse studied the Italian Masters, converting them in a Gothic manner to his
Flemish style. First in Flanders to paint Classical themes with nudes, he is also
known for his straightforward portraits.

JOHN CONSTABLE   *Dedham Mill*
British, 1776–1837   1820
                                  Oil on canvas
Among the most prominent landscapists of all time, Constable tried to capture
the evanescence of nature. Noted for his skies, particularly his clouds, he
painted with flecked color frequently applied with a palette knife.

JEAN-BAPTISTE CAMILLE COROT   *View of Grez-Sur Loing*
French, 1796–1875   1850–1860
                                  Oil on canvas
Corot's style underwent several changes. His most popular paintings were

Claude Monet, The Seine at Bougival. *Courtesy Currier Gallery of Art, Manchester*

executed in a gauzy atmospheric manner accented by small figures attired in bright accessories.

GIOVANNI BATTISTA TIEPOLO *The Triumph of Hercules*
Italian, 1696–1770 1761
Oil on canvas
Tiepolo is best known for his fantastic, airy, graceful frescoes. His early dark, Baroque style later developed into the lighter, more fragile Rococo.

PABLO PICASSO *Woman Seated in a Chair*
Spanish, 1881–1973 1941
Oil on canvas
Picasso's work, undergoing many stylistic changes, exerted the greatest influence on modern art. The series of seated women, painted during World War II, expressed Picasso's contempt for mankind's current inhumanity.

GEORGES ROUAULT *The Wounded Clown*
French, 1871–1958 1939
Oil on masonite
Rouault's paintings, with somber outlines encasing vibrant color, are influenced by his youthful career in a stained-glass factory. Although chiefly a painter of religious subjects, he identified with man's oppression and painted profane works also of prostitutes, clowns, etc.

HILAIRE GERMAIN EDGAR DEGAS *Dancers*
French, 1834–1917 ca. 1890
Pastel on paper
Although Degas exhibited with the Impressionists, he deviated from their tenets. He painted ballet dancers, women at work and in domestic settings. As his eyesight deteriorated, he turned to pastels, an easier medium to control.

FRANCO-FLEMISH *The Visit of the Gypsies*
Tournai late 15th c.
Tapestry
From mid- to late-15th century, Tournai was a major center of tapestry production. The tapestries were usually executed in monumental style and grandeur.

FACILITIES

Special Gallery Tours for adults and student groups may be arranged in advance by calling the Currier Gallery of Art, Department of Education.

Changing Exhibitions are regularly featured.

Special Events such as *Lectures, Films* and *Concerts* are held frequently with no admission charge.

The *Library* is open by appointment for students and researchers.

The *Sales Desk* carries a small selection of art catalogs and postcards.

Hours: Tuesday, Wednesday, Friday, Saturday, 10 A.M. – 4 P.M.; Thursdays, 10 A.M. – 10 P.M. with special Thursday evening programming; Sunday, 2 P.M. – 5 P.M.. *Closed:* Mondays, national holidays, Thanksgiving, Christmas.

Admission: Free.

NEW JERSEY

CAMDEN

CAMPBELL MUSEUM
Campbell Pl.
Camden, NJ 08101
Tel: (609)964–4000

The museum, supported by the Campbell Soup Company, houses a collection of tureens, bowls and ladles from 500 B.C. to the present with fine examples of Chinese Export ware, the forerunner of porcelain. The majority of items on display were made in the 18th century in Western Europe, where the decorative arts received abundant attention and financial encouragement from royal and wealthy persons.

SAMPLING THE COLLECTION

CHINESE
Ch'ing Dynasty, Ch'ien Lung Period, 1735–1796

Animal Head Tureen with Stand
ca. 1760
Hard-paste porcelain

Hard-paste porcelain, durable and inexpensive, was developed in China before the 9th century. In the 18th century Europeans often commissioned the Chinese to copy Western objects. This tureen blends an Oriental art form with an Occidental idea.

PORTUGUESE
Rato, Brunetto Period, 1767–1771

Tureen with Fish Cover
Faïence (tin-enameled earthenware)

Brunetto founded the Rato factory, near Lisbon. He introduced this Turin style of earthenware which continued to be popular into the 19th century. This tureen was appropriate for an area abounding in fishing villages.

ENGLISH
Chelsea, Red Anchor Period, 1752–1756

2 Rabbit Tureens
Soft-paste porcelain

These are two of several rabbit soup tureens produced from the same mold. There were slight variations due to handling and firing. No two were painted alike. About seven still exist.

ENGELBART JOOSTEN
Dutch, 18th c.

Tureen
1772
Silver

Elaborate tureens in silver were the special treasures of great dinner services. Sometimes a service had four tureens. This is one of a pair Joosten made for Assuer Jan Baron Torck and his wife.

FACILITIES

Related *Loan Exhibitions* are arranged from time to time.

Films relevant to the museum's collection are presented.

A *Catalog* of the collection is the only item for sale and costs $5.

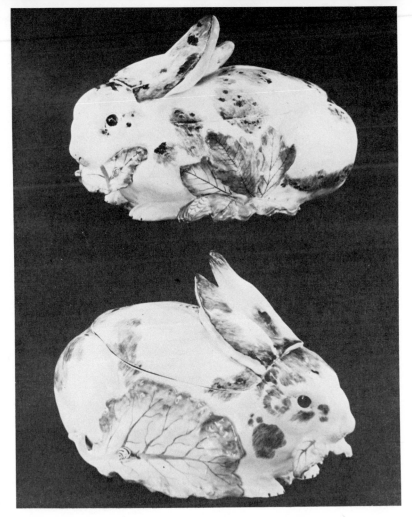

Tureens. *Courtesy Campbell Museum, Campbell Place, Camden*

Hours: Monday–Friday, 9:30 A.M.–5 P.M. *Closed:* Saturday, Sunday, holidays, as well as Good Friday, day before July 4, day after Thanksgiving.

Admission: Free.

MONTCLAIR

MONTCLAIR ART MUSEUM
3 South Mountain Ave.
Montclair, NJ 07042
Tel: (201)746–5555

The museum, founded in 1912, is housed in a Neoclassic building in a heavily treed setting where 50 varieties are identified and labeled. The American painting collection includes art from the 18th into the 20th century. The Gallery of American Indian Art, on the upper level, presents art and artifacts of the seven major North American Indian cultural groups. Special collections from other periods and cultures include textiles, silver, ceramics, decorative arts, European paintings, Japanese prints and one of the finest collections of Chinese snuff bottles in the United States.

SAMPLING THE COLLECTION

Works from the permanent collection are usually, but not always, shown in one of the galleries.

JAMES A. MCNEILL WHISTLER   *The Sea*
American, 1834–1903   ca. 1865
Oil on canvas

Whistler used color with great restraint, concentrating on tonal relationships. At this time in his career he was much influenced by Japanese prints.

EDWARD HOPPER   *Coast Guard Station*
American, 1882–1967   1927
Oil

Influenced both by the Impressionists and the Ashcan School, Hopper's realistic paintings of America's towns and cities are spare, melancholy evocations of the isolation and loneliness he saw.

JOHN SINGLETON COPLEY   *Portrait of Elizabeth Allen*
American, 1738–1815   *Stevens*
ca. 1760
Oil

Copley, the foremost Colonial portraitist, taught himself largely by copying Old Masters. His early portraits, including this canvas, are influenced by English mezzotints, but show a strong interest in the portrayal of character.

MARY CASSATT   *Le Jeune Mariée*
American, 1845–1926   ca. 1875
Oil

Exterior view. Courtesy Montclair Art Museum, Montclair

Although opposed by her family, Cassatt settled in Paris and continued to paint. Befriended by the Impressionists, particularly Degas, she promoted their ideas among Americans and became this country's most renowned woman painter.

ADOLPH GOTTLIEB   *Spectre of the Sea*
American, 1903–1974   1947
    Oil

Gottlieb, a founder of Abstract Expressionism, was influenced by the writings of Freud and the paintings of Dali. His work of this period is noted for the use of geometric shapes and also contains a suggestion of Realism.

FACILITIES

Gallery Talks on current exhibitions are offered on Sunday afternoons.

A *Morning Lecture Series* brings distinguished artists or art historians to lecture on aspects of American art.

Temporary Exhibitions gathered from the museum's collection and *Loan Exhibitions* organized from other institutions are regular features of the museum's program.

A *Saturday Night Series* offers jazz, film, dance, poetry and other related arts.

Concerts are held on Sunday afternoons in March and November featuring soloists and chamber music groups.

Children's Workshops based on current exhibitions are offered periodically on Saturday afternoons.

Vacation Programs for children offered during school holidays include puppetry, dance, music and storytelling.

Art Classes for adults and children are offered in a variety of media.

The *Museum Shop* carries books, postcards and handcrafted objects from all over the world.

The *Library* houses an art reference collection of over 8,000 books, exhibition catalogs, periodicals and a lending collection of 13,000 color slides. Open: Tuesday–Friday, 10 A.M.–12 P.M., 1 P.M.–5 P.M. Saturday, 10 A.M.–1 P.M. Closed: Sundays, Mondays.

Hours: Tuesday–Saturday, 10 A.M.–5 P.M.; Sunday, 2 P.M.–5 P.M. *Closed:* Mondays, July–August, New Year's, Thanksgiving, Christmas.

Admission: Free.

NEWARK

NEWARK MUSEUM
49 Washington St.
Newark, NJ 07101
Tel: (201)733–6600

History, science and artworks are housed in the museum's three-story building. Newark's oldest schoolhouse (1784) is located in the sculpture garden behind the building, set on an acre of trees and grass. Also in the garden is the Newark Fire Museum, where antique firefighting equipment may be viewed. The Ballantine House, entered through the museum, contains five rooms restored in High Victorian taste. The 1800 house, on the second floor, features the kitchen and parlor of a Federal home. The science exhibits are on the third floor.

SAMPLING THE COLLECTION

JOSEPH STELLA
Italian/American, 1877–1946

The Bridge
#5 panel of the series:
"New York Interpreted"
1922
Oil on canvas

Joseph Stella, The Bridge. *Collection of the Newark Museum, Newark*

Stella was influenced by Italian Futurism. Linear forms of brilliant color mark his work. He painted many versions of the Brooklyn Bridge.

JOHN SINGLETON COPLEY   *Portrait of Mrs. Joseph Scott*
American, 1738–1815   (Freelove Olney)
     ca. 1765
     Oil on canvas

This portrait was painted before Copley departed the Colonies for England. His understanding of paint enabled him to convey textures with great skill and his native talent gave life to his portraits.

     Tibetan Buddhist Altar
     1935
     Reproduction

This altar and ritual articles although not copied from any specific one typifies those in a small meditation room of a monastery or fine home. The altar was the place of worship and the heart of the Tibetan home.

ARTS OF AFRICA

The collection includes masks, figural carvings and applied arts from the area south of the Sahara, including the Guinea coast eastward over the Cameroons, Congo and northern Angola. It shows how these objects were used in their traditional cultures.

THE EUGENE SCHAEFER COLLECTION OF ANCIENT GLASS

The collection consists of over 1,000 pieces. The glass, assembled not for its beauty alone but to exemplify almost every known shape and process, developed from earliest Egyptian times to the dissolution of the ancient world.

FACILITIES

Guided Tours, Lectures, Films and *Gallery Talks* are all offered.

Changing Exhibitions from the American painting and sculpture collection are regularly featured.

The *Library* of art and science reference books is available for use on the premises.

The *Sales Shop* sells jewelry, cards, publications, books, toys, Tibetan wool rugs, textiles and reproductions priced from 25¢ to $200.

Hours: Every day, 12 P.M.–5 P.M. *Closed:* July 4, Thanksgiving, Christmas, New Year's.

Admission: Free.

NEW JERSEY HISTORICAL SOCIETY
230 Broadway
Newark, NJ 07104
Tel: (201)483–3939

The society, devoted to New Jersey and American history, presents exhibits on transportation and industry, household utensils, textiles, decorative arts, jewelry and Indian arts as well as paintings, drawings and prints. There is iconography of New Jersey with views of all 567 towns before 1875; the first map of the state and its charter signed by King Charles II in 1664; a portrait of General George B. McClellan of Civil War fame and equipment invented and perfected by Thomas Alva Edison of West Orange (1890–1920).

SAMPLING THE COLLECTION

GILBERT STUART
American, 1755–1828

Portrait of Vice-President
Aaron Burr
1792
Oil

Stuart was best known for his portraits. He was mostly interested in the faces of his subjects, paying scant attention to their backgrounds.

ELIAS BOUDINOT
American, 1706–1770

Teapot
1750
Silver

Boudinot was a successful Philadelphia silversmith. Little of his work remains today. Teapots were unknown until the end of the 17th century and few American pots made prior to 1750 survive.

JOHN WATSON
British, 1685–1768

Miniatures
1715

Portrait miniatures were very popular in the 18th century. With the introduction of ivory at the time, the whole art was changed. The white background was effective with watercolors or oil.

AMERICAN
New Jersey,
Batsto Ironworks

Cipher
1780
Iron

This cipher, with the initials *G.W.*, was most likely made to represent the arms of George Washington. Its design is similar to the escutcheon of the British Washington family.

AMERICAN

250 Drawings
ca. 1791–1815
Pencil, ink, wash

About half the drawings were made by Robert Fulton. The rest involve Benjamin Henry Latrobe, Charles Stoudinger, Chancellor Livingston, Boulton and Watt (England) and others. Subjects include steam-pumping engines and rolling mills, steamboats and other means of mechanical propulsion, the Philadelphia Waterworks, canals, submarines and other devices for undersea warfare.

FACILITIES

Guided Tours, Lectures, Films and *Gallery Talks* are all offered. Call for further information.

A *Library* containing books, manuscripts, maps, pamphlets, broadsides and newspapers pertaining to New Jersey history and genealogy is available for use on the premises.

The *History Shop* offers among its most popular items: wooden models of butter churns; rolling pins; mortars and pestles and irons all moderately priced.

Hours: Monday–Saturday, 12 P.M.–4:15 P.M. For research in library and/or museum collections: Monday–Saturday 9:15 A.M.–4:15 P.M. *Closed:* national holidays.

Admission: Free.

NEW BRUNSWICK

RUTGERS UNIVERSITY ART GALLERY
Voorhees Hall, Hamilton St.
New Brunswick, NJ 08903
Tel: (201)932–7237/7096

In 1966, the gallery was organized to house the fine arts collection assembled over a period of 200 years. Containing more than 5,000 paintings, prints, drawings, sculptures and decorative art objects, the permanent collection spans the history of art. Highlights are its 19th-century French and American prints; American paintings from the 18th century to the present; English paintings from the 18th and 19th centuries and a group of medieval paintings and tapestries.

SAMPLING THE COLLECTION

The paintings listed below are sometimes in storage and consequently not always on view.

PIETER CLAESZ, THE ELDER   *St. Dominic and the Virgin*
Flemish, ca. 1499–1576   ca. 1570
    Oil on panel
Claesz and his contemporaries, Gossaert (Mabuse) and Brueghel, were interested in the common man and realism. Claesz's mostly religious paintings were filled with rugged peasant types.

CENTRAL ITALIAN (?)   *Susanna and the Elders*
    2nd half of 15th c.
    Oil on gesso panel
Oil on panel was a Flemish technique introduced in Italy. Painters discovered the Classic past and chose their subjects from mythology or religion. These they portrayed with an emphasis on individualism and realism.

Interior Gallery. *Courtesy Rutgers University Art Gallery, New Brunswick*

BENJAMIN WEST   *Rinaldo and Armida*
American, 1738–1820   1766
                                     Oil on canvas
West settled in England in 1763, becoming painter to the court and president
of the Royal Academy. He helped train many important American artists and
was successively in the vanguard of Classicists, Realists and Romantics.

WALT KUHN   *Pine at Five O'clock*
American, 1880–1949   1945
                                     Oil on canvas
Kuhn commenced his varied career as a cartoonist. Heavily influenced by
Fauvism, he departed from Realism to try other styles. He painted circus figures
and later turned to landscapes and still lifes.

CHARLES SHEELER   *Boneyard*
American, 1883–1965   1945
                                     Oil on canvas
Originally an architectural photographer, Sheeler was converted to modern art
by Cézanne's work. His first paintings emphasized folk art and architecture and
then shifted to contemporary industrial scenes, using bright colors and becoming more abstract.

CLAUDE MONET   *Portrait of a Man*
French, 1840–1926   1862
                                     Oil on canvas
Monet painted this portrait at the outset of his career, and at that time was
studying in Paris. He was already meeting artists with whom he would develop
Impressionism

FACILITIES

Group Tours may be arranged. Call at least one week in advance.

Lectures are offered.

Temporary Exhibitions culled from the art gallery's collection or *Loan Exhibitions* from other institutions are regular features of the art gallery's program.

A *Saturday Children's Program* is available. For information call (201)932–
7096.

A *Sales Desk* offers catalogs of exhibitions, posters and cards. Prices, $1–$8.

Hours: Monday–Friday, 10 A.M.–4:30 P.M.; Saturday–Sunday, 12 P.M.–5 P.M.
         Closed: Easter weekend, Thanksgiving weekend, Christmas weekend.

Admission: Free.

PRINCETON

ART MUSEUM, PRINCETON UNIVERSITY
Princeton, NJ 08544
Tel: (609)452–3787

The museum is one of the oldest university museums in the nation. The original
structure opened in 1889; the present building was completed in 1966. The
collection, which tends to reflect the curriculum of the Department of Art and
Archaeology and which is not static in display, ranges from ancient to contemporary times; it focuses on the Mediterranean regions, Western Europe, China,

the United States and the pre-Columbian world of Central and South America. It is particularly strong in Greek and Roman antiquities; medieval European sculpture, painting, stained glass and metalwork; Renaissance painting from Italy and Northern Europe; French 18th- and 19th-century painting and sculpture; Chinese paintings and bronze ceremonial vessels; prints and drawings (these seen only by appointment). The Putnam Memorial Collection of contemporary monumental sculpture is located throughout the campus; the group of 20 pieces includes works by Gaston Lachaise, Alexander Calder, Henry Moore, Louise Nevelson and Arnaldo Pomodoro.

SAMPLING THE COLLECTION

CHINESE
Western Chou Dynasty,
1027–770 B.C.

Kuang
Bronze

Various subscribers made it possible to acquire Chester D. Carter's important collection of Chinese bronze ritual vessels of the Shang, Chou and Han dynasties. "The Sackler Kuang at Princeton," the gift of Dr. Arthur M. Sackler, is a superb example of a wine container in animal form, covered with stylized ornament.

Chinese Ritual Bronze Vessel. *Courtesy Art Museum, Princeton University, Princeton*

CHINESE
Sung Dynasty, A.D. 960–1279

Statue of Kwan Yin
mid-13th c.
Painted wood

The life-size statue represents the Buddhist deity as serenely seated in the pose known as "royal ease." Compared with other images of the popular embodiment of the virtue of mercy that can be dated, the style of the Princeton example is placed toward the close of the Sung Dynasty.

LI KUNG-NIEN
Chinese, early 12th c.

Winter Landscape
Ink painting on silk

Dr. DuBois S. Morris, a Princeton alumnus, presented to the university at the time of its bicentennial in 1947 the paintings he collected while living in China. The treasure in this group is this rare, early landscape.

MEXICAN
Mayan Culture, Late Classic Period,
ca. 600–900

Vase
Pottery

The cylindrical jar is an outstanding example from a group of funerary vases painted with scenes that reflect lost texts written on perishable materials. The complicated mythic cycle they represent prepared the deceased for the journey into the underworld.

GREEK

Zeus Hurling a Thunderbolt
ca. 460 B.C.
Bronze

The statuette represents the god poised, arms outstretched and about to release the bolt. In small scale, it is a fine example of the style of monumental Greek sculpture of the period between the Persian Wars and the age of Phidias.

ROMAN SYRIAN

Mosaic Pavements
2nd–6th c.
Stone

Princeton University was part of a team that excavated Antioch-on-the-Orontes in the 1930s. Numerous houses and public buildings were uncovered, their floors offering an unusual sequence of styles of mosaic work through several centuries. Figured scenes, often mythological, and ornamental patterns are represented in the selected group brought to Princeton.

FRENCH

The Martyrdom of St. George
1st half of 13th c.
Stained glass

The panel is from one of the windows of the Cathedral at Chartres that was replaced in the 18th century by clear glass. It once belonged to Viollet le Duc, the 19th-century architect involved with the restoration of many churches in France; he seems to have been the one responsible for reconstructing, with old and new glass, the panel as we see it now.

FRENCH

Statue of a Saint
ca. 1515–1525
Limestone

The statue, a fine example of late French Gothic style, is probably from the workshop of the unidentified sculptor, working in the province of Champagne, who carved the St. Martha in the Church of the Madeleine in Troyes. The attributes that would identify "The Princeton Saint" with certainty are missing, but it, too, may be Martha.

ALBRECHT DURER
German, 1471–1528

Holy Family with Hares
Woodblock

The block is the one cut by the artist himself for printing the composition on paper. The versatile and influential Dürer is best known for his graphic works, but it is usually only the printed impression that has survived.

GUIDO DA SIENA
Italian, 13th c.

The Annunciation
Painting on wooden panel

Originally, the panel was one of a series of scenes of the life of Christ in the wings of an altarpiece in the church of San Domenico in Siena. For so large a commission, Guido had assistants working under his direction; it is generally believed that *The Annunciation* is by the Master's hand.

ANTHONY VAN DYCK
Flemish, 1599–1641

The Mocking of Christ
Oil on canvas

Royal patronage, such as that of Charles I of England, not only enhanced Van Dyck's reputation as a portrait painter but made such work an expediency. There is, however, a considerable group of paintings that show a less well known interest in religious subjects on the part of the famous artist.

CLAUDE MONET
French, 1840–1926

Waterlilies and Japanese Bridge
1899
Oil on canvas

When Monet settled in Giverny, he created a garden and lily pond. His constant study of their light and color is caught on the numerous canvases he painted. Princeton's painting is of the Japanese bridge that still arches over the pond.

CHARLES WILLSON PEALE
American, 1741–1827

Elias Boudinot IV
Oil on canvas

Boudinot, a resident of Princeton and a trustee of the college, was the first president of the Continental Congress. When unpaid troops made Philadelphia uncomfortable for the new government, Boudinot moved the administration to the college's Nassau Hall, which became the nation's capitol for a few months. Family portraits (including the one by the eminent Peale), furniture, silverware, chinaware and other furnishings, are exhibited in two rooms.

FACILITIES

Temporary Exhibitions culled from the museum's collection or *Loan Exhibitions* from other institutions are regular features of the museum's program.

Hours: Tuesday–Saturday, 10 A.M.–4 P.M.; Sunday, 1–5 P.M. (academic year); 2 P.M.–4 P.M. (summers). *Closed:* Mondays, national holidays.

Admission: Free.

TRENTON

NEW JERSEY STATE MUSEUM
205 West State St.
Trenton, NJ 08625
Tel: (609)292-6300

The modern three-level museum building, overlooking the Delaware River, was dedicated in 1965. Collections and exhibitions relate to art, history, natural science and archeology/ethnology, with emphasis primarily but not exclusively on New Jersey.

SAMPLING THE COLLECTION

The works below may not always be on view; they are shown on a rotating basis.

THOMAS EAKINS   *The American Army Crossing*
American, 1844–1916   *the Delaware*

                                The Battle of Trenton
                                1892–1895
                                Bronze reliefs

Eakins first became impressed with Realism when traveling in Spain, where he viewed the paintings of 17th-century masters. His subsequent interest in Realism remained with him for the rest of his life.

GEORGIA O'KEEFFE   *East River from the Shelton*
American, b. 1887   1927–1928
                                Oil on canvas

O'Keeffe's early work was abstract but during the 1920s she returned to realism in Cubist-Realist style.

ARTHUR DOVE   *After the Storm, Silver and*
American, 1880–1946   *Green (Vault Sky)*
                                1922
                                Oil and metallic paint on
                                wood panel

Dove was interested in the power of color or form to produce a visual experience. His later paintings became increasingly geometric, though never totally abstract.

MAX WEBER   *Fleeing Mother and Child*
Russian/American, 1881–1961   1913
                                Oil on canvas

Weber's early work is done in both representational and abstract styles. Paintings in the 1920s and 1930s show movement away from the abstract and toward the use of color in the manner of Cézanne.

FACILITIES

Changing Exhibitions are regularly featured.

The *Museum Shop* offers museum-related items at nominal cost.

A *Recorded Telephone Message* covering ongoing exhibitions and programs may be dialed around the clock (609)292–6464.

Various Locations A variety of *Performing Arts Programs* are held on Sunday afternoons.

Auditorium *Children's Theater* is presented irregularly throughout the year with nominal admission. For information call (609)292–6310.

Auditorium *Weekend Movies* of interest to family and adult groups are offered without charge. No age restriction.

Planetarium The *Planetarium* presents free public lectures daily during July and August, and at 2 P.M., 3 P.M. and 4 P.M. each Saturday, Sunday and holiday of the year. Admission tickets are distributed in the lobby first come, first served 30 minutes before each show. Children under 7 not admitted.

Lower Level A *Lunchroom* is serviced by a battery of vending machines stocked with snacks and light refreshments.

Hours: Monday–Friday, 9 A.M.–4:45 P.M.; weekends and most holidays, 1 P.M.–
          5 P.M.

Admission: Free.

NEW YORK

ALBANY

ALBANY INSTITUTE OF HISTORY AND ART
125 Washington Ave.
Albany, NY 12210
Tel: (518)463-4478

The institute was founded in 1791. In addition to paintings of the upper Hudson River by Hudson River artists, it contains paintings by early Dutch primitive artists and two reconstructed interiors, a Dutch room and the Hanrahan Room, an 18th-century paneled parlor.

Exterior view. Courtesy Albany Institute of History and Art, Albany

SAMPLING THE COLLECTION

EDWARD LAMSON HENRY
American, 1841–1919

*First Railroad Train on
the Mohawk and Hudson Road*
1892–1893
Oil on canvas

A popular artist in his day, Henry was a historical painter. This is a large panorama of the primitive "De Witt Clinton" being readied for its first trip from Albany to Schenectady.

115

Main **Hallway**	THOMAS COLE American, 1801–1848	*Lake Winnepesaukee* Oil on canvas

This panoramic view of the lake is typical of Cole's romantic style. He was the principal painter of the Hudson River School.

Upstairs, **Round** **Gallery**	POSSIBLY PIETER VANDERLYN Dutch, ca. 1687–1778	*Pau de Wanderlaer* ca. 1730 Oil on canvas

One of 40 portraits painted in the Hudson Valley and attributed to the Schuyler Limner. His style was crude and powerful.

Ariaantje Coeymans
1723
Oil on canvas

This woman, dressed in gray, domed buildings in the background, is also attributed to Vanderlyn.

FACILITIES

Guided Tours are provided by the Women's Council.

Lectures, Films, Gallery Talks and *Concerts* are offered frequently. Call for program information.

Changing Exhibitions are regularly featured.

The *Luncheon Gallery* serves light lunches with homemade soups and desserts. Open 11 A.M.–1:30 P.M.

The *Sales Shop* has items priced for children and other quality material for collectors, including antique jewelry and fine handmade articles. Priced accordingly. Open Tuesday–Saturday, 10:30 A.M.–4 P.M.; Sunday, 2 P.M.–4 P.M.

Hours: Tuesday–Saturday, 10 A.M.–5 P.M.; Sunday, 2 P.M.–5 P.M. *Closed*: Monday, national holidays.

Admission: Free. A donation is appreciated.

BINGHAMTON

ROBERSON CENTER FOR THE ARTS AND SCIENCES
30 Front St.
Binghamton, NY 13905
Tel: (607)772–0660

The Roberson Center, opened in 1954, is a multifaceted complex, housing in addition to a fine arts collection, historical and scientific displays, educational facilities and an extensive program of performing arts. The Keith Martin Wing, designed by Richard Neutra, was erected in 1968. The first of four buildings projected for the future, it contains Roberson's permanent collection. This collection was formerly quartered in the Binghamton Museum of Fine Arts and is now considerably expanded. The Metropolitan Museum of Art in New York City has made available a long-term loan of some 300 artifacts from Ancient Near East, Egypt, Cyprus, Greece and Rome, plus arms and armor and European decorative arts. An art museum and science wing are being planned. Attached to the center is the Roberson Mansion, designed by Edward Vosbury and completed in 1909 in Italian Renaissance style. It contains the historical collection. Its restored room settings are a reminder of the wealth and taste of the people who created the "Parlor City." Additionally the collections contain 19th- and 20th-century American paintings and sculpture; furnitu re and decorative arts, including porcelain, timepieces and pressed glass; and Mexican, Eskimo and African paintings, prints, sculpture and artifacts.

SAMPLING THE COLLECTION

FRENCH — *Diptych* — Martin Wing, 2nd Floor, Metropolitan Collection

Ivory

A diptych, usually an altarpiece, is a pair of hinged panels. Ivory—hard, durable and easily polished—was valued highly. Exportation from Paris, the center of ivory carving, helped to spread the Parisian Gothic style throughout Europe.

FRENCH — *Chasse* — Martin Wing, Metropolitan Collection

Limoges — mid-13th c.

Copper with champlevé enamel

A chasse was used for liturgical purposes. Champlevé was a method of decorating enamel. The background, usually copper, was hollowed out and filled with glassy colored pastes, then fired until fused to the metal.

GREEK — *Jug* — Martin Wing, Metropolitan Collection

Corinth — ca. 7th c.

Clay painted with slip

Corinth was well known during this period for its bronzes, terracottas and ceramics, especially vases. They were crafted with balance, proportion and naturalism as is shown by the griffins, lions, gazelles, birds and rosettes encircling this jug.

CYPRIAN — *Head of a Man* — Martin Wing, Metropolitan Collection

ca. 500 B.C.

Limestone

Cypriot sculptors used clay and limestone that hardened with exposure to air. They worked with knives, giving their pieces a linear quality. Concentrating on the face and indifferent to bodily form, their sculpture tended to be abstract.

GEORGE INNESS — *Autumn Landscape* — Martin Wing, Roberson Collection

American, 1825–1894 — 1875

Oil on canvas

Influenced at first by the Hudson River School, Inness later combined art and religion in landscapes depicting the meadows and woods of the North Atlantic states in all moods.

FACILITIES

Changing Exhibitions in art, science and history are regularly featured.

The *Museum Shop* carries reasonably priced international handcrafts. Items are **Main Lobby** selected by the museum's art curator and are mostly one-of-a-kind. There are hand-embroidered tapestries, authentic folk jewelry, woven wall hangings, miniatures, folk art, ancient Egyptian and pre-Columbian jewelry and items that reflect the exhibitions and programs at the center. A children's table has handmade items under $1.

The *Two Rivers Gallery/Randall House* is housed in the newly expanded **Museum Shop** Museum Shop. It sells and rents contemporary art and fine crafts representing artists from the Eastern Seaboard in a variety of media. Included are paintings, prints, photographs, drawings, sculpture, blown glass, stained glass, pottery, weavings and jewelry.

Two Rivers Gallery, 1st Floor   The *Antiques Exchange* of the Two Rivers Gallery sells selected antiques from private collectors. The merchandise changes from small collectibles to furniture and includes glassware, silver, wood carvings, quilts, porcelain and paintings. Wednesday–Friday, 10 A.M.–5 P.M. Saturday, Sunday, 12 P.M.–5 P.M. *Closed:* Mondays, Tuesdays.

Martin Wing, 2nd Floor   The *Sears-Harkness Theater* presents lectures, films, plays, concerts and dance programs.

Hours: The Roberson Center Galleries: Tuesday–Friday, 10 A.M.–5 P.M.; Saturday, Sunday, 12 P.M.–5 P.M. *Closed:* Mondays, New Year's, Memorial Day, July 4, Labor Day, Thanksgiving, Christmas.

Admission: Free. Donations are welcome.

UNIVERSITY ART GALLERY, STATE UNIVERSITY OF NEW YORK AT BINGHAMTON
Fine Arts Bldg. S.U.N.Y. Binghamton
Vestal Parkway
Binghamton, NY 13901
Tel: (607)798–2634

This three-room University Art Gallery was founded in 1967 and contains paintings, sculpture, graphics, decorative arts and archeological material.

SAMPLING THE COLLECTION

LEONARD BASKIN   *King Priam*
American, b. 1922   1961
                                        Pen and ink wash
Baskin is a sculptor, printmaker and book illustrator. His themes usually concern man's struggle with some universal emotion. This is one of four Baskins in the collection, including a portfolio of 60 illustrations of *The Iliad.*

LOVIS CORINTH   *Die Waffen des Mara*
German, 1858–1925   1914
                                        Lithograph
Steeped in Dutch and Flemish traditions, yet influenced by Impressionism, Corinth made the transition from Realism to Expressionism. His literary, religious and mythological themes were expressed with vigor and earthiness. The gallery owns 20 important drypoints and etchings by Corinth.

COIN COLLECTION 269 B.C.–A.D. 361

Approximately 100 Roman coins are displayed as examples from this period.

WEDGWOOD COLLECTION

Josiah Wedgwood (1730–1795) manufactured earthenware in England under a translucent glaze. He called it creamware or Queensware. Stoneware or Jasperware, later products, were produced in black or pale colors. Antique and Classical designs have always been used.

FACILITIES

Hours: Monday–Friday, 9 A.M.–5 P.M.; Saturday, Sunday, 1 P.M. –5 P.M.
Closed: National holidays.
Admission: Free.

BROOKLYN

BROOKLYN MUSEUM
188 Eastern Parkway
Brooklyn, NY 11238
Tel: (212)638–5000

The museum, opened in 1897, was designed by McKim, Mead and White. Only one portion of the ambitious construction plans was ever completed. It was to be a "Museum of Everything for Everybody" with 28 departments housing multitudinous examples from art to zoology. The building has undergone numerous changes along with the shifting emphasis of the collection. In the 1930s, all but the art-related collections were dispersed to other Brooklyn institutions.

Façade of the Brooklyn Museum. *Courtesy Brooklyn Museum, Brooklyn*

The museum consolidated its holdings, becoming an art museum that concentrated on collecting original works of quality rather than reproductions. The five-story museum has major collections of Egyptian, Classical, Oriental, Middle Eastern and African art as well as art from the Americas and the South Pacific; European and American paintings and sculpture; prints and drawings; costumes; textiles; decorative arts; two dozen American period rooms, ranging in time from 1715 to the present; and a sculpture garden of ornaments from demolished New York buildings.

SAMPLING THE COLLECTION

1st Floor *PRIMITIVE ART AND NEW WORLD CULTURES*

BRITISH COLUMBIAN *Thunderbird Mask*
Vancouver Island, Kwakiutl Indian late 19th c.
Painted wood
The Kwakiutl created masks with movable and hinged parts for use at firelit ceremonials in the winter. When opened, the huge eagle head displays brilliantly colored mythological figures.

AMERICAN *Robe*
Plains Indian late 19th c.
(Probably Shoshone) Painted elk skin
The men painted their animal skin robes with narrative pictures. This one depicts the Sun Dance, the major religious festival. Trade pigments, applied with a porous bone tool, had succeeded natural colors.

AMERICAN *Kachina Doll and Mask*
New Mexico, late 19th c.
Zuni Indian Cotton fabric, fiber, wool and
feathers; painted wood and leather
Zuni "masked gods" reside beneath a sacred lake returning to dance in performances of past deeds. The priests acting these roles supposedly acquire the gods' spirits. If pleased, the gods make rain.

CENTRAL MEXICAN *Mask*
Teotihuacán 200–600
Dark green stone
This mask was probably attached to a cult figure or used as a burial mask. It is perceptively fashioned but because its teeth and inlaid eyes are missing it also has an impersonal aspect.

MEXICAN *Lienzo of Ihuitlán*
Oaxaca, Mixtec Culture 1500–1550
Painted cotton cloth
Because of its fine execution and genealogical information concerning the area's ruling families, this rare pictorial manuscript, completed about 30 years after the Conquest, is outstanding among the museum's five examples.

EASTERN MEXICAN *Quetzapcoatl*
San Vicente Tancuayalab 900–1250
Limestone
Maya-speaking people inhabited the Huasteca. Isolated from the main Mayan population their postclassic art reveals little Mayan influence. This renowned life-size statue demonstrates the late Huastec style.

Mesoamerican installation. *Courtesy Brooklyn Museum, Brooklyn*

PERUVIAN   *The Paracas Textile*
Cabeza Larga, Paracas Necropolis   late 1st c. B.C.–early
                                         1st c. A.D.
                                         Cotton with wool decoration
Notables were wrapped for burial in abundant yardage of cotton cloth containing luxurious woolen mantles and other grave furnishings. This complexly
wrought mantle is unequaled except for one in Sweden.

MELANESIAN   *Canoe Prow*
New Guinea, Sepik River   early 20th c.
                                         Wood
Outstanding Sepik sculpture exhibits strong human and animal forms depicting
supernatural forces. Several figures are frequently combined. The wood, originally painted but now gray and worn, makes this sculpture even more dramatic.

AFRICAN   *Royal Portrait of Bom Bosh*
Central Congo,   Wood
Bushongo (Kuba) Tribe
Highly stylized royal likenesses associated each ruler with a symbolic object.

Bom Bosh, a mid-17th-century warrior king, is identified by a drum with a severed hand carved in relief.

ORIENTAL ART

NORTHERN IRANIAN   *Fragment of a Carpet*
Tabriz   ca. 1550
                                     White cotton warps
                                     and wefts, senna knots
Rugs of this period are very rare. They generally contain medallion designs in vivid colors with naturalistic floral and animal decorations.

INDIAN   *Zummurad Shah in His Tent*
Agra   1567–1587
                                     Opaque watercolor and gold
                                     on cotton
Indian Mughal painting was mostly a court art depicting secular subjects for the first time. This scene portrays an episode from a Persian romance and is similar to Iranian miniature painting.

NEPALESE   *Indra*
                                     probably 14th or 15th c.
                                     Gilt copper set with gems
The myths and art of Nepal are often concerned with Indra. He is the Buddha of one of the Six Spheres of Existence and is often portrayed seated in repose.

CAMBODIAN   *Masculine Figure*
First Ankor Period, late   Brown sandstone
9th–12th c.
Khmer art of Cambodia was influenced by the culture of India. This figure is most likely a deified guardian.

CHINESE   *Duck-Shaped Vessel*
Late Chou Period, 600–221 B.C.   Cast bronze
Bronze cups and wine vessels were modeled since the Shang Dynasty and used mostly in burial sites. This later piece was probably used in the home or at banquets.

CHINESE   *Oviform Jar*
Yüan Dynasty, 1260–1368   14th c.
                                     Porcelain with blue underglaze
                                     painting
Porcelain, decorated in cobalt blue with a transparent glaze, is called "Chinese blue and white" and is the most popular ceramic ornamentation. Fourteenth-century Yüan porcelain is a marred blackish blue.

HSUEH CH'UANG   *Orchid, Bamboo and Thorn*
Chinese, fl. 14th c.   Ink on paper
To the Mongol-dominated Chinese of the Yüan Dynasty, orchid painting was synonymous with princeliness and symbolized loyalty. Bamboo represented the complete gentleman while the thorn probably referred to the difficulties under occupation.

KIM MYONG-KUK (YUN TAM)   *Painting of a Local Korean God*
Korean, Li Dynasty, 1392–1910   Ink on paper
Kim Myong-kuk's paintings were influenced by frequent diplomatic visits to Japan. Po Dai, the local god of good fortune, is rendered in swift, graceful brushwork with frugality of line.

JAPANESE
Kamakura Period, 1185–1333

Taizokai Mandara (Womb-world)
Paintings in color and gold on silk

Pictures containing geometric patterns of Buddhist deities made them easier to fathom than did writings. These were the primary works in the Shingon temples, a sect brought to Japan from China.

KAIHO YUSHO
Japanese, 1533–1615

Drying Fish Nets
(One of a pair of screens)
Color on paper, pasted over
with gold foil

Momoyama artists painted screens used as walls which were portable to enliven the vast gloomy interiors of stone castles. Gold leaf was often used to brighten these spaces and mirror additional light.

JAPANESE
Edo Period, 1615–1868

Screen
17th c.
Colors and ink on paper
with gold embossing

During this period an urban population encouraged genre painting by specialists in screen decoration. Beautiful and easygoing women were the prime subjects of these compositions.

IKE-NO-TAIGA
Japanese, 1723–1776

Scroll of Calligraphy

In calligraphy, each brush stroke contributes to complete the harmony. No error may be corrected once made. Ike-no-Taiga, an excellent calligrapher in childhood, emboldened his style in maturity.

PRINTS AND DRAWINGS   **2nd Floor**

The Print Room is opened by appointment and selections from it are rotated for exhibition.

ALBRECHT DURER
German, 1471–1528

St. Eustace
1501
Engraving

Dürer's harmonious composition of this conversion scene is elaborately detailed. Fastidiously formed and richly shaded, it demonstrates his superb draftsmanship.

FRANCISCO GOYA Y LUCIENTES
Spanish, 1746–1828

What a Golden Beak
(from *Los Caprichos,* plate #53)
1799
Aquatint and etching

The museum's 87 Goya prints include the entire *Caprichos* series. Goya executed these scathing social commentaries even though he was an esteemed painter to the Spanish court. This one ridicules the medical profession.

HONORE DAUMIER
French, 1808–1879

Enfoncé Lafayette . . . Attrapé
Mon Vieux
Lithograph

Daumier, a gifted painter, earned his living as a caricaturist. Political satires caused his imprisonment. His outstanding lithographs were marked by a diversity of blacks and a feeling for line and three-dimensionality.

JAMES A. MCNEILL WHISTLER
American, 1834–1903

Drouet
1859
Drypoint

Whistler believed this to be one of his best prints although he was only twenty-five years old when it was executed. The body is sketchily drawn with emphasis on the large head.

WINSLOW HOMER
American, 1836–1910

Eight Bells
1887
Etching

Homer's prints, seeming too harsh to a romantic public, were not immediately acclaimed. *Eight Bells* demonstrates a directness of draftsmanship. The unique composition places the precisely linear figures to the right.

HENRI DE TOULOUSE-LAUTREC
French, 1864–1901

Portrait of the Countess Adéle de Toulouse-Lautrec
1882
Charcoal

This portrait of Toulouse-Lautrec's mother was accomplished at the outset of his career. At his family's estate in southern France, he drew portraits of relatives and of the household staff.

PIERRE BONNARD
French, 1867–1947

La Blanchisseuse
1896
Lithograph in color

Bonnard's color lithographs were unsuccessful when they first appeared, etchings being the acceptable medium of the day. He was influenced by Japanese prints and endowed his ordinary subjects with dignity and grace.

GEORGES ROUAULT
French, 1871–1958

Le Conducteur de Chevaux
1910
Lithograph in color

This was Rouault's first lithograph in color. In his later religious themes, he renounced the older traditions of printmaking to adopt a style similar to that of the German Expressionists.

EMIL NOLDE
German, 1867–1956

South Sea Islander
1915
Lithograph in color

Nolde, a German Expressionist, turned to graphics late in his career but, even so, accounted for about 600 prints. This lithograph of a native youth was inspired by a trip to Melanesia.

ARSHILE GORKY
Armenian/American, 1904–1948

Study for "They Will Take My Island"
1944
Crayon

Executed in his last years, this exploratory drawing is all linear motion. Fantastic floating shapes are more detailed than in previous work, a combination of Surrealism and Abstraction.

3rd Floor *ANCIENT ART*

EGYPTIAN
Mohamerieh, near Edfu, Early
Predynastic Period

Bird Deity
ca. 4000 B.C.
Painted pottery

The earliest art in the Nile Valley was sculpture in the round. The birdlike appearance of this stylized female statuette depicts the spirit of the dead.

EGYPTIAN
Saqqarah, Old Kingdom,
Dynasty VI, 2420–2258 B.C.

Methethy as a Mature Man
ca. 2340 B.C.
Wood covered with gesso and painted

Unlike most idealized Egyptian sculpture, the face of Methethy, an estate administrator, is wise and lifelike. The eyes, still intact, allow the viewer an insight into the man's character.

EGYPTIAN
Hierakonpolis, Middle Kingdom,
Dynasty XII, 2000–1786 B.C.

King Sesostris III
1878–1843 B.C.
Black granite

The realistic fashioning of pharaoh's face distinguishes this sculpture. Unlike idealized portrayals of earlier times, Sesostris III observes his god harshly with energetic strength. Conversely, his body is executed in idealized style.

EGYPTIAN
New Kingdom, Dynasty XVIII,
1570–c. 1342 B.C.

King Amenhotep III
ca. 1415 B.C.
Diorite

Amenhotep III is compared to Louis XIV for his luxurious life-style. He introduced grace and charm to the modeling of male sculpture. Under his influence the style continued to increase in richness and variety.

EGYPTIAN
Thebes, Tomb No. 81, New
Kingdom, Dynasty XVIII, 1570–
ca. 1342 B.C.

Lady Thepu
ca. 1400 B.C.
Painting on gesso over mud
plaster

Egyptian painting had reached its peak. *Lady Thepu,* a prominent mature woman, is portrayed in her youth clothed like all great ladies of her day.

ASSYRIAN
Nimrud, Iraq

Assur-nasir-pal II, King of Assyria
ca. 880 B.C.
Alabaster

From the northwest palace of the king come 12 large friezes, the most important set of reliefs in the United States. This one depicts the king in procession.

EGYPTIAN
Karnak, New Kingdom,
Dynasty XXX, 405–332 B.C.

Wesir-wer's Head
ca. 360 B.C.
Green schist (metamorphic slate)

The head was most certainly modeled from life. Restraint in sculpturing the features resulted in a simple facial composition, typical of this period.

EGYPTIAN
Mitrahineh (Memphis),
Late Ptolemaic Period

The "Brooklyn Black Head"
ca. 80 B.C.
Black diorite

Egyptian and Greek influences dominate this portrait sculpture. The grand proportions, the pillar inscription and the frontality come from Egyptian art; the hairstyle, wide-open eyes and unbalanced features derive from Greece.

ITALIAN
Vulci, Attic

Amphora with the Death of Orpheus
ca. 470 B.C.
Red-figured pottery

Mediterranean countries used amphorae for food and wine storage and for transportation. Glossy black glazes cover the background of red-figure amphorae allowing the figures to remain the original red of the clay.

DECORATIVE ARTS   **4th Floor**

AMERICAN
New York, Brooklyn Flatlands

The Jan Martense Schenck House
ca. 1675

This faithfully reconstructed 17th-century two-room house is fitted with the simple furniture possessed by early New York settlers of Dutch background.

AMERICAN   *High Chest*
New England   1680–1710
                                  Walnut veneer
In earlier days, furniture production was akin to house construction, the results coarse and inelegant. The veneer, fine legs and stretchers of this piece demonstrate the new refined style.

PAUL DE LAMERIE   *Tray*
British, 1688–1751   ca. 1720
                                  Silver
De Lamerie created detailed Baroque and Rococo silver. This piece, executed before he turned to the Rococo, was influenced by French silverwork, the then prevailing English style.

JOSIAH WEDGWOOD 1730–1795
AND THOMAS BENTLEY (?)–1780   *Plaque with Four Muses and Apollo*
British   ca. 1775
                                  Blue and white Jasperware
Some time after 1770, Josiah Wedgwood, in partnership with Thomas Bentley, produced "ornamental" pieces. Jasperware, although created in other soft hues, is most familiar in blue gray.

HENRY WILL   *Inkstand*
American, New York,   Pewter
ca. 1736–1802
The inkstand contained letter writing material. Pewter, a popular Early American silver substitute, was cheap and easy to produce but soft and easily damaged. Very few pewter inkstands are extant.

ATT. TO HENRY WILLIAM STIEGEL   *Sugar Bowl*
American, Pennsylvania, 1729–1785 1765–1774
                                  Sapphire-blue glass
Deep blue color and diamond-molded designs typify the glass inspired by English and continental manufacturers. So skilled was Stiegel in duplicating foreign ware that his pieces are often mistaken for them.

DAVID SPINNER   *Pie Plate*
American, Pennsylvania,   ca. 1800
1758–1811   Red earthenware with sgraffito
                                  decoration
Red earthenware Pennsylvania produced pottery, glazed in yellow, brown and green and scratched with designs, was desirable until replaced by less costly manufactured pieces. Popular prints and familiar adages supplied the themes.

TUCKER AND HEMPHILL   *Pitcher*
American, Philadelphia,   1832–1838
Pennsylvania, 1825–1838   Porcelain
The French-style porcelain from this factory is imitative of Empire designs from Sèvres.

AMERICAN   *Parlor, the Robert J. Milligan House*
Saratoga, New York   ca. 1853
This gracious early Victorian parlor, furnished in Rococo revival style, belonged to an upper-class home whose owners were influenced by notions of a Renaissance villa.

JOHN HENRY BELTER   *Bed*
American, New York, 1804–1863   ca. 1860
                                  Rosewood
Belter's elaborate Rococo revival furniture of laminated rosewood, made him the most celebrated manufacturer of furniture during Victorian times.

Parlor, the Robert J. Milligan House. *Courtesy Brooklyn Museum, Brooklyn*

HOUSE OF WORTH
French

Dress
1880s
Silk moiré, chiffon, satin

Worth, an outstanding Parisian couturier, was trained in a draper's shop and studied museum portraits. His background inspired lavish styles and an ability to handle fabrics.

PAINTING AND SCULPTURE   **5th Floor**

CLAUDE MONET
French, 1840–1926

The Doge's Palace
1908
Oil on canvas

Monet's later paintings were done in series, becoming more abstract as the landscapes became more dissolved in brilliant light and atmospheric vapor.

JOHN SINGLETON COPLEY   *Mrs. William Eppes*
American, 1738–1815   (Abigail Pickman)
                                ca. 1769
Copley was the outstanding American portraitist of his day, rivaling the best artists of Europe. His works are insightful, forcefully drawn and of glowing color.

FREDERIC EDWIN CHURCH   *South American Landscape*
American, 1826–1900   1873
                                Oil on canvas
Rather than travel to Europe to learn from the past, Church became fascinated with the wilderness of the Western Hemisphere. He made two trips to South America. This painting is the result of one.

THOMAS EAKINS   *William Rush Carving His*
American, 1844–1916   *Allegorical Figure of the Schuylkill*
                                River
                                1908
                                Oil on canvas
Eakins, a Realist, only painted a nude if it was meaningful and had a logical relationship to actuality. He painted William Rush and his nude female model in a series.

WINSLOW HOMER   *The Turtle Pond*
American, 1836–1910   1898
                                Watercolor on paper
In his later years Homer turned to watercolors. He painted many light-filled tropical scenes most often pitting man against nature.

WILLIAM GLACKENS   *Nude with Apple*
American, 1870–1938   1910
                                Oil on canvas
Glackens, a member of "The Eight," believed that life was the motive force in art. To this end, he integrated the color and animation of the city into his work.

GASTON LACHAISE   *Standing Woman*
French/American, 1882–1935   1932
                                Bronze
The standing female nude was Lachaise's favorite theme. His sensual interpretations often offended the public.

FACILITIES

Gallery Talks, Lectures and *Symposia* are offered throughout the year.

Discovery Days explore and explain the museum's holdings and include special programs, guided gallery tours and related activities emphasizing different parts of the collection.

Information Desk   *Gallery Tours* by trained guides are available Wednesdays 1 P.M.

Temporary Exhibits culled from the museum's collection or *Loan Exhibitions* from other institutions are regular features of the museum's program.

1st Floor   *Concerts, Poetry* and *Theater Readings* take place on Sundays.

1st Floor   The *Cafeteria* serves lunches, snacks and tea. Open: Wednesday–Saturday, 10 A.M.–4:30 P.M. Sundays, holidays, 11 A.M.–4:30 P.M.

1st Floor   The *Gallery Shop* is well stocked and carries items from around the world from antiques to museum reproductions. Prices range from 10¢ to $1,000. The varied assortment includes pewter reproductions from the museum's collection, such as the inkstand, $125 (see section on Decorative Arts); a pair of Chinese opera marionettes, hand-painted in Taiwan, $5; slate trivets, $7.50 each; and a set of coasters, $20, incised with Egyptian hieroglyphs; and solid glass paper-weights handblown by a leading American craftsman, $10. There are also art books, posters, exhibition catalogs, children's books, greeting and note cards and postcards.

The *Art Reference Library* contains books, periodicals, exhibition catalogs and **2nd Floor** documentary materials. Open: Wednesday–Friday, 1 P.M.–5 P.M.

Films on art or related subjects are often screened. **3rd Floor**

The *Paintings Study Gallery* is open weekdays by appointment. The museum's **5th Floor** inventory of over 1,000 pictures is listed in a location file and may be viewed on sliding or rotating panels.

For Children in 1st through 7th grades there is a program called "What's Up" familiarizing them with the museum's collections through looking, drawing and creative dramatics.

Parking may be found either at meters in front of the building or for 50¢ in the lot behind the museum.

Hours: Wednesday–Saturday, 10 A.M. –5 P.M.; Sunday, 12 P.M.–5 P.M.; Holi-
         days, 1 P.M.–5 P.M. *Closed:* Mondays, Tuesdays, New Year's, Christ-
         mas.

Admission: Suggested donation: Adult, $1.50; students with I.D. or G.O.
             cards, 50¢. Free to senior citizens and children under 12 accom-
             panied by an adult.

BROOKLYN CHILDREN'S MUSEUM
**145 Brooklyn Ave. at
St. Marks Ave.
Brooklyn, New York 11213
Tel: (212)735–4432**

The museum is the oldest children's museum in the world. It was established in 1899 in a Victorian mansion on its present site. Conceived and executed by Hardy, Holzman, Pfeiffer Associates, the innovative building invites the child to examine its structural properties as well as its 50,000 artifacts. The architects have transported objects in daily use and incorporated them into the building's composition. Thus, a blue porcelainized grain silo is converted into a fire escape; a superhighway sign heralds the museum's name; stadium bleachers become seats for the open-sky theater; steel gothic-beams are transformed into rooftop benches; and huge corrugated pipes are remade into People Tubes. With the exception of one corner opening onto a sunken courtyard, the rein-forced concrete structure is entirely underground in order to preserve Brower Park, the site of its location.

SAMPLING THE COLLECTION

PARTICIPATORY ACTIVITIES

These activities change daily and involve the visitor, the instructor and objects from the museum's collection. Instructors select a topic and appropriate objects relating to it. They then set up "Focus Activities" at various locations in the museum's Participatory Learning Environment. Visitors explore without guides whichever Focus Activity interests them in cultural history, natural history or technology. Items range from mineral specimens, to musical instruments, to

African masks, to animal specimens, to primitive tools and to larger permanent exhibits such as an indoor windmill.

PARTICIPATORY LEARNING ENVIRONMENT

One large open learning space is divided into four levels with a connecting ramp, each representing the classic elements of air, earth, fire and water. A stream of water with locks, dams and waterwheel runs through the ramp. Major exhibits include a steam engine on the fire level, a windmill on the air level and a greenhouse on the earth level.

FACILITIES

The *Children's Resource Library* contains films, books, magazines, slides, video equipment, records, etc., and is maintained for children only.

The *Take Home Collection* permits the borrowing of such objects as shells, stuffed animals and African musical instruments for a two-week period. They are loaned out in kits containing additional information on the object borrowed.

Storytelling Sessions become creative experiences when held in conjunction with craft programs in which the child constructs items pertaining to the story.

The *Marketplace* sells unusual craft and educational items related to the museum's programming. Prices are inexpensive, ranging from 5¢ to $12. Currently popular items are a twirl hand drum from Taiwan; seahorses and blowfish; a map puzzle; and modeling clay.

Hours: Wednesday–Monday, 1 P.M.–5 P.M. *Closed:* Tuesdays.

Admission: Free.

BUFFALO

ALBRIGHT-KNOX ART GALLERY
1285 Elmwood Ave.
Buffalo, NY 14222
Tel: (716)882-8700

In 1962, an international award-winning modern wing was added to the distinguished 1905 Neoclassical museum. They form a unique union of sensibilities recognized as one of the most successful museum structures anywhere. Several galleries and a very pleasant restaurant in the addition open onto an impressive glass courtyard housing a sculpture garden. The museum's special strength and interest lies in its collection of 19th- and 20th-century American, European and Latin American works.

SAMPLING THE COLLECTION

For the location of all items, it is necessary to check the "Location File" at the Information Desk because installations are subject to change.

PAINTINGS

PAUL GAUGUIN
French, 1848–1903

Yellow Christ
1889
Oil on canvas

Spirit of the Dead Watching
1892
Oil on canvas

During the years of these paintings, Gauguin was searching for a simpler culture where he could paint in the Synthesist style he developed.

JOAN MIRO
Spanish, b. 1893

Carnival of Harlequin
1924–1925
Oil on canvas

Miró, an Abstract Surrealist, paints with great humor. He uses a brilliant palette to create his fanciful figures.

GEORGIA O'KEEFFE
American, b. 1887

Black Spot #3
1919
Oil on canvas

O'Keeffe is often frugal in her selection of color and form. She sometimes paints in a series over a long period of time.

HENRI MATISSE
French, 1869–1954

La Musique
1939
Oil on canvas

Matisse was the leader of the Fauvists, a group who first exhibited in 1905. Though his work underwent several stylistic changes, an emphasis on color was always present.

JACKSON POLLOCK
American, 1912–1956

Convergence
1952

Pollock dripped paint on large canvases without the aid of brushes or tools, creating works that lack finite boundaries. Roundly criticized at first, today he is considered an important mid-20th-century painter.

SCULPTURES

AUGUSTE RODIN
French, 1840–1917

Eve
1881
Bronze

Rodin introduced Impressionism to sculpture, modeling his naturalistic pieces with light and shadow. He was the most important sculptor of the 19th century.

PABLO PICASSO
Spanish, 1881–1973

Woman's Head
1909
Bronze

Picasso modeled this head during his early Cubist period. The study of Negro sculpture had helped free him from the traditional expression of purely representational art.

HENRI MATISSE
French, 1869–1954

Reclining Nude I
1907
Bronze

Matisse, best known for his paintings, also created sculpture. The reclining

Auguste Rodin, Eve. *Courtesy Albright-Knox Art Gallery, Buffalo*

nude, a popular theme since antiquity, was simplified and stylized by Matisse in his choice of materials and poses.

ANTOINE PEVSNER
Russian/French, 1886–1962

Construction in the Egg
1948
Bronze doré

Pevsner, with his brother Gabo, were the founders of Constructivism. He incorporated industrial materials and methods and believed that motion in space was essential.

DAVID SMITH
American, 1906–1965

Cubi XVI
1963
Stainless steel

Smith first worked in a car factory. His welded sculptures are an extension of this interest. The *Cubi* series, among his most important, are geometric shapes that soar into space, reflecting the sky and surroundings.

TONY SMITH
American, b. 1912

Cigarette
1967
Cor-Ten steel

Smith was a principal influence on Minimal sculpture, and trained as an architect. His geometric, black-painted, steel works are large and severe and sometimes allude to real subjects.

ANTHONY CARO
British, b. 1924

Georgiana
1969–1970
Painted steel

Caro's sculptures are based on Constructivism. He uses prefabricated metal forms welded and riveted into massive assemblages and painted in vivid colors.

FACILITIES

Temporary Exhibitions culled from the art gallery's collection or *Loan Exhibitions* from other institutions are regular features of the art gallery.

An ongoing program of *Tours, Lectures, Gallery Talks, Concerts* and *Films* is offered. Call for schedule and program information.

An *Art Reference Library* is available for use on the premises, Tuesday–Friday, 2 P.M.–5 P.M.; Sunday, 1 P.M.–3 P.M.

The *Children's Activity Center* is open Saturday and Sunday, 2 P.M.–4 P.M. and caters to children up to 8 years of age. It contains a library of art-oriented books. A special activity is offered from 2:30 P.M. to 3:30 P.M., such as creative writing, puppetry; even musicians are invited to play for the children.

The *Garden Restaurant,* a pleasant eating facility, looks out on the sculpture garden of the glass-enclosed courtyard. Open Tuesday–Saturday, 10:30 A.M.– 4:30 P.M.; Sunday 12 P.M.–4:30 P.M.

The *Gallery Shop* sells cards, stationery, posters, catalogs of exhibitions, books on art for adults and children, small sculpture, jewelry, toys, calendars and much more.

Hours: Tuesday–Saturday, 10 A.M.–5 P.M.; Sunday, 12 P.M.–5 P.M. *Closed:* Mondays, New Year's, Thanksgiving, Christmas.

Admission: Free. Voluntary contribution boxes are at each entrance.

COOPERSTOWN

FENIMORE HOUSE, ADMINISTERED BY
THE NEW YORK STATE HISTORICAL ASSOCIATION
Lake Rd.
Route 80
Cooperstown, NY 13326
Tel: (607)547-2533

Cooperstown was founded in 1786 by the father of James Fenimore Cooper (1789–1851). Fenimore House, a stately stone building of the 1930s, was established as a museum in 1945. Located on the site of the author's former home, it is a repository for art, furniture and memorabilia pertaining to the Cooper family and to the early years of Cooperstown's history. It includes family portraits by Gilbert Stuart (1755–1828) and John Wesley Jarvis (1780–1840); other American paintings; portrait busts by John Henri Isaac Browere (1790–1845), a group of bronzes done from life masks of famous early Americans such as Thomas Jefferson, James Madison, John Adams, DeWitt Clinton, Martin Van Buren and others, and a collection of American folk art consisting of paintings, sculpture, furniture and textiles.

Exterior view. Courtesy New York State Historical Association, Cooperstown

SAMPLING THE COLLECTION

BENJAMIN WEST   *Robert Fulton*
American, 1738–1820   Oil

West, a portraitist, settled in England, where fellow Americans, including Fulton, came to study under him. He was the first to introduce modern dress on his subjects in his historical canvases.

GILBERT STUART   *Joseph Brant*
American, 1755–1828   1786
                                 Oil
Stuart was the leading portraitist in Federal America. Working in London in 1786, he painted this educated American Indian Mohawk chief who had come to England on a fund-raising mission.

ASHER BROWN DURAND   *The Hudson River*
American, 1796–1886   Oil on canvas
Durand was a prominent member of the Hudson River School of painting. His naturalistic, poetic landscapes were some of the first in America to be painted outdoors.

THOMAS COLE   *The Last of the Mohicans*
American, 1801–1848   Oil
Cole was the leading painter of the Hudson River School of landscape artists. Cooper's tale lends itself to Cole's dramatic and romantic interpretations of primeval landscapes.

WILLIAM SIDNEY MOUNT   *Eel Spearing at Setauket*
American, 1807–1868   Oil on canvas
Mount lived and worked on his native Long Island, recording its daily rural life in realistic and perceptive genre scenes.

EDWARD HICKS   *Peaceable Kingdom*
American, 1780–1849   Oil on canvas
Hicks, an itinerant preacher, coach and house painter was a self-taught folk artist. He painted the *Peaceable Kingdom* over 25 times, taking his theme from the Bible.

GRANDMA MOSES
(ANNA MARY ROBERTSON MOSES)   *Sugaring Off*
American, 1860–1961   Oil
Grandma Moses commenced painting at the age of seventy-six. In naïve style she completed over 2,000 pictures of rural life in New York State as she recollected it from her youth.

FACILITIES

Guided Tours are available.

The *Fenimore Book Store* sells books on art, folk art, architecture, decorative arts, furniture, antiques and crafts.

Hours: *May 1–October 31:* Daily, 9 A.M.–7 P.M. *Fall and Spring:* Slightly reduced schedule. *Winter:* More reduced schedule.

Admission: Adults, $2.50; children (7–15), $1.25; under 7, free.

EASTHAMPTON

GUILD HALL OF EASTHAMPTON
158 Main St.
Easthampton, NY 11937
Tel: (516)324-0806

Guild Hall is a cultural and educational center attracting over 80,000 visitors each year to its museum, theater and other programs. The museum's permanent

Exterior view. Courtesy Guild Hall of Easthampton, Easthampton

collection consists of works by major artists of the area. Its changing exhibitions feature established artists or innovative themes. Because the collection is rotated, the following works may not always be on view.

SAMPLING THE COLLECTION

JAMES BROOKS
American, b. 1906

Floxurn
1955
Oil on canvas

Executed in Brooks's mature style, which developed in the 1950s, this Abstract Expressionist work has the warm, subdued tones found in nature.

WILLEM DE KOONING
American, b. 1904

Wah Kee Spareribs
1972
Lithograph

This work contains strong figurative elements in a powerful and stark framework of a black and white image. De Kooning is an artist of the Easthampton area.

WARREN BRANDT
American, b. 1918

The Checker Game
1967
Oil on canvas

This work is in the soft, sunny colors introduced by the Impressionists and depicts a sympathetic interior in complete harmony with the rosy coloration of the work.

CHILDE HASSAM
American, 1859–1935

Little Old Cottage,
Egypt Lane, Easthampton
1917
Oil on canvas

The Easthampton subject matter and fine painterly quality of this canvas by the American Impressionist make it one of Guild Hall's most popular paintings.

FACILITIES

Changing Exhibitions are regularly featured.

John Drew Theater presents professional theater nightly during July and August. *Concerts, Films, Lectures, Dance* and *Community Theater* are presented during the remainder of the year. Call or write for schedule and admission price.

The *Museum Shop*'s most popular items are the posters by well-known regional artists such as Willem de Kooning, Saul Steinberg, James Rosenquist, Jimmy Ernst and Paul Davis. They are sold in both signed and unsigned editions. Prices range from $15 to $400. Also featured are handcrafted articles from $1 to $150.

Hours: *May–September:* Monday–Saturday, 10 A.M.–5 P.M.; Sunday, 2 P.M.–5 P.M. *Rest of year:* Tuesday–Saturday, 10 A.M.–5 P.M.

Admission: Free.

ELMIRA

ARNOT ART MUSEUM
235 Lake St.
Elmira, NY 14901
Tel: (607)734-3697

The museum, founded in 1911, is quartered in an 1833 Greek Revival-style home built for John Arnot, Sr. The rooms are still intact. His son, Matthias, added a gallery on the north side to house his art collection. The original collection was built around 72 European paintings and some sculpture, the most noteworthy from the 16th to the 18th century. The trustees have continued to add to the collection, mostly American works, while maintaining the high standards of its founder.

SAMPLING THE COLLECTION

These works are on display from June through September. The remainder of the year is devoted to changing exhibitions.

JOHANNES (JAN) BRUEGHEL   *A Dutch Fair*
Flemish, 1568–1625   1613
                                       Oil on copper
Jan was the younger son of Pieter Brueghel, the Elder. Known as "Velvet Brueghel," he was a popular painter of still lifes and landscapes which he composed with careful detail.

CLAUDE LORRAIN   *Ulysses Discovering*
French, 1600–1682   *Himself to Nausicaa*
Claude lived and worked in Rome for most of his life, painting successfully for European nobility. He was an accomplished landscape painter greatly influencing later landscapists, especially the English.

GUSTAVE COURBET   *A Mountain Stream*
French, 1819–1877   Oil on canvas
A revolutionary in art as well as in politics, Courbet turned from the academicism of his teachers to evolve a naturalistic style. He died in Switzerland, whence he fled after meddling in French politics.

THEODORE (PIERRE-ETIENNE)
ROUSSEAU   *An Autumn Evening*
French, 1812–1867   Oil on wood
Rousseau was a founder of the Barbizon School. He painted detailed represen-
tations of nature. This school met with great opposition from the establishment
but was the precursor of Impressionism.

JEAN FRANCOIS MILLET   *The Apple Gatherers*
French, 1814–1875   1851
                                             Oil on canvas
Millet, a member of the Barbizon School, painted the hardships of peasant life
as well as landscapes. His subjects affronted the public. It was only toward the
end of his career that he met with approval and wealth.

THOMAS COLE   *Autumn in the Catskills*
American, 1801–1848   1827
                                             Oil on wood
Cole was the leader of the Hudson River School, a group of American landsca-
pists who depicted the wonders of nature in a romantic style.

FACILITIES

Changing Exhibitions are regularly featured.

The *Museum Shop* offers prints and postcards, art calendars, miniatures, sculptures, and paintings by regional artists, for sale or rent. Each month a different
artist's work is featured.

Hours: Tuesday–Friday, 10 A.M.–5 P.M.; Saturday, 9 A.M.–5 P.M.; Sunday, 2 P.M.–
         5 P.M.   *Closed:* Mondays, national holidays.

Admission: Free.

FLUSHING

QUEENS COLLEGE ART COLLECTION
Paul Klapper Library
Kissena Blvd. & Long Island Expressway
Flushing, NY 11367
Tel: (212)445-7500, ext. 243

The museum was founded in 1957. Its collection contains Near Eastern, Oriental, Western and contemporary art; graphics; paintings; sculpture; ancient and
antique glass and prints.

SAMPLING THE COLLECTION

PHILIPS WOUWERMAN   *A Dutch Horseman's Game*
Dutch, 1619–1668   ca. 1650
                                             Oil on canvas
Wouwerman, a prolific painter of landscapes and genre scenes, peopled his
paintings with finely drawn figures usually including horses. His cool color
harmonies account for part of his great popularity.

ANDREA SANSOVINO   *Christ at the Column*
Italian, 1460–1529   ca. 1525
                                    Bronze and wood
Sansovino is an important transitional figure from the Early to the High Renais-
sance in Italy. This figure is placed in a carved wooden tabernacle.

ANTOINE LOUIS BARYE   *Crouching Jaguar Devouring Hare*
French, 1795–1875   1850
                                    Bronze
Most of Barye's Romantic sculptures were of animals warring with other
animals or men. Although he studied them only in the zoo, he was able to
translate their wild and ferocious qualities into bronze.

BRITISH COLUMBIAN   *Ceremonial Rattle*
Kwakiutl Indian   19th c.
                                    Wood
This tribe, native to the coast of British Columbia, has long been known for its
clever wood carvings and bold use of paint. Development of secret societies
led to rituals and carvings connected with their ceremonies.

FACILITIES

Changing Exhibitions are regularly featured.

Hours: Monday–Friday, 9 A.M.–5 P.M. Some evenings until 8 P.M. *Closed:*
         Saturdays, Sundays, New Year's, Thanksgiving, Christmas, Human
         Rights Day.

Admission: Free.

FREDONIA

MICHAEL C. ROCKEFELLER ARTS CENTER GALLERY
State University College
Fredonia, NY 14063
Tel: (716)673–3537

The gallery, sponsored by the college's Art Department, is housed in its Arts
Center. It is a contemporary building accommodating classrooms and studios.

SAMPLING THE COLLECTION

WILLIAM KING   *Words*
American, b. 1925   1974
                                    Stainless steel
These three figures are in the midst of a conversation or intellectual debate.
King's elongated and somewhat anonymous figures are a cynical expression of
life today.

RICHARD STANKEIWICZ   *Untitled Sculpture*
American, b. 1922   1972
                                    Cor-Ten steel

This piece, of modest size, is an example of acrobatic balance between geometric cylindrical shapes for which Stankeiwicz is noted.

FACILITIES

Tours of the gallery may be arranged with advance notice.

Hours: The gallery attendants are students. Therefore, the viewing schedule changes every semester. Check with gallery.

Admission: Free.

GLENS FALLS

HYDE COLLECTION
161 Warren St.
Glens Falls, NY 12801
Tel: (518)792-1761

Built in 1912 in the Florentine style of the Renaissance, Hyde House was intended to be not only a home but, eventually, a setting for the collection of paintings, sculpture, furniture and books assembled by Mr. and Mrs. Louis Fiske Hyde. In 1963 the collection was opened to the public. It includes works of art from the 5th century B.C. through the 20th century. Cunningham House, located next door, is the educational annex of the Hyde.

SAMPLING THE COLLECTION

Library REMBRANDT HARMENSZ VAN RIJN *Portrait of Christ*
Dutch, 1606–1669 Oil on canvas
Rembrandt, essentially a portrait painter, remained exactly that even when he turned to religious subjects. In time his palette became more subdued; light and shadow conveyed his insightful interpretations of the sitter's character.

Music Room PETER PAUL RUBENS *Head of a Negro*
Flemish, 1577–1640 Oil on panel
Rubens was the leading exponent of northern Baroque art. He combined bold use of color, flowing brushwork and luminous skin tones to idealize his subjects.

East Hall LEONARDO DA VINCI *Study for the Mona Lisa*
Italian, 1452–1519 ca. 1500
Silver point (overworked
later in other medium) on
grounded paper
Mona Lisa is one of Leonardo's few completed works, most of which were finished by pupils or left undone. It is important for its sfumato technique, pale tones softly graded into dark ones by blurring the outlines.

Mrs. Hyde's WINSLOW HOMER *St. John's River*
Room American, 1836–1910
A Good One, Adirondacks

Forebodings
all late 1800s watercolors

Music Room. *Courtesy Hyde Collection, Glens Falls*

Homer and Eakins were the foremost American Realist genre painters of their day. Homer's watercolors, influenced by those of the English style, were energetically expressed. Masculine viewers were attracted to his subjects: the sea, fishing, hunting.

FACILITIES

Lectures and *Concerts* are offered without charge. Call for program information.

A *Library* of art books is available for use on the premises.

The *Sales Shop* carries reproductions of works in the collection, notepaper, slides, catalogs and booklets, coloring books, jewelry and sculpture.

Hours: Tuesday–Wednesday, Friday–Sunday, 2 P.M.–5 P.M. Mornings by appointment only for special groups. *Closed:* Mondays, Thursdays, holidays.

Admission: Free.

HEMPSTEAD

EMILY LOWE GALLERY, HOFSTRA UNIVERSITY
Hempstead Turnpike
Hempstead, NY 11550
Tel: (516)560-3275,6

Exterior view. Courtesy Emily Lowe Gallery, Hofstra University, Hempstead

Established in 1963, the gallery has an extensive permanent collection including African, Oceanic, pre-Columbian, Japanese and Indian sculpture, American prints and European painting of the 18th, 19th, and 20th centuries.

SAMPLING THE COLLECTION

Special Collections of the Library, Not Always on View

JEAN FRANCOIS MILLET
French, 1814–1875

Retreat from the Storm
ca. 1846–1848
Oil on canvas

Millet's paintings of peasant life were executed in a sentimental academic style. He became an important member of the Barbizon School of landscape painting even though his figures were always central to his work.

PAUL GAUGUIN
French, 1848–1903

Portrait of a Woman or Model Juliette
ca. 1880
Oil on canvas

This painting in bright pastel tones was done in Gauguin's early Impressionist manner. It was prior to the nonnaturalistic style he adopted in Brittany and continued to use while living in the South Seas.

FACILITIES

Loan Exhibitions organized by the gallery and from other institutions are regular features of the gallery's program.

Special Events, such as *Lectures, Films, Gallery Talks, Concerts,* and *Dance Recitals* are offered. Call for information.

The *Sales Shop* carries posters and exhibition catalogs priced from $1 to $14.95.

Hours: Tuesday–Wednesday, 10 A.M. to 9 P.M.; Thursday–Friday, 10 A.M.–5 P.M.; Saturday–Sunday, 1 P.M.–5 P.M. *Closed:* Mondays; national holidays; school vacations.

Admission: Free.

HUNTINGTON

HECKSCHER MUSEUM
Prime Ave.
Huntington, NY 11743
Tel: (516)351-3250

Situated in a pleasant park with a pond, this one-story Greek Revival limestone museum, founded in 1920, contains four galleries. Two are devoted to the permanent collection, works that span the 16th through the 20th centuries with major emphasis on 19th- and 20th-century American artists.

SAMPLING THE COLLECTION

LUCAS CRANACH, THE ELDER
German, 1472–1553

Virgin, Child, St. John the Baptist and Angels
1534
Oil on canvas, transferred from panel

Cranach was an engraver, woodcutter and painter. He combined a careful technique with a certain liveliness in his figures and landscapes. He painted mostly religious and classical subjects.

GUSTAVE COURBET
French, 1819–1877

Depth of the Forest
Oil on canvas

Courbet was a Realist painter, an iconoclast whose genre scenes, still lifes, portraits, seascapes and landscapes were executed with simple naturalism. Later, concentrating on landscapes frequently peopled with erotic nudes, he dismayed a prudish public.

GEORGE GROSZ
German/American, 1893–1959

American Tourists in Berlin
(Trio)
1928
Ink and watercolor on paper with gelatin glaze

Eclipse of the Sun
1926
Oil on canvas

Circus Rider
1928
Oil on canvas

Grosz was a principal exponent of Dadaism, a movement mirroring the cynicism bred by World War I. His satirical works criticize reactionary attitudes. *Eclipse of the Sun* is considered by some Grosz's most important oil.

THOMAS EAKINS
American, 1844–1916

The Cello Player
Oil on canvas, mounted
on board

Eakins was influenced by 17th-century Spanish Realists. Incurring a scandal for posing a nude male model before a mixed class and disparaged for his realism, Eakins was mostly unappreciated until after his death.

FACILITIES

Temporary Exhibitions organized from the museum's collection and from other institutions, as well as *Loan Exhibitions* are regular features of the museum's program.

The *Cottage* serves as educational center for the museum and includes a library and teacher resource center.

A *Sales Desk* carries some postcards of art in the collection at 15¢, and catalogs of exhibitions from $1 to $8.

Hours: Tuesday–Friday, 10 A.M.–5 P.M.; Saturday and Sunday, 1 P.M.–6 P.M. *Closed:* Mondays.

Admission: Free.

ITHACA

HERBERT F. JOHNSON MUSEUM OF ART
Central Ave.
Cornell University
Ithaca, NY 14853
Tel: (607)256-6464

This contemporary-style university museum designed by I. M. Pei offers dramatic views of Lake Cayuga and the surrounding area. The museum's collections are especially strong in Asian art and in 19th- and 20th-century painting, with major holdings in the graphic arts. The George and Mary Rockwell Galleries of Asian Art are located on a separate floor and contain mostly ceramics, sculpture and paintings. Another floor is devoted to the Print and Photograph Collections, approximately 7,200 items in all. Other floors are reserved for the installation of American and European objects.

SAMPLING THE COLLECTION

It is impossible to give the location of the objects listed below because the collections are frequently rotated.

Exterior view. Courtesy Herbert F. Johnson Museum of Art, Ithaca

JAPANESE Late Heian Period, 898–1185	*Standing Amida Buddha* 12th c. Carved wood, assembled black technique, with traces of gilding

A purely Japanese art developed during the Heian Period when intercourse with China had been severed. Buddhism was undergoing changes, with emphasis on the emotional, human side of the religion rather than otherworldly aspects.

CHINESE	*Seated Kuan Yin* 11th c. or later Carved wood with polychrome

Kuan Yin was an Indian import, one of the Bodhisattvas of Mahayana Buddhism. A Bodhisattva is a being who has led such a virtuous life, he is qualified to become Buddha.

ARTHUR G. DOVE American, 1880–1946	*Alfie's Delight* 1929 Oil on canvas

One of America's first Abstractionists, Dove's work always retained something of reality and was based on mainly natural shapes.

CHARLES FRANCOIS DAUBIGNY   *Fields in June*
French, 1817–1878   1874
                                   Oil on canvas
Daubigny was a member of the Barbizon School. Landscapes became major
themes instead of merely backgrounds in Classical paintings. Daubigny was the
only one to paint outdoors and was a decided influence on the Impressionists.

CIRCLE OF GHEERAERDTS–DE
CRITZ   *Bess Throckmorton—*
Flemish, act. 1550–1640   *Lady Walter Raleigh*
                                   ca. 1592
                                   Oil on canvas
The de Critz and Gheeraerdts families established workshops in England where
they produced portraits of Elizabethan society in which clothing and accesso-
ries were faithfully reproduced.

FERNAND LEGER   *Still Life*
French, 1881–1955   1936
                                   Oil on canvas
Léger worked in many media. Commencing as an architect, he was influenced
by several movements before evolving his own brand of Cubism.

ALBERTO GIACOMETTI   *Walking Man II*
Swiss, 1901–1966   1959–1960
                                   Bronze edition 5/6
Commencing as a Surrealist sculptor, Giacometti is best known for his at-
tenuated, isolated figures, evocations of today's alienated world.

FACILITIES

Changing Exhibitions are regularly featured.

Group Tours of the galleries and of special exhibitions may be arranged by
calling the museum two weeks in advance.

The *Sales Desk* carries cards from 15¢ to 35¢.

Hours: Tuesday–Sunday, 10 A.M.–5 P.M. *Closed:* Mondays, December 24,
         January 14, Memorial Day, July 4, Labor Day.

Admission: Free.

MANHATTAN

AMERICAN CRAFT MUSEUM
44 West 53rd St.
New York, NY 10019
Tel: (212)397-0630

The museum, formerly the Museum of Contemporary Crafts, was founded in
1956 as part of the American Craft Council, the first museum in the country to
be devoted entirely to crafts. Since 1979 it has occupied its present location in
an award-winning building whose façade still remains untouched. On the first
two floors, simple, versatile exhibition space is developed by open walls and
carefully placed alcoves. Observation decks provide surprise views of works

below. Since its inception the museum has presented over 4,000 works by celebrated American and foreign craftspeople, as well as those by new talent, in changing exhibitions. Included have been contemporary, functional and sculptural works in clay, glass, fiber, wood and metal. Although the museum concentrates on these exhibitions, it does maintain a permanent collection on the fourth floor of over 300 20th-century craft objects available for viewing by appointment. Selections from this collection are shown each summer.

SAMPLING THE COLLECTION

GERTRUD NATZLER *Bowl*
Austrian/American, 1908–1971 1956
Earthenware, crater glaze

OTTO NATZLER
Austrian/American, b. 1908
The Natzlers used simple unaffected shapes in their ceramics thrown on the wheel by Gertrud and glazed by Otto, who developed glazes over years of experimentation.

MERRY RENK *Wedding Crown*
American, b. 1928 1968
Yellow gold, wire, cultured pearls
Renk lives and works in San Francisco. She refers to her work as "organic" and it has been described as deceptively simple and natural looking.

Merry Renk, Wedding Crown. *Courtesy American Crafts Council, New York*

FACILITIES

Lectures, Demonstrations and other *Living Events,* related to the theme of the current exhibition, are presented in informal programs.

The *Sales Desk* carries books and catalogs.

Hours: Tuesday–Saturday, 10 A.M.–5 P.M.; Sundays, holidays, 11 A.M.–5 P.M.

Admission: Adults, $1; children under 16, students and senior citizens, 50¢.

ASIA HOUSE GALLERY OF THE ASIA SOCIETY, INC.
725 Park Ave.
New York, NY 10021
Tel: (212)751–3210

At the time that this guide was being compiled the Asia Society's new eight-story building was under construction. It was designed by Edward Larrabee Barnes and is composed of two shades of red granite. The gallery occupies the main floor where its barrel-vaulted ceiling rises to the second floor and additional exhibition space. On view will be, for the first time, a permanent collection in addition to the three exhibitions of Asian art and, generally, one of vintage photographs it exhibits annually. Works are borrowed from public and private collections in the United States and abroad. Previous exhibitions have included such shows as *The Last Empire: Victorian Photographs of India; Southeast Asian Ceramics;* and *Masterworks in Wood: China and Japan.*

FACILITIES

Lectures, Tape-Slide Lectures and *Films* related to the theme of each display are usually presented.

The *Sales Desk* carries exhibition catalogs and postcards of some of the pieces included in the loan exhibitions.

Hours: Tuesday–Saturday, 10 A.M.–5 P.M.; Sunday, 1 P.M.–5 P.M. Open one evening; call to verify. *Closed:* New Year's, Thanksgiving, Christmas.

Admission: A voluntary contribution is suggested.

THE CLOISTERS
Fort Tryon Park
New York, NY 10040
Tel: (212)923–3700

The Cloisters, opened in 1938, is an adjunct to the Metropolitan Museum of Art. A modern building in medieval style, it overlooks the Hudson River from its location in Fort Tryon Park and is solely concerned with the arts of the Middle Ages. The building contains architectural components from various European structures including portions from five cloisters, a chapter house, a Romanesque chapel and apse and Gothic doorways, all ranging from the 12th through the 15th centuries. The collection is rich in tapestries, ivories, illuminated manuscripts, stained glass, panel paintings, sculpture and metalwork. The medieval

Exterior view. Courtesy The Cloisters, New York

gardens on display include a Herb Garden planted with over 200 species grown in the Middle Ages.

SAMPLING THE COLLECTION

GREEK	*The Chalice of Antioch* between A.D. 350–500 Gilded silver	**Treasury**

Discovered in 1910, this is one of the earliest surviving Christian chalices.

FRANCO-FLEMISH	*The Unicorn Tapestries* ca. 1499	**Tapestry** **Hall**

These tapestries are notable for their design, color and pictorial realism. They compose one of the outstanding sets of late medieval textiles in existence.

ROBERT CAMPIN Flemish, ca. 1378–1444	*The Merode Altarpiece* ca. 1425	**Spanish** **Room**

Complex symbolism and fastidious detail along with a great sense of composition and space contribute to make this devotional triptych an accepted early Flemish masterwork.

ENGLISH	*The Bury St. Edmunds Cross* 1150–1190 Walrus ivory	**Romanesque** **Hall**

The figures on this cross, made for the abbot of the celebrated monastery, proclaim the coming of Christ based on evidence from the Old Testament.

Ground   MODELED AFTER FRENCH GOTHIC   *Gothic Chapel*
Floor   14th c.
Austrian stained-glass windows and 13th- and 14th-century tomb monuments are installed in the chapel.

FACILITIES

A *Tour* of the Cloisters' collection, free of charge, is given each Wednesday at 3 P.M.

Special Concerts are announced well in advance. Programs of recorded medieval music are played daily.

The *Bookshop* offers postcards, books, posters, reproductions of museum pieces, jewelry and slides.

Hours: Tuesday–Saturday, 10 A.M.–4:45 P.M.; Sunday, holidays, 12 P.M.–4:45 P.M.

Admission: Pay-what-you-wish.

COOPER-HEWITT MUSEUM
THE SMITHSONIAN INSTITUTION'S
NATIONAL MUSEUM OF DESIGN
2 East 91st St.
New York, NY 10028
Tel: (212)860–6868

In 1859, Peter Cooper founded Cooper Union, a free school, library and lecture forum. He had wished to open a museum as well, but could not afford to at that time. It was not until 1897 that his three Hewitt granddaughters established the museum, not the general one envisioned by their grandfather, but one devoted to decorative arts. It was closed in 1963 for lack of sufficient operating funds, but an interim "Committee-to-Save" kept the collections intact. In 1968 they were entrusted to the Smithsonian Institution and since that time the museum has been known by its present name. In 1972, Andrew Carnegie's six-story mansion with a neo-Georgian exterior, on upper Fifth Avenue, was deeded to the Smithsonian as a home for the Cooper-Hewitt Museum. The property includes an adjoining town house and a garden, one of the few remaining on Fifth Avenue. Renovation necessary to open as a public building required four years; the museum reopened in 1976. The building is now a National Historic and City Landmark.

The museum's collection objects come from around the world, span 3,000 years of history and contain drawings and prints; wallpaper; textiles and lace; ceramics; glass; furniture and woodwork; metalwork and jewelry; advertising, fashion, interior, home furnishing, architectural, urban and industrial design resources.

The exhibitions change periodically, relate to some aspect of design or the decorative arts or architecture. But the museum has a dual purpose: In addition to its exhibitions it offers data for the study of design; it makes a wealth of reference material easily available to researchers, scholars and students.

Because of the great number of objects owned by the museum it is never possible to show many of them at one time, although something from the

Louis-Gustave Taraval, Triumphal Arch with the Royal Swedish Coat of Arms. *Courtesy of Cooper-Hewitt Museum, the Smithsonian Institution's National Museum of Design, New York*

museum's permanent holdings is included in a current exhibition whenever collection items fit the theme of the show. In 1979 a new Decorative Arts Gallery was opened on the main floor of the museum for exhibition of objects from the museum's own collections. In its first months it showed rare objects in separate exhibitions of porcelain and of glass. Furniture and other decorative arts objects will be featured in future exhibitions in this gallery.

SAMPLING THE COLLECTION

EARTHENWARE, STONEWARE, PORCELAIN AND GLASS

The collection encompasses the field from antiquity to the present, with special strength in its 18th- and 19th-century group of European porcelain figurines. Classical, Oriental and European earthenware include examples of Italian majolica; German stoneware; French, German and Italian faïence and wall and stove tiles. Highlighting the glass collection are a Nevers figurine; Irish candelabra and a chandelier; German and Bohemian engraved goblets and covered cups; cameo-cut French and English pieces; three Italian glass birdcages and leaded glass panels from Rheims Cathedral.

FURNITURE, ARCHITECTURAL WORK AND HARDWARE

The collection, largely 18th-century French, of wall panels, trophées, frames, doors, boxes and architectural elements is unequaled, except for those in Paris. The furniture, primarily Western European and American, demonstrates the structural and stylistic evolution from the 17th century to the present. A glass desk by Djo Bourgeois displayed in the 1929 Paris Exposition and Marcel Breuer's chromium steel and canvas chair show that mediums other than wood were used in furniture production.

WALLPAPER AND BANDBOXES

More than 6,000 examples, exceeded only by a West German museum devoted solely to wallpaper, illustrate the development of wall coverings from Spanish and Dutch tooled leather hangings to contemporary wallpapers and polyplastics. Also included are documented fragments from special American houses, and many wallpaper-covered bandboxes.

FABRICS: WOVEN, PRINTED, EMBROIDERED

This sizable collection includes many techniques, cultures and periods, among which are exceptional examples of Egyptian, Islamic, Mediterranean and Near Eastern textiles, ranging from the 3rd through the 15th centuries, and woven silks from Christian Europe from the 14th through the 18th centuries. The pattern-dyed fabrics are outstanding, and include techniques from many countries and periods. Embroidery figures prominently, especially in men's highly styled 18th- and early 19th-century waistcoats and a good-size group of samplers.

METALWORK—MINOR METALS

Iron, steel, copper, brass, bronze and pewter are well represented. A large collection of Japanese sword guards is evidence of the skill of the Far Eastern craftsmen. European gilt bronze furniture mounts from the 18th century through the Empire are featured, as is English and American hardware. Additionally, there are iron locks, keys and sundry hardware of previous periods and a group of wrought-iron articles that include an 18th-century balcony, and two German lantern brackets, along with French overdoors and window grilles.

GOLDSMITHS' WORK AND JEWELRY

Seventeenth- and 18th-century German presentation pieces, French Rococo items and 18th- and early 19th-century English objects are included in the collection of silversmiths' and goldsmiths' work. The museum houses examples of 18th- and early 19th-century snuff, patch and comfit boxes and silver, some of it peasant work, from China, Turkey, Russia, Scandinavia, Central Europe, Mexico and the United States. From the 20th century are various Austrian, English and American articles. The jewelry collection, which ranges from ancient to contemporary times, has been assembled with an eye toward design and diversity, rather than monetary value, and materials other than precious metals and stones have been utilized. Especially outstanding are the European and American 19th-century jewels with examples by two prominent goldsmiths, the Castellani of Rome and Carlo Guiliano of London.

MISCELLANEA

An entertaining but valid look at the past is provided by this amusing collection, which contains sand, tinsel and feather pictures; birdcages; pressed flowers; straw-work; boxes, Valentines, candy Christmas-tree ornaments and examples of packaging and paper folding, along with theater designs and precinema toys, such as peep shows; sand toys; zoetropes; anamorphoses and shadow puppets.

DRAWINGS AND PRINTS

With nearly 50,000 examples of original drawings, limited largely to architecture, design and ornament, the museum's collection is one of the most important in the world. The 18th- and 19th-century Italian designs for architecture and decoration are notable, as are the thousands of French designs for textiles and decoration and over 200 prints by the Tiepolo family. Additionally, there are American wood engravings; North European woodcuts and engravings by Schongauer, Dürer, Van Leyden and Rembrandt; drawings for theater, scenery and costumes; wall and ceiling decoration; architectural ornament, furniture, festival decoration, lighting fixtures, metalwork, jewelry, garden plans and ecclesiastical furnishings. The 19th-century American drawings include the largest number of Winslow Homer drawings in the world, over 2,000 sketches by Frederic Edwin Church and many drawings by Daniel Huntington, Elihu Vedder and Thomas Moran.

FACILITIES

Gallery Tours of current exhibitions are offered.

Saturday Tours to restorations, museums and other nearby places are frequently arranged.

Lecture Series and *Weekend Seminars* on a variety of design-related topics by prominent authorities are sponsored. Occasional attendance on a single admission basis is permitted.

The *Library* has a comprehensive reference collection of design and decoration and contains the most complete group of books on textile arts in America. It includes many old and rare books as well. It also houses an encyclopedic picture collection and archives of color, pattern, textiles, symbols, interior design and advertising.

Hours: Tuesday, 10 A.M.–9 P.M.; Wednesday–Saturday, 10 A.M.–5 P.M.: Sunday, 12 P.M.–5 P.M. Closed: Mondays, major holidays.

Admission: $1.50; senior citizens, students over 12, $1. Free: Tuesday evenings.

MUSEO DEL BARRIO
1230 Fifth Ave.
New York, NY 10029
Tel: (212)831–7272

The museum, founded in 1969, now occupies its second home on the first two floors of a multistory building it shares with two children's schools and a community center. A pleasant courtyard facing Central Park alternates as a sculpture garden and an outdoor assembly for concerts. Turning left, one enters the bright white-walled galleries where reconstructed interiors contain flexible installation space to accommodate a variety of exhibitions. The permanent collection, of which only a small portion is on view, is composed of 20th-century paintings and sculpture by Puerto Rican and Latin American artists; drawings, woodcuts and especially serigraphs mainly by Puerto Rican but including Latin American artists; pre-Columbian shards, bones and ritual objects;

and Santos. Still being readied are a planetarium, a terrarium and visual, tactile and sound areas especially for children where they may handle objects freely.

SAMPLING THE COLLECTION

Santos
Polychrome wood

These religious/folk art objects were created for home devotion. Although the exhibit area contains a large School of Burgos crucifix from Spain carved in the 17th century, the majority of the pieces are from Puerto Rico and are from the 19th and 20th centuries. The collection includes pieces from Mexico, Colombia, Guatemala, Argentina and the Philippines. It is the largest publicly held collection of Puerto Rican Santos in the continental United States.

Group of St. Anthonys. *Courtesy John Betancourt, Photographer, Museo del Barrio, New York*

FACILITIES

Guided Audio Tours are available.

Changing Exhibitions are regularly featured.

The *Library* houses books by Spanish and Puerto Rican authors; videotapes of Hispanic culture and history and Puerto Rican and Latin American information. Tuesday–Thursday, 10 A.M.–12 P.M.: 2 P.M.–4 P.M.

Puerto Rican 16-mm *Films* are screened.

The *Café* is an eating area serving up to 30 people.

The *Museum Shop* sells catalogs; posters; prints; postcards; crafts, reproductions and T-shirts. Prices range from 5¢ for cards to $350 for original prints and drawings.

Hours: Tuesday–Friday, 10:30 A.M.–4:30 P.M.; Saturday–Sunday, 11 A.M.–4 P.M. *Closed:* Mondays.

Admission: Free. Voluntary contributions.

FRICK COLLECTION
1 East 70th St.
New York, NY 10021
Tel: (212)288–0700

Henry Clay Frick, the industrialist, bequeathed his residence and art collection, assembled over a 40-year period, to a Board of Trustees, enabling them to create a center for art studies and related subjects. The 18th-century European-style house, containing French and English rooms of the same period, was erected in 1913–1914. In 1935, after some alteration, the home, retaining much of its original flavor, was opened to the public. An extension and garden were completed in 1977.

SAMPLING THE COLLECTION

Only the main floor is open to visitors. The works listed below are removed or relocated from time to time.

JOHANNES (JAN) VERMEER	*Officer and Laughing Girl*	**South Hall**
Dutch, 1632–1675	1655–1660	
	Oil on canvas	

Fewer than 40 of Vermeer's paintings survive. They are marked by balance, order, serenity and a splendid handling of color and light which seem to preserve them in timelessness.

JEAN HENRI RIESENER	*Sécretaire*	**South Hall**
French, 1734–1806	1790	
	Mahogany with gilt bronze mounts	

Riesener was the leading Paris furniture maker of the late 18th century. His late style was known for its restrained Classicism, although the marquetry became richer and the ormolu mounts finer.

THOMAS GAINSBOROUGH	*The Mall in St. James's Park*	**Dining Room**
British, 1727–1788	1783	
	Oil on canvas	

Exterior view. Courtesy Frick Collection, New York

Gainsborough's real interest was in landscape painting, although his livelihood was derived from portraiture. His later landscapes, composed in his studio, modified nature in restrained green, brown and silvery tones.

Living Hall GIOVANNI BELLINI *St. Francis in Ecstasy*
Italian, Venetian, ca. 1430–1516 ca. 1480
Tempera and oil on poplar panel
Bellini's religious and mythological figures dominate his poetic landscapes. Celebrated for his treatment of color and light and for graceful execution, he influenced two generations of painters, including Titian and Giorgione.

West REMBRANDT HARMENSZ VAN RIJN *Self-Portrait*
Gallery Dutch, 1606–1669 1658
Oil on canvas
Rembrandt painted approximately 60 self-portraits spanning his career. His insightful, probing eye observed his own countenance as candidly as others, bequeathing to us a composite picture of his character and face.

Oval JEAN-ANTOINE HOUDON *Diana the Huntress*
Room French, 1741–1828 1776–1795
Terracotta

Although Houdon, one of France's finest sculptors, fashioned Neoclassical themes such as *Diana,* he is best known for portrait sculptures of celebrated contemporaneous figures, of which the collection owns two.

FACILITIES

Illustrated Lectures are given Wednesday, Thursday, Saturday afternoons, October–May.

An *Introductory Lecture* is presented Tuesday–Friday, 11 A.M. during the lecture season.

Chamber Music Concerts are presented occasionally on Sunday from fall through spring.

The *Sales Desk* carries postcards, prints, books, slides and greeting cards, 15¢–$50.

Restrictions permit only children over 10 to be admitted to the collection. Those under 16 must be accompanied by an adult.

Hours: *September–May:* Tuesday–Saturday, 10 A.M.–6 P.M. Sundays, February 12, Election Day, 1 P.M.–6 P.M. *Closed:* Mondays, July 4, Thanksgiving, December 24 and 25, Tuesdays during June–August.

Admission: Weekdays, adults, $1; students, senior citizens, 50¢; Sundays, $2.

GREY ART GALLERY AND STUDY CENTER
33 Washington Pl.
New York, NY 10003
Tel: (212)598–7603

The New York University Art Collection was established in 1958 and contained works of modern American and European artists. The gallery was opened in 1975 to house this collection along with the Ben and Abby Grey Foundation's gift of contemporary Near and Far Eastern Art. Located in NYU's Main Building in Washington Square, the gallery is in the center of Greenwich Village at the edge of SoHo in a historic section of the city. The building itself contained studios occupied by Winslow Homer and George Inness. The architects maintained the integrity of the original structure while modernizing it with lighting and smoked mirror. Movable panels permit redesigning of the gallery space to accommodate a variety of exhibitions. The gallery organizes several loan exhibitions each year such as *The Paintings of Louis Comfort Tiffany* and *Life: The First Decade* and co-organizes exhibitions with other institutions, which have included *The Decorative Designs of Frank Lloyd Wright* and *American Imagination and Symbolist Painting.* Generally, one exhibition each year features works from the collection of over 3,000 items.

SAMPLING THE COLLECTION

THE BEN AND ABBY GREY FOUNDATION COLLECTION OF CONTEMPORARY ASIAN AND MIDDLE EASTERN ART

This pioneer collection of representative examples of modern art from Iran, Turkey, India, Japan, U.S.S.R., Pakistan, Lebanon, Greece and Israel includes paintings, sculpture, drawings and prints. The abstract, symbolic and representational works being produced in this area of the world depict a culture still alien to the ordinary Westerner.

THE NEW YORK UNIVERSITY ART COLLECTION

This collection's special strength lies in its 20th-century European and American art. From Albert Gleizes' *Paysage* (1923–1924) to Willem de Kooning's *Woman with a Green and Beige Background* (1966), it outlines the major currents of Western modern art. Earlier American painting is represented by painters whose styles developed during the 19th and early 20th centuries and include such artists as Winslow Homer and Everett Shinn.

FACILITIES

Films, Lectures and *Demonstrations* are frequently offered. Call for schedule. The *Information Desk* sells catalogs and posters of past Grey Art Gallery exhibitions.

Hours: Tuesday and Thursday, 10 A.M.–6:30 P.M.; Wednesday, 10 A.M.–8:30 P.M.; Friday, 10 A.M.–5 P.M.; Saturday, 1 P.M.–5 P.M. *Closed*: Sundays, Mondays, holidays.

Admission: Free.

HISPANIC SOCIETY OF AMERICA
Broadway at 155th St.
New York, NY 10032
Tel: (212)926–2234

The museum was opened in 1930. The collections are representative of the culture of the Iberian Peninsula from prehistoric days to the present century and include paintings, sculpture and decorative arts.

SAMPLING THE COLLECTION

Central **Court** **Arcade**	HISPANO-MORESQUE	*Container for Musk, Camphor* *and Ambergris* ca. 966 Ivory with gilt-silver mounts

This cylindrical and elegantly decorated container by a skilled carver of the Court of the Caliphs at Córdoba bears a Kufic inscription likening its domed cover to a maiden's breast.

Central **Court** **Balcony**	ROMAN Tiermes	*A Pair of Trullae, or Saucepans* 1st–2nd c. Silver

These examples of Roman silverwork display a relief design on their handles incorporating animal and human forms representative of Bacchic symbols.

Central **Court** **Balcony**	SPANISH Toledo or Córdoba	*Hebrew Bible* 15th c. Gold and body colors on vellum

The workmanship and illumination of this well-traveled Bible reflects late Gothic and Early Renaissance motifs of its period, near-coincident with the expulsion of the Jews from Spain.

FRANCISCO GOYA Y LUCIENTES	*Portrait of the Duchess of Alba*	**Central**
Spanish, 1746–1828	1797	**Court**
	Oil on canvas	

A formal but deeply personal portrayal inscribed by the artist "Goya Alone." Goya retained for years this record of his stay with the duchess at her estate in southern Spain.

JOAQUIN SOROLLA	*The Provinces of Spain*	**Sorolla**
Spanish, 1863–1923	1912–1919	**Room**
	Oil on canvas	

Sorolla sought to project the psychology and the pictorial quality of Spain's varied regions. He depicted the sun, sea and life in a "decoration" over four yards high and seventy-five yards long.

FACILITIES

A *Slide-Illustrated Commentary* on the collection with recorded (33-½ LP) and printed text in English and/or Spanish is available ($5 for U.S. educational institutions and $25 for individual purchasers).

Group Visits by appointment only.

The *Library* with its manuscripts, books, photographic references and clipping files is an important research center on Spanish and Portuguese art, history and literature. Library hours: Tuesday–Friday, 1 P.M.–4:30 P.M. Saturday, 10 A.M.–4:30 P.M. *Closed:* When museum is closed (see below) and August; December 24–January 1.

The *Sales Desk* carries books on the collections, books and articles by society members, postcards, note cards, color prints and color slides.

Hours: Tuesday–Saturday, 10 A.M.–4:30 P.M.; Sunday, 1 P.M.–4 P.M. *Closed:* Mondays, New Year's, February 12, February 22, Good Friday, Easter, May 30, July 4, Thanksgiving, December 24, 25, 31.

Admission: Free, but voluntary contributions are welcome.

INTERNATIONAL CENTER OF PHOTOGRAPHY
1130 Fifth Ave.
New York, NY 10028
Tel: (212)860–1777

The center, established in 1968, occupies the Audubon House, a former town house erected in 1915 and now a New York City Landmark. This red brick Federal-style building houses the only New York City museum devoted entirely to photography. It is concerned with the appreciation, preservation and development of great photographs. Changing exhibitions have included the works of such masters as Lewis W. Hine (1874–1940), Henri Cartier-Bresson (b. 1908),

Exterior view. Courtesy International Center of Photography, New York

Gordon Parks (b. 1912), Clarence John Laughlin (b. 1905) and of younger photographers, some of whose work has never been publicly shown before. These exhibitions encompass a wide range of historical, contemporary, thematic and experimental photography. The center is also a meeting place for those interested in photographic techniques and discussion.

FACILITIES

Lectures and *Open Forums* are conducted throughout the season.

Films of historic and educational interest are screened. Call for program information.

The *Bookstore* carries a wide range of photographic publications, posters and photographs from around the world.

Hours: Tuesday, 11 A.M.–8 P.M.; Wednesday–Sunday, 11 A.M.–5 P.M. *Closed:* Mondays.

Admission: General, $1.50; students, 50¢; senior citizens, free.

JAPAN HOUSE GALLERY
333 East 47th St.
New York, NY 10017
Tel: (212)832–1155

Japan House is the headquarters for the Japan Society founded in 1907 to further relations between Japan and the United States. The four-story building was designed by Japanese architect Junzo Yoshimura. Mainly American materials were used although it is finished in Japanese style. A bamboo staircase ascends over a reflecting pool, graced by green plants, to the exhibition space on the mezzanine level which is accessible to the Japanese garden. The ambience is one of serenity and quiet inviting the visitor to enjoy the three major exhibits mounted each year. There is no permanent collection. Past shows have included *Japanese Art Swords; Japanese Packaging; Ukiyo-e Prints; Nara Ehon: Illuminated Manuscripts of Medieval Japan;* and *Chanoyu: Japanese Tea Ceremony.*

Exterior view. Courtesy Japan House Gallery, New York

FACILITIES

Lectures; classical and contemporary *Dance* programs; *Dramatic Presentations; Concerts* of electronic and classical music; and *Poetry Readings* are presented from time to time. Call for program information.

Japanese-made *Films* or those about Japan are regularly screened. Call for program information.

The *Library* contains books on Japanese art and history. Books are available for use on the premises.

The *Sales Desk* carries exhibition catalogs; posters; postcards and notepaper.

Hours: Open only during exhibitions. Daily, 11 A.M.–5 P.M. Friday, 11 A.M.–7:30 P.M.

Admission: Suggested contribution is $1.50 although any amount is accepted.

JEWISH MUSEUM
1109 Fifth Ave.
New York, NY 10028
Tel: (212)860–1888

The museum, established in 1904 as part of the library of the Jewish Theological Seminary of America, has been located on its present site in a former mansion since 1947. A building was added in 1963. It is devoted to collecting, preserving and interpreting art objects of Jewish life. The permanent collection is composed of ceremonial objects, paintings, prints, drawings, sculpture, textiles, decorative arts, coins and medals.

SAMPLING THE COLLECTION

3rd Floor   POLISH   *Torah Shield*
Breslau   late 17th c.
                                 Silver partly gilt
The Torah, the most sacred Jewish possession, is a parchment scroll inscribed with the first five books of the Bible. The shield contained an interchangeable central panel inscribed with the Sabbath or holy day on which a particular scroll would be used.

3rd Floor   EGYPTIAN   *Head of an Official*
New Kingdom, Dynasty XVIII-XX,   ca. 1000 B.C.
1567–1085 B.C.   Granite
Sculpture of this period captured the essence of the subject for eternity. Celebrated personages were usually depicted lifesize to show their importance. This head was owned by Sigmund Freud.

3rd Floor   ENGLISH   *Tray (Wedding Gift)*
Staffordshire   mid-18th c.
                                Salt-glaze stoneware,
                                painted in Delft
Salt-glaze stoneware produced a white or cream-colored pitted glaze. In the mid-18th century, Delft potters enameled the ware achieving colors Oriental in feeling, the Dutch being the only Europeans allowed into Japanese ports.

Exterior view. Courtesy Jewish Museum, New York

FACILITIES

Changing Exhibitions are regularly featured.

Special Events, including *Lectures, Symposia, Concerts* and *Films* are scheduled during the year on topics relating to exhibitions or particular Jewish themes.

The *Museum Shop* carries adaptations by Boehm porcelains of ceremonial objects in the permanent collection; coins and jewelry, graphics by noted artists commissioned for the museum; books on Jewish art, history and culture; contemporary ceremonial objects from the museum's workshop; posters; toys; Israeli crafts and Jewish Museum catalogs. Prices range from $5 to $525. The shop closes half an hour earlier than the museum.

Hours: Monday–Thursday, 12 P.M.–5:00 P.M.; Sunday, 11 A.M.– 6:00 P.M.
   Closed: Fridays, Saturdays, Jewish holidays.

Admission: Adults, $2; children 6–16 and students with I.D. cards, $1; senior citizens pay-as-you-wish.

METROPOLITAN MUSEUM OF ART
Fifth Ave. at 82nd St.
New York, NY 10028
Tel: (212)535–7710

Four city blocks long and containing three floors of paintings and art objects, the Metropolitan Museum of Art is still growing. Established in 1870 and housed in its present quarters since 1880, its vast collections are divided among 19 curatorial departments. Over two million visitors flock annually to its 300 galleries. For anyone who loves museums, the Metropolitan is a thrilling place to visit—again, and again, and again.

SAMPLING THE COLLECTION

(Gallery sites are not listed for all works because either the gallery is being reconstructed or is not specifically numbered.) Please note that curatorial departments are listed alphabetically with the galleries contained in each in numerical order.

AMERICAN DECORATIVE ARTS

The American Wing possesses outstanding yet typical examples in the field of American decorative arts. With 35 rooms in all, the items are presented in chronological order. The collection's holdings range from the Colonial period of the 17th century to the early 20th century. There are 950 pieces of furniture, 850 pieces of silver, 200 pieces of pewter, 1,900 pieces of glass, 600 examples of textiles and 650 ceramics.

American Wing, 1st Floor   FRANK LLOYD WRIGHT   *Living Room from F. W. Little*
       1869–1959   *House*
       Wayzata, Minnesota
       1912–1914

Two styles of furniture are represented here. The first related to that designed for Wright's earlier Prairie homes is stained dark brown. The later, simpler, more straightforward design has a blond finish.

American Wing, 2nd Floor   PENNSYLVANIA   *Powel Room*
       Philadelphia   1765

This room and its furnishings, epitomizing the Chippendale style, belonged to the last Colonial Mayor of Philadelphia. The furniture is mainly from Philadelphia, where some of the most celebrated cabinetmakers worked.

American Wing, 2nd Floor   NEW YORK   *Van Rensselaer Entry Hall*
       Albany   1760s

Van Rensselaer's great manor house is an example of Georgian architecture at its very best. It was particularly known for its entry hall which extended from the front to the rear and was papered with a rare custom-painted paper.

American Wing   *AMERICAN PAINTINGS AND SCULPTURE*

The museum's collection of American paintings and sculpture is thought to be the best in the country; it covers almost all periods of American art.

GILBERT STUART   *George Washington, 1795*
1755–1828   Oil on canvas

Stuart painted many portraits of George Washington. This is one of the first he did and it was done from life.

THOMAS COLE
1801–1848

The Oxbow (The Connecticut River near Northampton)
1836
Oil on canvas

With its sweeping vista and detailed forefront, this romantic yet realistic canvas, exalting the American countryside, typifies the style of the Hudson River School landscape artists, of which Cole was a founder.

GEORGE CALEB BINGHAM
1811–1879

Fur Traders Descending the Missouri
ca. 18th c.
Oil on canvas

Sold at first in a lottery for $75, this is an example of the Western genre scenes that Bingham did so well.

THOMAS EAKINS
1844–1916

Max Schmitt in a Single Scull
1871
Oil on canvas

Technical skill, perspective, precise workmanship and his ability to treat color make this one of the finest landscapes of its time.

Thomas Eakins, Max Schmitt in a Single Scull. *Courtesy Metropolitan Museum of Art, and Gift of George D. Pratt, 1934*

ALBERT PINKHAM RYDER
1847–1917

Moonlight Marine
Oil on wood panel

Ryder was drawn to the sea which he often depicted, endowing these paintings and his landscapes with supernatural, wondrous properties prefiguring the work of the 20th-century Abstract Expressionists.

JOHN SINGER SARGENT   *Madame X—Mme Pierre Gautreau*
1856–1925   Oil on canvas
Sargent considered this his best painting although, when it was first exhibited, it was not well received. The subject's dress was thought too daring and her skin tones strange.

WINSLOW HOMER   *The Gulfstream*
1836–1910   1899
                                        Oil on canvas
For many years Homer lived by the shore in both the West Indies and New England, where he painted naturalistic and striking marine scenes picturing the sea as both friend and foe.

2nd Floor, *ANCIENT NEAR EASTERN ART*
Ancient Near
Eastern Art   Countries from the eastern Mediterranean seacoast in the west, to Afghanistan in the east, from Turkey and Southern Russia in the north, to the Persian Gulf and Arabia in the south, form the boundaries from where the ancient Near Eastern Art was found. Two galleries house the items that range from the 6th millennium B.C. to the Arab conquest in the 7th century A.D.

MESOPOTAMIAN   *Figure of Gudea*
Ur   2100–2000 B.C.
                                        Diorite
Sculpture in Lagash, a Sumerian city-state, adhered mostly to one kind typified by the governor's statue. Usually of diorite and of large dimensions, the cap and eyebrows were in linear designs.

ELAMITE   *Head of a Ruler*
Akkad   2000 B. C.
                                        Copper
An early example of the technique of solid casting for huge objects. The hollow eye sockets were once inlaid.

SOUTHERN IRANIAN   *Collection of Sassanian Silver*
                                        and Gold
                                        3rd and 4th c. A.D.
Western forms and styles were closely imitated in these objects but the expansion to the east led to the appearance of many Indian and Central Asian elements.

Main Floor *ARMS AND ARMOR*

The Metropolitan's collection of arms and armor is the greatest in the United States and one of the most inclusive in the world. Comprising about 15,000 items, its galleries surround the spacious Equestrian Court. The pomp and pageantry of the knights in armor under flying heraldic banners stir the imagination.

Gallery 1,   ENGLISH   *Armor of George Clifford*
Equestrian   ca. 1590
Court   The darkened blue background is a handsome setting for the etched and gilded decoration. It was made in Greenwich in the foremost English armory of the 16th century.

GERMAN   *Wheellock Pistol of Emperor*   **Gallery 4,**
                                Charles V   **Equestrian**
Wheellock guns made it easier to reload quickly. A piece of pyrite was struck **Court**
by a revolving wheel creating a spark.

Wheellock Pistol. *Courtesy Metropolitan Museum of Art, Bequest of William Henry Riggs, 1914*

GERMAN   *Parade Rapier of Christian II,*   **Gallery 7,**
                                Duke of Saxony   **Equestrian**
                                1606   **Court**
                                Steel, gilt, bronze, jewels,
                                seed pearls, traces of enamel
The hilt was signed by Israel Schuech of Dresden. The blade was made by the
most famous Toledo swordsmith, Juan Martinez.

THE COSTUME INSTITUTE   **North Wing,**
                                                                  Ground Floor
The public can see only the exhibition currently on view. The institute presents
an annual exhibition in its ten galleries. A special subject is always surveyed.
The material is from the permanent collection with additions sometimes borrowed from outside. The institute has approximately 30,000 articles of clothing.

DRAWINGS   **2nd Floor**

Drawings are very perishable. They fade or darken easily when exposed to too
much light. Therefore, the public can only see the exhibition currently on view.
The department owns examples from almost every national school. The Italian
and French material is outstanding.

EGYPTIAN ART   **North Wing,**
                                                                  Main Floor
The Egyptian Art Department of the Metropolitan is one of the most important
in the world. It has items of great significance from every period of ancient

Egyptian history. Many of the valuable holdings are from excavations. There are large numbers of articles with recorded histories.

North Wing,
Main Floor

Temple of Dendur
ca. 1st c.
Sandstone

Once on the west bank of the Nile, Dendur was endangered by flooding from the lake forming behind the Aswan High Dam. A gift from the Egyptian government in recognition of $16 million from the United States to save Nubian monuments, the temple's façade, with two columns, conceals three rooms. A pylon stands before it.

Main Floor,

Models from the Tomb of Meketre
Dynasty XII, 2050 B.C.

Private tombs briefly substituted painted models for wall decorations. Meketre,

Temple of Dendur. *Courtesy Metropolitan Museum of Art, Gift of Arab Republic of Egypt, 1968*

the king's chancelor and great steward, made his inspection tours in boats. Two barques await his funeral while other models depict domestic activities.

Sphinx of Sesostris III   **Main Floor,**
Early Dynasty XVIII   **Egyptian Art**
Diorite

The head of the king set upon the mighty body of a lion suggests the grandeur of Sesostris.

Seated Figure of Hatshepsut   **Main Floor,**
Early Dynasty XVIII, ca. 1495 B.C.   **Egyptian Art**

Believed to be from the queen's own chapel, this was one of about 200 statues placed in pairs to grace the approach to the temple of the queen at Deir el Bahri.

Pectoral from the Lahun Treasure   **Main Floor,**
Dynasty XII, ca. 1880 B.C.   **Egyptian Art**
Gold with semiprecious stones

This is thought to be the finest piece of Egyptian jewelry in existence. The back is almost as marvelous as the front.

EUROPEAN PAINTINGS

2nd Floor
European
Paintings

The Metropolitan houses one of the world's great collections of European paintings dating from the late Middle Ages to the early 20th century. Among the most famous galleries are Italian and northern Renaissance, Dutch 17th century, Spanish and French, particularly the Impressionist and Post-Impressionist galleries.

TITIAN (TIZIANO VECELLIO)   *Venus and the Lute Player*
Italian, Venetian, ca. 1490–1576   Oil on canvas

The subject matter of this great painting has frequently been questioned. Nonetheless, this work shows the artist's feeling for texture and rich detail.

STEFANO DI GIOVANNI SASSETTA   *Journey of the Magi*
Italian, Sienese, ca. 1400–1450   1430s
Tempera on wood

This panel was originally the upper section of an Adoration of the Magi. The artist's style still adheres to the Gothic although Florence had for some time been enthralled by the Renaissance.

REMBRANDT HARMENSZ VAN RIJN   *Aristotle Contemplating the*
Dutch, 1606–1669   *Bust of Homer*
1653
Oil on canvas

This painting, conjured from the artist's imagination, is of a renowned poet being praised by a renowned philosopher. It illustrates Rembrandt's dramatic use of light and shadow.

JOHANNES (JAN) VERMEER   *Young Woman with a Water Jug*
Dutch, 1632–1675   ca. 1663
Oil on canvas

This painting is typical of Vermeer at his best. His use of light is singular. He was probably the first painter to use daylight as a means of illumination.

NICHOLAS POUSSIN   *The Rape of the Sabine Women*
French, 1594–1665   ca. 1636–1637
Oil on canvas

Although Poussin lived and worked mostly in Rome, he introduced Classical painting to France. Abandoning religious themes he turned to mythological ones rendered in suppressed color in a logical, precise style.

JEAN ANTOINE WATTEAU   *Mezzetin*
French, 1684–1721   Oil on canvas
Watteau was an admirer of commedia dell'arte and his dreamy paintings frequently reflected this. He was a great influence on the transition of French painting from Classicism to Rococo.

CLAUDE MONET   *Terrace at Sainte-Adresse*
French, 1840–1926   Oil on canvas
This work was painted early in Monet's career. Considered a leader among the French Impressionists, Monet always worked out-of-doors, creating a new method for the depiction of color and light.

PIERRE AUGUSTE RENOIR   *Mme Charpentier and Her*
French, 1841–1919   *Children*
                                         1878
                                         Oil on canvas
Renoir was an Impressionist who most often painted people, especially women and children. The showing of *Madame Charpentier and Her Children* established his popularity as a painter.

HILAIRE GERMAIN EDGAR DEGAS   *Woman with Chrysanthemums*
French, 1834–1917   1865
                                         Oil on canvas
Degas painted Parisian life—shopgirls, ballet dancers, the underworld. He had the Impressionist's skill of modeling with light.

JAN VAN EYCK   *Crucifixion and Last Judgment*
Flemish, ca. 1380–1441   early 15th c.
                                         Tempera and oil on canvas
                                         transferred from wood
These panels were painted as two parts of a triptych. Unlike the symbolism which dominated religious works at the time, Van Eyck gives us a more naturalistic depiction of this subject.

PIETER BRUEGHEL, THE ELDER   *The Harvesters*
Flemish, ca. 1525–1569   1565
                                         Oil on wood
This is the summer panel of one of five paintings portraying the seasons. Brueghel's landscapes were joyous settings for the masses of Flemish people he painted both at work and play.

EL GRECO (DOMENICOS
THEOTOCOPOULOS)   *View of Toledo*
Spanish, 1541–1614   Oil on canvas
This is the first real landscape in Spanish art. El Greco took the liberty of rearranging the setting to suit his artist's eye.

DIEGO RODRIGUEZ DE SILVA Y
VELAZQUEZ   *Juan de Pareja*
Spanish, 1599–1660   1650
                                         Oil on canvas
While purchasing paintings for Philip IV in Rome, Velázquez executed this portrait of his assistant to call attention to himself as a painter. It was purchased in 1970 for $5,592,000.

FRANCISCO GOYA Y LUCIENTES   *Majas on a Balcony*
Spanish, 1746–1828   Oil on canvas
Goya painted what he saw with boldness. He did not prettify his subjects. Majas
were street women whose manner of dress became popular even with the
upper classes.

EUROPEAN SCULPTURE AND DECORATIVE ARTS

Complete rooms from palaces and great houses, furniture, European decorative **European**
arts and sculpture from the Renaissance to 1900 make up the collection of this **Arts,**
department. It is one of the largest in the entire museum.   **Gallery 25A**

These 19th-century rooms and galleries are reassembled in the museum as they **Western**
originally appeared. The room from the Hotel de Varengeville comes from **Gallery 25B**
France and was designed in 1935. It is paneled in gold and white.

The room from the *Palais Paar* was built some thirty years later and has predom- **Main Floor,**
inantly blue woodwork. It is Viennese.   **Gallery 56**

SPANISH   *Patio from Velez Blanco*
   1506–1515
More commonly known by the name of its donor, the Blumenthal Patio, an
open-air loggia from a castle in southeastern Spain, combines the finest Renaissance architecture with traces of the Gothic.

TULLIO LOMBARDO   *Adam*   **Main Floor,**
Italian, ca. 1455–1532   ca. 1495–1499   **Gallery 56**
   Marble
Adam was carved for the Venetian Doge, Andrea Vendramin. The whiteness
of the marble, its smoothness and the fact that it was the first large-scale nude
since Classical times make this an important sculpture.

ANTONIO CANOVA   *Perseus Carrying the Head*   **Head of the**
Italian, 1757–1822   *of Medusa*   **Great**
   1804–1808   **Hall,**
   Marble   **Stairs**
One of two sculptures of Perseus that Canova modeled after the Apollo Bel-
vedere. He became the most celebrated of the Neoclassical sculptors.

FAR EASTERN ART

The Far Eastern Art Department houses material from Japan, China, Korea and
a small number of outstanding sculptures from India and Southeast Asia. The
objects range in date from the 2nd millennium B.C. through the 19th century
A.D. In all, the collection comprises some 30,000 items. Of particular interest
in this department are the Chinese Garden Court and Ming Furniture Room.
These two spaces were made in the People's Republic of China in 1979 and
shipped to New York. They evoke the beautiful traditional architecture of
16th-century China with its subtle colors and quiet, enclosed gardens. The Ming
Dynasty Furniture Room houses the famous collection of Ming furniture and
domestic objects. Flanking the Garden Court are two galleries which display a
selection of the museum's great collection of Chinese painting.

CH'U TING   *Summer Mountain*   **2nd Floor**
Chinese, Sung Dynasty,   late 10th c.
A.D. 960–1279   Handscroll
Taoism and Confucianism, oriented toward nature, played an important role in
this period during which Chinese landscape painting originated. It was one of
the greatest Oriental contributions to painting.

Francisco de Goya, Majas on a Balcony. *Courtesy Metropolitan Museum of Art.*
Bequest of Mrs. H. O. Havemeyer, 1929, H. O. Havemeyer Collection

CHINESE   *Standing Buddha*   **2nd Floor,**
Northern Wei Dynasty, A.D. 386–535   Gilt bronze   **Sackler**
This is the largest and probably most significant statue of its period to be **Gallery**
unearthed to date. The way in which the Buddha's robe is modeled is particularly fascinating.

CHINESE   *Buddhist Mural*   **2nd Floor,**
Yüan Dynasty, 1260–1368   early 14th c.   **Sackler**
This impressive mural was intended for the illiterate worshiper. Surrounding a **Gallery**
large figure of Buddha are many divine, mythological and symbolic figures.

GREEK AND ROMAN ART

The museum has a huge collection of Greek and Roman art but is outstanding
in several areas: Cypriot art, painted Greek vases, Roman portrait busts and
Roman wall paintings. With the exception of Athens, it has the most renowned
collection of original Attic sculpture. Its collection of ancient glass is the most
significant in the world. The collection spans the period from the 3rd millennium
B.C. to A.D. 313.

ROMAN   *Frescoes from Boscoreale*   **Greek and**
                    1st c. B.C.   **Roman Art,**
These three sections from a wall painting from a villa not far from Pompeii were **Gallery 8**
cut from a larger wall. They are preserved so well because they were buried
in the same volcanic eruption that destroyed Pompeii.

POTTER EUXITHEOS AND
PAINTER EUPHRONIOS   *Calyx-Krater*   **Greek and**
Greek   ca. 500 B.C.   **Roman Art,**
                  Terracotta   **Gallery 10**
This vase brought to new heights the technique of red figure painting which was
an innovation from the earlier black figures depicted against a pale background.

ISLAMIC ART   **2nd Floor**

Generous gifts and bequests along with some purchases and objects from
excavations combine to give the Metropolitan the greatest selection of Islamic
art in the world. The collection contains objects from Spain in the West to India
in the East.

IRANIAN   *Mihrab*   **Islamic Art,**
                    1354   **Gallery 4C**
All prayer niches pointed toward Mecca and were always the most ornate part
of a mosque. In this one, bits of glazed faïence, individually fired, provide
intense color.

IRANIAN   *The Houghton Shah-Nameh*   **Islamic Art,**
                  early 16th c.   **Gallery 6**
The museum possesses 78 miniatures of a manuscript that contained 258. It is
the story of the people of Iran up to the time of the Arab conquest and was
created for the reigning shah.

SYRIAN   *Nur-ad-Din Room*   **Islamic Art,**
                  1707   **Left of**
Peace and harmony prevailed in the upper-class Syrian home. This winter **Gallery**
reception room, furnished with divan cushions, contains an inner courtyard **Entrance**
with splashing fountain and a paneled reception room enhanced by open
niches.

Mihrab. *Courtesy Metropolitan Museum of Art, Harris Brisbane Dick Fund*

EGYPTIAN   *Simonetti Carpet (Mamluk)*   **Gallery 5**
                                  late 15th c.
                                  Wool
This carpet combines contemporary geometric patterns with older Egyptian
designs. It is considered one of the best of its kind in existence.

THE ROBERT LEHMAN COLLECTION   **Main Floor**

A collection of wide variety from the Middle Ages to the present represents Mr.
Lehman's personal choice. A garden court is at its center surrounded by galleries. Some of the rooms of his home have been reassembled and contain
furniture, decorative objects, tapestries and carpets. It is really a museum within
a museum, having its own library and seminar rooms.

GIOVANNI DI PAOLO   *Expulsion from Paradise*   **Red Velvet**
Italian, 1399–1482   ca. 1445   **Room**
                                 Tempera and oil on wood
This intensely personal interpretation of an oft-used theme is essentially Gothic
in style, although most of Giovanni's contemporaries were experimenting with
the new knowledge of the Renaissance.

SANDRO BOTTICELLI   *Annunciation*   **Red Velvet**
Italian, ca. 1444–1510   Tempera and oil on wood   **Room**
Botticelli was a Florentine painter favored by Lorenzo the Magnificent. Many
of his paintings adorned the walls of Florentine buildings. This is a panel from
one of his splendid altarpieces.

PETRUS CHRISTUS   *St. Eligius as a Goldsmith*   **Flemish**
Flemish, ca. 1410–1472   1449   **Room**
                                 Tempera and oil on wood
The care and detailed workmanship that characterized Christus's work is apparent in this painting. In all likelihood it was commissioned by the goldsmith's
guild of Antwerp.

EL GRECO (DOMENICOS   **Sitting**
THEOTOCOPOULOS)   *St. Jerome as a Cardinal*   **Room**
Spanish, ca. 1548–1625   ca. 1600–1610
This idealized representation of St. Jerome is a late painting of El Greco's and
is testimony to the strong influence of his Byzantine background.

JEAN AUGUSTE DOMINIQUE   **Special**
INGRES   *Princesse de Broglie*   **Gallery**
French, 1780–1867   1853
                                 Oil on canvas
It took Ingres more than a year to finish this portrait. The sensuous look of the
gown shows to great advantage against the severity of the background.

MEDIEVAL ART   **Main Floor**

The important phases of medieval art are all on view here. Outside of Europe,
there is no other collection to equal this one of more than 4,000 articles. It
contains objects from the 4th to 16th centuries, commencing with the early
Christian and ending with the Gothic period. Its selection of enamels, ivories,
tapestries and sculpture is outstanding.

CAROLINGIAN   *Virgin Enthroned*   **Medieval Art,**
                                 early 9th c.   **Medieval**
                                 Ivory   **Treasury**
The weaver's distaffs in the left hand are evidence that this is a sculpture of the
Virgin Mary. The Virgin was supposedly weaving when she received the angel
of annunciation.

Medieval Art, **Gallery 1**	CONSTANTINOPLE	*The David Plates* A.D. 613–629/30 Silver

These six Byzantine plates depicting the life of David show the Classical influence still present at this date.

Medieval Art, **Gallery 2**	FRENCH	*Virgin and Child Enthroned,* *School of Auvergne* late 12th c. Polychromed oak

An exceptionally fine example of wood sculpture from the Romanesque period. This subject was a common one and known as the Throne of Wisdom.

Medieval Art, **Gallery 2**	FRENCH	*St. Germain-des-Prés Window* ca. 1245 Stained glass

Presented in a chapellike setting, this window from the Abbey of St. Germain-des-Prés is characteristic of French Gothic stained glass. It depicts stories from the life of St. Vincent of Saragossa.

Medieval Art, **Gallery 3**	FRANCO-FLEMISH	*The Annunciation Tapestry* early 15th c. Wool and remains of metallic thread

This tapestry is a rare example in the international Gothic style displaying curved fluid patterns, soft colors and naturalistic handling of the theme. Tapestries were used as decorations for feasts, holidays and in battle tents.

Medieval Art, **Gallery 4**	FRENCH Burgundy	*Virgin and Child* 15th c. Limestone, painted and gilded

This sculpture from the church in Poligny shows great feeling in contrast to the austerity with which the subject is often presented. It retains its original polychromy.

2nd Floor	*MUSICAL INSTRUMENTS*

Nearly 4,000 instruments comprise this collection with many from primitive cultures. It is possible to study art styles through the centuries by observing the decoration of the pieces. From time to time many are used in demonstrations or in concerts.

Musical **Instruments,** **Gallery 11**	ITALIAN	*Spinettina* 1540

This instrument was made for Eleonora d'Este, Duchess of Urbino. It is in excellent condition and is playable. The decoration is of certosina, painting, carving and intarsia.

Musical **Instruments,** **Gallery 11**	BARTOLOMMEO CRISTOFORI Italian, 1655–1731	*Pianoforte* 1720

This is one of three extant pianos made by Bartolommeo Cristofori, the inventor of the piano. Although it is probably the most renowned instrument in the collection, it is a very plain piece with a simple black body.

Musical **Instruments** **after Gallery** **18—** **Unmarked**	ITALIAN	*Gilded Harpsichord* mid-17th c.

Harpsichords were large instruments, the precursors of the piano. Because of their size they easily lent themselves to ornate decoration. This one is richly Baroque.

PRIMITIVE ARTS

New quarters in the south wing of the building are being planned for this department. It is hoped that the collection of more than 4,000 items ranging over the entire field of primitive arts, will be ready for viewing sometime in the early 1980s. Meanwhile the collection remains in storage.

PRINTS AND PHOTOGRAPHS   2nd Floor

The public may see only the exhibition currently on view. However, this department contains a broad spectrum of material. Not only prints and photographs but illustrated books, drawings (mostly preparatory designs), posters, silhouettes and trade cards are included. The Print Study Room is open to the public by appointment.

TEXTILE DEPARTMENT

This department is closed to the public. Objects may only be viewed by special arrangement with the curator.

20th-CENTURY ART   2nd Floor

Spanning the years from 1900 to the present, this department's greatest strength lies in American art. Paintings, drawings, sculpture and decorative arts are all accorded space. One-man shows of the best in contemporary art are occasionally installed.

EDWARD HOPPER	*The Lighthouse at Two Lights*	**2nd Floor,**
American, 1882–1967	1929	**20th-c. Art**
	Oil on canvas	

Hopper painted in the Northern European manner, modeling with light. Bleak, lonely, solitary, spare are adjectives that best describe his work.

PABLO PICASSO	*Gertrude Stein*	**2nd Floor,**
Spanish, 1881–1973	1906	**20th-c. Art**
	Oil on canvas	

This painting is important in spanning the artist's evolution from representational painting to Cubism. It is especially evident in the face which was painted from memory.

JACKSON POLLOCK	*Autumn Rhythm*	**2nd Floor,**
American, 1912–1956	1950	**20th-c. Art**
	Oil on canvas	

Pollock's Action Paintings, achieved by dripping and tracking paint on canvas, met with initial opposition but are now an accepted step in the ongoing progression of 20th-century art.

DAVID SMITH	*Becca*	**2nd Floor,**
American, 1906–1965	Stainless steel	**20th-c. Art**

In this late work, named for his daughter, Rebecca, we see how Smith was influenced by Cubism. His sculpture kept pace with the greatest of postwar American developments in painting.

HILAIRE GERMAIN EDGAR DEGAS	*Ballet Dancer*
French, 1834–1917	1880–1881
	Bronze

Best known as a painter, Degas also modeled figures in wax to be cast later in bronze. The *Ballet Dancer* is thought to be his finest bronze.

FACILITIES

The museum offers a wide variety of free activities, introductory tours, gallery talks (some in Spanish), films and lectures. The Information Desk in the Great Hall provides current information on all museum activities.

Special Exhibitions are featured each year. They consist of several major shows of national or international origin.

North Wing, Main Floor	The *Auditorium* is one of the most popular in the city, the 708-seat Grace Rainey Rogers Auditorium is a showcase for lectures and musical events by top-notch artists. Tickets for these can be purchased singly or in series from the auditorium office.
Main Floor	The 185,000-volume *Library* is not open to the public but can be used by any serious student.
South Wing, Ground Floor	The *Junior Museum* has a snack bar (open during museum hours), sales desk and art reference library. Its own auditorium provides free talks, films and special events. The frequent treasure hunts in which the children must seek out particular objects from the museum's collections are very popular.
South Wing, Main Floor	The *Fountain Restaurant* has tables that surround an enormous reflecting pool with sculptures by Carl Milles. The cafeteria is open for lunch daily and for dinner on Tuesday evenings when the museum remains open until 8:45.

Leading off the Great Hall are the museum's *Sales Shops.* To the south is a gift shop and to the north there is a series of shops on several levels. Included here is a wide range of books, cards, slides, posters and prints; gifts; reproductions and items for children.

Hours: Wednesday–Saturday, 10 A.M.–4:45 P.M.; Tuesday, 10 A.M.–8:45 P.M.; Sundays, holidays, 11 A.M.–4:45 P.M. *Closed:* Mondays.

Admission: Pay-what-you-wish, but you must pay something. Suggested admission: Adults, $3; young people, senior citizens, $1.50; and children under 12, free.

MUSEUM OF AMERICAN FOLK ART
49 West 53rd St.
New York, NY 10019
Tel: (212)581–2474

The museum, founded in 1961, is housed in a small building. Two galleries, connected by a sales area, display selections from the permanent collection. A new home is actively being sought in order to give greater exposure to the collection of American 18th- and 19th-century folk sculpture, painting and decorative arts.

SAMPLING THE COLLECTION

Because of the rotating nature of the collection, the following items may not always be on view.

Interior Gallery. *Courtesy Dia Stolnitz, Photographer, Museum of American Folk Art, New York*

ARTIST UNKNOWN   *Flag Gate*
                                           ca. 1876
                                           Wood and metal painted
This gate, executed for the patriotic celebration of the American Centennial, still
has its hinge and hook.

ARTIST UNKNOWN   *Father Time*
                                           ca. 1910
                                           Wood and metal painted
The original purpose for which this folk sculpture was intended is uncertain. The
right arm moves so that the sickle strikes the hanging bell.

ARTIST UNKNOWN   *Gabriel Weathervane*
(Possibly New England)   ca. 1840
                                           Sheet iron polychromed
Fairly complex executions of weathervanes, representing figures or animals are
extant from this period.

FACILITIES

Lectures and *Gallery Talks* are held from time to time.

Changing Exhibitions are regularly featured.

The *Museum Shop* has a unique selection of books on folk art, often stocking
out-of-print or difficult to find titles. Note cards are popular, as are handcrafted
items by contemporary craftsmen.

Hours: Tuesday, 10:30 A.M.–8 P.M.; Wednesday–Sunday, 10:30 A.M–5:30
         P.M. *Closed:* Mondays, Labor Day, Christmas.

Admission: Adults, $1; senior citizens and students, 50¢; children under 12,
             free. Free for everyone on Tuesday evenings, 5:30 P.M. to 8 P.M.

MUSEUM OF THE AMERICAN INDIAN
HEYE FOUNDATION
Broadway at 155th St.
New York, NY 10032
Tel: (212)283–2420

The museum, founded in 1916, is a scientific research and educational institution. It houses a collection of an estimated four and a half million objects,
representing the cultures of Native Americans from the Arctic to Tierra del
Fuego and from the Atlantic to the Pacific. The specimens include objects of
the most artistic to the most ordinary household goods.

SAMPLING THE COLLECTION

1st Floor   AMERICAN   *Wampum Belt*
                   Pennsylvania   1683
Wampum, polished shells, were strung on belts and used for ornamentation,
money and ceremonial pledges. This belt, presented to the chiefs by William
Penn, established peace and the occupation of eastern Pennsylvania by the
Colonists.

AMERICAN	*Money*	**2nd Floor**
California, Yurok Indians	19th c.	
	Obsidian	

Large chipped blades of obsidian volcanic glass were used as money and as symbols of high status.

AMERICAN	*Figurine*	**2nd Floor**
	A.D. 1200–1600	
	Stone	

Thomas Jefferson was once the owner of this figurine.

AMERICAN	*Chilkat Shoulder Blanket*	**2nd Floor**
Alaska, Northwest Coast,	19th c.	
Tlingit Tribe	Cedar bark, mountain	
	goat, dog hair	

These blankets, made in the village of Chilkat, are usually black, blue-green yellow-brown, have shredded bark fringe on the sides and bottom and symbolic and naturalistic abstract designs. The back hung straight and the sides were gathered up in front.

PERUVIAN	*Mantle*	**3rd Floor**
Paracas Peninsula	400–100 B.C.	

Mantles of fabulous color and patterns, well preserved in arid soil, were used to wrap the dead. Ancient craftsmen, familiar with all types of modern weaves, used approximately 190 colors.

MEXICAN	*Plaque*	**3rd Floor**
Oaxaca, Mayan Culture	A.D. 550–950	
	Jade	

The Mayans of this time used no metal but were outstanding craftsmen in stone. They created many extraordinary jade pieces; jewelry, plaques, figurines and more.

MEXICAN	*Necklace*	**3rd Floor**
Oaxaca, Sola de	A.D. 1250–1500	
Vega, Mixtec Culture	Gold	

The Mixtecs introduced gold-working techniques into Mexico, making Oaxaca the celebrated center of production. Craftsmen, unequaled in skill and taste, fashioned jewelry in symbolic designs.

MEXICAN	*Sculpture of Xipe Totec*	**3rd Floor**
Tepepan, Aztec Culture	A.D. 1507	
	Stone	

Aztec sculpture can be awesome and gruesome. Naturalistic, stolid pieces, although three-dimensional, often appear four-sided, evidence of the stone block from which they originated. Xipe Totec is the fearsome God of Spring.

FACILITIES

The *Library* contains books, monographs, journals and other items relating to the collection.

The *Photographic Archives* house prints, negatives and slides, from early photographs to modern photos of specimens in the collection.

The *Museum Shop* is well stocked with silver jewelry, pottery, Kachina dolls, sculptures, textiles, beadwork, paintings in oil, acrylic and other mediums, cloth hangings, books about Indians, postcards, slides, greeting cards, posters, rugs and much more. Prices range from 10¢ for postcards to $2,000 for necklaces.

Hours: Tuesday–Saturday, 10 A.M.–5 P.M.; Sunday, 1 P.M.–5 P.M. *Closed:* Mondays, major holidays.

Admission: Adults, $1.25; students and senior citizens with I.D. cards, 75¢.

MUSEUM OF THE CITY OF NEW YORK
Fifth Ave. at 103rd St.
New York, NY 10029
Tel: (212)534-1672

The museum first opened in 1923 in Gracie Mansion, today the home of New York City's Mayor. In 1932, it moved to its present quarters, built in the style of a Colonial Georgian home, popular in 18th-century New York. It re-creates the varying life-styles of the most diverse city in the world from a small Dutch settlement of the 1630s to that of contemporary life. The collection contains costumes, displayed against a background of period rooms from 1690 to 1906; silver; furniture; paintings; decorative arts; toys; dolls and theatrical items on view in changing exhibitions. The second floor Marine Gallery is rich in American marine memorabilia with material stressing New York City as a major port of the world. A gallery housing old fire-fighting equipment is located on the ground floor.

SAMPLING THE COLLECTION

Main Floor,   *The Big Apple*
South Hall   A multimedia audiovisual exhibition of the history of New York City from 1524 to the present. Objects from the collections are spotlighted during the 20-minute film.

Main Floor,   GILBERT STUART   *Portraits of George Washington*
South Hall   American, 1755–1828
Stuart painted Washington from life three times. He made several replicas of which the museum owns two. The Athenaeum Head, the best known, was so named because the original was owned by the Boston Athenaeum. The other, in a standing position, is known as the Landsdowne Portrait.

2nd Floor,   AMERICAN   *Figurehead of Andrew Jackson*
Marine   1834
Gallery   Wood
This imposing figurehead once gazed down from the U.S.S. *Constitution* ("Old Ironsides"). The head, now replaced, was sawed off by an irate sailor protesting that Jackson, an Army man, was also Chief of the Navy.

3rd Floor,   AMERICAN   *Stettheimer Dolls' House*
Toy Gallery,   1925
This 10-room dollhouse, with working elevator, is one of several on view. Carrie Walter Stettheimer was hostess to many celebrated artists who decorated the house with miniature copies of their work. There are statues by Gaston Lachaise, paintings by Gela Archipenko and Marcel Duchamp's *Nude Descending a Staircase.*

3rd Floor   DUNCAN PHYFE   *Drawing Room*
American, 1768–1854   early 19th c.

Stettheimer Dolls' House. *Courtesy Museum of the City of New York*

Duncan Phyfe was one of the foremost cabinetmakers of his time whose studio was in New York City. Most of the furniture was made by him. The woodwork is from an old New York home.

| AMERICAN | *John D. Rockefeller Rooms* | **5th Floor** |
| New York City | 1880s | |

Furnished in Victorian manner in the style of Charles Eastlake, the bedroom and dressing room of Mr. and Mrs. Rockefeller are richly ornate. Reassembled from the Rockefeller home, they afford us a close-up view of a very special way of life.

FACILITIES

Guided Tours as well as *Recorded Tours* of the museum are available.

Sunday Walking Tours through the city are conducted from April through October on various Sundays. $3 each tour.

Changing Exhibitions are regularly featured.

The *Theater and Music Collection* features temporary exhibitions of historic and contemporary theatrical material.

For *Children* the replica of Fort Amsterdam, on the main floor, is exciting to explore.

The *"Please Touch"* demonstrations for children 6–12 are offered on Saturday afternoons from November to April and cost $1.

Puppet Shows are presented on Saturdays from November to April. Call for program information.

Concerts are held on Sunday afternoons from November to April. No charge.

The *Sales Shop* offers items from 5¢ magazines to a variety of more expensive goods that include postcards of old New York scenes; miniature household objects and dolls; books relating to the city and to the theater and, especially for children, articles costing under $1, such as totem poles, quill pens and miniature wooden shoes.

Hours: Tuesday–Saturday, 10 A.M.–4:45 P.M.; Sundays and holidays, 1 P.M.–5 P.M. Open on holidays that fall on Monday and closed the following Tuesday. *Closed:* Mondays, Christmas, January 1.

Admission: Free.

MUSEUM OF MODERN ART
11 West 53rd St.
New York, NY 10019
Tel: (212)956-6100

The museum was founded in 1929 "to help the public to enjoy, understand and use the visual arts of our time." The collections range from 1880 with the Impressionists to the present. The museum opened in the existing building in 1939, was enlarged in 1964 and again in 1966 with the acquisition of the erstwhile Whitney Museum adjacent to it. Plans are underway for a 40-story apartment house to be built on top of the present structure which will also afford the museum additional space. Housed on the second and third floors and in the Sculpture Garden is an outstanding collection of 20th-century art. There, too, are drawings and prints; the architecture and design collection and the Edward Steichen Photography Center, first to elevate photography to the status it enjoys today.

SAMPLING THE COLLECTION

2nd Floor

PABLO PICASSO · *Les Demoiselles d'Avignon*
Spanish, 1881–1973 · 1907
Oil on canvas

This transitional painting is considered the first Cubist picture. Of monumental size, with distorted, angular and crowded figures that are painted against a jagged background, it still retains its shocking quality.

Ma Jolie
1911–1912
Oil on canvas

Confining his palette to browns, tans and grays, Picasso explored Cubism in greater depth than in *Les Demoiselles d'Avignon*. Horizontal and vertical lines conceal the subject, which refers to a popular song and his amour of the time.

VINCENT VAN GOGH   *The Starry Night*   **2nd Floor,**
Dutch, 1853–1890   1889   **Gallery 1**
                          Oil on canvas
While in southern France, van Gogh painted "a star-spangled sky." Whirling
brush strokes of heavy impasto express his agitation shortly before his suicide.

PIET MONDRIAN   *Broadway Boogie-Woogie*   **2nd Floor,**
Dutch, 1872–1944   1942–1943   **Gallery 8**
                         Oil on canvas
Mondrian likens his painting style to boogie-woogie music. ". . . destruction of
melody which is the equivalent of destruction of natural appearance, and
construction through the continuous opposition of pure means—dynamic
rhythm."

HENRI MATISSE   *The Red Studio*   **2nd Floor,**
French, 1869–1954   1911   **Gallery 11**
                         Oil on canvas
Circling a red field, in complex arrangement, Matisse painted his various possessions and works of art in small scale, approximating their actual color. By
excluding himself, he suggests that the significance of his life lies in his creations.

ANDREW WYETH   *Christina's World*   **2nd Floor,**
American, b. 1917   1948   **Gallery 16**
                         Tempera on gesso panel
This is the most familiar painting of several Wyeth made of his crippled neighbor. His penetrating realistic style, meticulously detailed, projects a sense of
nostalgia and sadness.

JACKSON POLLOCK   *One (Number 31, 1950)*   **3rd Floor**
American, 1912–1956   1950
                         Oil and enamel
This title derives from the painting's all-over design denoting unity. Although
Pollock's "drip paintings" suggest a lack of control he did, indeed, direct the
splatters and drips, incorporating the accidental to advantage.

SALVADOR DALI   *The Persistence of Memory* **3rd Floor,**
Spanish, b. 1904   1931   **Gallery 4**
                         Oil on canvas
Dali's paintings rely heavily on dreams and the irrational. His precisely executed
limp watches reject modern formalist art and reach into the past along with his
choice of color, size and other symbolic detail.

FACILITIES

Tours with accoustiguides are available.

Temporary Exhibitions culled from the museum's collection or *Loan Exhibitions* from other institutions are regular features of the museum's program.

Gallery Talks, Lectures, Concerts, and *Special Events* are often featured.

The *Reference Library* contains, in addition to books, catalogs, magazines and
gallery notices on modern trends since the Post-Impressionists.

Classic Films are screened regularly. Call (212)956-7078 for program informa-   **1st Floor,**
tion.   **Auditorium**

The *Garden Restaurant* looks out on the Sculpture Garden. It serves lunch and   **1st Floor**
tea daily and dinner on Thursdays.

Two Bookstores, one in the lobby, the other at 23 West 53rd Street, stock
books, cards, posters, reproductions, slides, design objects, gifts and toys.

3rd Floor   The *Abby Aldrich Rockefeller Print Room* has 10,000 prints available for viewing by appointment.

North Wing   The *Lillie P. Bliss International Study Center* houses art from the museum's collection that is not on view in the galleries. It is available for study on easily accessible storage racks.

Checkroom   *Baby Carriers* and *Wheelchairs* are available.

Hours: Friday–Tuesday, 11 A.M.–6 P.M.; Thursday, 11 A.M.–9 P.M. *Closed:* Wednesdays, Christmas.

Admission: $2.50; full-time students with current identification, $1.50; children and senior citizens, 75¢; Tuesday: Pay-what-you-wish.

NEW MUSEUM
65 Fifth Ave.
New York, NY 10003
Tel: (212)741–8962

The New Museum, founded in 1977, is located in a large gallery space donated by the New School. It organizes and mounts exhibitions of the work of lesser-known living artists, presenting to the public new, provocative art—painting, sculpture, photography, graphic arts and related video, film and performance —in a critical and scholarly context. Exhibitions that provide exposure for art of the previous decade are changed approximately every two months.

Interior Gallery. *Courtesy Warren Silverman, Photographer, the New Museum, New York*

FACILITIES

Tours of the collection are available.

Lectures and symposia are conducted. Call for program information.

A *Sales Desk* carries exhibition catalogs from each show; they usually cost about $3.75. Exhibition posters are also for sale.

Hours: Weekdays, 12 P.M.–6 P.M.; Wednesday, 12 P.M.–8 P.M.; Saturday, 1 P.M.–5 P.M. *Closed:* Sundays and weekends during August.

Admission: Free.

NEW-YORK HISTORICAL SOCIETY
170 Central Park West
New York, NY 10023
Tel: (212)873–3400

The society's first home was Federal Hall, where "it was organized in 1804 to collect and preserve material pertaining to the history of the United States, and of New York State in particular. . . ." It is the second-oldest historical society in the nation. The present building, completed in 1938, is its eighth home. Its collection is composed of Americana; objects of New York City and State; American portraits; 19th-century American landscapes and other paintings; and a library.

SAMPLING THE COLLECTION

FRENCH   *The Beekman Coach*   **2nd Floor**
                                    1770s
The coach was sometimes drawn by four horses with a coachman and two footmen in attendance. Once elegantly painted, the Beekman coat of arms still graces the exterior.

JOHN JAMES AUDUBON   *Birds of America*   **2nd Floor**
American, 1785–1851   1827–1838
                             Watercolor drawings
The society owns 433 of 435 watercolors Audubon painted for *Birds of America*. Some of these with memorabilia and a set of engravings from the original drawings are on view.

INTERNATIONAL   *Paperweights*   **2nd Floor**
                             Glass
The collection comprises 549 paperweights, simple to complex. The Sinclair Collection contains 439 European classic paperweights plus related glass (1845–1855) and American examples from mid-19th century to early 20th century.

THOMAS COLE   *Course of Empire*   **4th Floor**
American, 1801–1848   1836
                             Oil on canvas
Cole was the leader of the Hudson River School. His allegorical romantic landscapes, sometimes painted in series, were dramatic and filled with fantasy. This apocalyptic pastoral vista is one in a series of five.

The Beekman Coach. *Courtesy New-York Historical Society, New York*

FACILITIES

Guided Tours may be arranged through the Education Department.

Changing Exhibitions are regularly featured.

Lectures are offered occasionally.

Concerts are held Sundays at 2:30 P.M. from November through April. Admission $1. Students, senior citizens, 50¢.

Movies and Story Hours are available for children at no charge. Call for further information.

The *Library* is one of the most important reference libraries of American history in the United States containing almost 600,000 volumes, manuscripts, maps, prints and photographs. Hours: Tuesday–Saturday, 10 A.M.–5 P.M. Admission $1 per day.

The *Sales Desk* carries postcards, greeting cards, catalogs, posters, prints, New York City guidebooks and maps from 10¢ to $7.

Hours: Tuesday–Friday, 10 A.M.–5 P.M.; Saturday, 10 A.M.–5 P.M.; Sunday, 1 P.M.–5 P.M. *Closed:* Mondays, New Year's, Memorial Day, July 4, Labor Day, Thanksgiving, Christmas.

Admission: Discretionary admission fee for nonmembers. Recommended: Adults, $1.50; children, 75¢.

PIERPONT MORGAN LIBRARY
29 East 36th St.
New York, NY 10016
Tel: (212)685–0008

The library, designed by McKim, Mead and White, was completed in 1906 as a private repository for the books and art collection of Pierpont Morgan and was adjacent to the family's town house. It was opened to the public in 1924. In 1928, an annex was erected on the site of the former residence, doubling the library's size. The original structure is inspired by Italian Renaissance villas and is constructed of marble blocks fitted in Classical Greek manner. It is listed in the National Register of Historic Places and is also a National Historic Landmark. The original study of Pierpont Morgan (the West Room) and the library room (the East Room) in the 1906 building have been kept much the same as in Morgan's time. Gracing the walls are Old Masters paintings by such early Flemish and Italian painters as Hans Memling (c. 1435–1494) and Pietro Perugino (c. 1445–1523). On display also are ancient medieval and Renaissance sculpture, gold work and enamels of the Middle Ages and majolica, porcelain and faïence.

SAMPLING THE COLLECTION

MEDIEVAL AND RENAISSANCE MANUSCRIPTS

This extensive collection, some 1,000 manuscripts, consists of such choice items as the 13th-century *Old Testament Illustrations,* a volume once owned

East Room. *Courtesy Pierpont Morgan Library, New York*

by Shah Abbas the Great, King of Persia; an 11th-century Greek *Gospel Lectionary;* an important 10th-century illustrated Beatus *Apocalypse;* two 11th-century gospels illuminated in England; a 10th-century Greek illuminated manuscript of *Dioscorides, "De Materia Medica";* a 9th-century Reims *Gospels,* completely written in gold; and the *Missal of Abbot Berthold,* one of the finest extant 13th-century German manuscripts,which still has its original jeweled binding. Two outstanding examples from the 15th century are the celebrated *Hours of Catherine of Cleves* and the Prayerbook of *Michelino de Besozzo.*

OLD MASTERS DRAWINGS AND REMBRANDT ETCHINGS

The collection contains about 5,000 Italian, French, Flemish, Dutch, German and English drawings. Among the artists represented are Botticelli, Filippino Lippi, Parmigianino, Guercino, Tiepolo and Piranesi, Poussin, Boucher and Fragonard, Brueghel, Rubens and Van Dyck, Rembrandt and Ostade, Dürer, Gainsborough, West, Blake and Lawrence. The collection of Rembrandt etchings is the most extensive in the country.

EARLY PRINTED BOOKS

The library's collection of incunabula (books printed before 1500) is of unsurpassed quality, beginning with both paper and vellum copies of Gutenberg's 42-line Bible, plus a complete 42-line Old Testament on paper containing unique typesettings of a number of pages. Special strengths of the collection include: editions of William Caxton and other early English presses (the most important collection outside England); editions in vernacular languages, particularly French; illustrated editions; Bibles and liturgical printing; early editions of classical texts; books from rare presses and obscure printing towns illustrating the early spread of printing throughout Europe.

AUTOGRAPHS, MANUSCRIPTS, LETTERS AND DOCUMENTS

Thousands upon thousands of letters and hundreds of original manuscripts with special emphasis on the Italian Renaissance, the German Reformation, the Tudor and Stuart English periods, and the American Revolution and young Republic are included in the collection. Additionally, there is particularly notable manuscript material of La Fontaine, Bossuet, Voltaire, Dumas père, Lamartine, Sir Philip Sidney, Milton, Swift, Pope, Sterne, Gray, Horace Walpole, Cowper, Burns, Blake, Scott, Coleridge, Shelley, Keats, Byron, Southey, Jane Austen, the Brontës, the Brownings, Dickens, Thackeray, Wilkie Collins, Meredith, Morris, Ruskin, Kipling, Poe, Emerson, Hawthorne, Thoreau, Holmes, Longfellow, Mark Twain, Bret Harte and John Steinbeck.

BOOKBINDINGS

The collection of historically and artistically significant bookbindings is world famous and almost uniquely comprehensive, extending from late Classical times down to the present. Some of its special strengths are medieval jeweled bindings, gold-tooled bindings of the Renaissance and after, and bindings from the libraries of famous bibliophiles, most notably Jean Grolier.

MUSICAL MANUSCRIPTS

With the exception of the Library of Congress, the Morgan Library has the most extensive collection of musical autographs in America. The Gilbert & Sullivan collection is the largest in the world.

LATER PRINTED BOOKS

The library's collection is relatively small but very choice. Among its major emphases are the history of the book arts, monuments of the history of thought, and writings—including many presentation and association copies—of important English, American and continental authors.

EARLY CHILDREN'S BOOKS

The Morgan Library's collection, probably the most significant one in the United States, concentrates on English and continental children's literature through the 19th century. It features a great number of unique or very rare items. The printed books include the unique copy of the earliest known French children's book (ca. 1487), the manuscripts include the original text of Perrault's *Mother Goose,* and there are original drawings for book illustration from all periods.

ANCIENT WRITTEN RECORDS

The library possesses a superior collection of Assyrian and Babylonian seals (cylinders and stamps) in addition to cuneiform tablets, Egyptian, Greek and other papyri.

FACILITIES

Changing Exhibitions are regularly featured.

The *Reading Room* and *Print Room* are open for qualified research. Application must be made in advance.

Photographic Services include microfilms, photographs, color slides and ektachromes (for rental only) of original materials in the collections.

Lectures on the fine arts, iconography and archeology are given and also **Meeting** published in book form. **Room**

Hours: Tuesday–Saturday, 10:30 A.M.–4:45 P.M.; Sunday, 1 P.M.–4:45 P.M.
   Closed: Mondays, August, national holidays.

Admission: None set, but voluntary contributions are requested.

SOLOMON R. GUGGENHEIM MUSEUM
1071 Fifth Ave.
New York, NY 10028
Tel: (212)860–1300

The museum, opened in 1959, is one of modern architecture's most controversial buildings. Designed by Frank Lloyd Wright and cast in concrete, it faces Central Park. The structure has been regarded as both "a giant snail" and "the most beautiful building in New York." Its spiral shape encloses a curved cantilevered ramp running from the ground to the dome almost 100 feet above; 74 nichelike bays display the artworks. The permanent collection comprises over 4,000 paintings, sculptures and works on paper from the late 19th and 20th centuries. It reflects the development of modern art, from European Impressionism to contemporary American and international movements and is augmented by 75 works from the Justin K. Thannhauser Collection of Impressionist and Post-Impressionist works, including a concentration of Picassos.

SAMPLING THE COLLECTION

VINCENT VAN GOGH   *Mountains at Saint-Rémy*
Dutch, 1853–1890   1889
                                    Oil on canvas
Van Gogh painted this tormented landscape while hospitalized after his second breakdown. Distorted forms are executed in swirling brush strokes and intense color typifying his later works that so influenced German Expressionism.

Vincent van Gogh, Mountains at Saint-Rémy. *Courtesy Solomon R. Guggenheim Museum, New York*

PAUL CEZANNE   *The Clockmaker*
French, 1839–1906   1895–1900
                                    Oil on canvas
Cézanne's mature style concentrated on the underlying structure of his subject whether animate or inanimate. He painted in vibrating strokes of unmixed color, using light randomly and modeling his figures flatly.

FERNAND LEGER   *The Great Parade*
French, 1881–1955   1954
                                Oil on canvas
This large-scale canvas is the final version of *The Great Parade.* It is the culmination of such themes as Cyclists, Constructors, Country Outings and Circus pictures which had occupied Léger for over a decade.

PABLO PICASSO   *Mandolin and Guitar*
Spanish, 1881–1973   1924
                                Oil with sand on canvas
In the mid-1920s Picasso painted many large, colorful still lifes where the objects are placed on a table in front of an open window.

                                Woman with Yellow Hair
                                (Marie-Thérèse Walter)
                                1931
                                Oil on canvas
Between 1927 and 1935 Picasso painted a series of blond women inspired by the mother of his daughter, Maia, often portraying her asleep. They were rendered in sensuous curves in lavenders and purples suggesting sleepiness and introspection.

FACILITIES

Lectures by visiting scholars are frequently scheduled. Gallery talks by museum-trained guides are given Tuesday–Sunday at 11:30 A.M. and 2 P.M. and on Tuesday at 6:30 P.M.

Temporary Exhibitions selected from the museum's collection or *Loan Exhibitions* from other institutions are regular features of the museum's program.

Films on art are screened. Call for program information.

Performing Art Events are presented in the museum auditorium and rotunda on occasion.

Poetry Readings, sponsored by the Academy of American Poets, are given on selected Tuesday evenings.

The *Bookstore* carries a variety of exhibition catalogs; art books; original lithographs; prints; posters; slides; postcards; note cards and greeting cards.

The *Café* serves light lunches and refreshments. An outdoor terrace is open during the summer. Tuesday–Sunday, 11 A.M.–5 P.M.

Taped Tours of the Justin K. Thannhauser Collection, special exhibitions and **Admissions** the museum itself are conducted by museum curators and are available for rent. **Desk**

Hours: Wednesday–Sunday, holidays, 11 A.M.–5 P.M.; Tuesday, 11 A.M.–8 P.M.
         Closed: Mondays except holidays, Christmas.

Admission: $1.50; students with I.D. and visitors over 62, 75¢; group visits, arranged in advance for 10 students or more, 50¢ per person; children under 7, free; Tuesday evenings, 5–8 P.M., free.

STUDIO MUSEUM IN HARLEM
2033 Fifth Ave.
New York, NY 10035
Tel: (212)427–5959

Paul Cézanne, The Clockmaker. *Courtesy Solomon R. Guggenheim Museum, New York*

The museum, founded in 1968, is presently located in a loft building in central Harlem but will shortly move to a five-story structure donated by the New York Bank for Savings. It is at 144 West 125th Street, Harlem's most-trafficked thoroughfare, and is being readied for a 1981 opening. It will be known as the Museum of African-American Art. Plans are underway to enlarge the permanent collection and to expand the film library and archives to include classic Black films, films for children and original work by independent Black and third-world filmmakers. Additionally, photography exhibitions will be displayed in the newly created James van der Zee Wing named for the well-known photographer. The Gift Shop will be better stocked to offer a greater variety of items. The museum is the principal center for the study of Black art in America. A curatorial council of prominent figures in Black fine arts acts in an advisory capacity. The museum is devoted to the works of African and African-American painters, printmakers and photographers. Visitors may view the works in progress in the Artists-in-Residence program which provides young artists with studio space for a period of one to two years. Approximately ten exhibitions each year include group and one-man shows of Black artists as well as historical and other informative material. The permanent collection is presently in storage.

FACILITIES

Lectures, Seminars, Films, Concerts, Poetry Readings and *Dance Performances* are periodically presented.

The *Gift Shop* sells reproductions; books; posters; slides; catalogs and videotapes.

Hours: Tuesday–Friday, 10 A.M.–6 P.M.; Saturday–Sunday, 1 P.M.–6 P.M.
   Closed: Mondays, national holidays.

Admission: A contribution of $1.50 is suggested.

UKRAINIAN MUSEUM
203 Second Ave.
New York, NY 10003
Tel: (212)228–0110

The museum, opened in 1976, houses a collection that covers the major crafts in Ukrainian folk art: woven and embroidered textiles, woodwork, metalwork, ceramics and Easter egg painting.

SAMPLING THE COLLECTION

Costumes   **4th Floor**
late 19th c.–early 20th c.

Both men's and women's regional costumes are on view, including a wedding dress from the western Ukraine and an older woman's mourning costume from the central Ukraine. Embroidery was a mass phenomenon. Every girl embroidered her costume as well as ritual cloths, tablecloths, etc., for her trousseau. In one small item of dress one can find 10 to 15 different stitches and various colors. At this time new and brighter colors appear with the replacement of vegetable dyes with chemical ones. In southwestern Ukraine, gold and silver metallic thread is also used. The richest embroidery is found on women's costumes, especially the sleeves of blouses.

Woman's Costume, Village of Cherniatyn. *Courtesy Ukrainian Museum, New York*

FACILITIES

Guided Tours are available by advance arrangement (minimum of 10, maximum of 35).

Lectures are given, some in Ukrainian, some in English, on Ukrainian arts and crafts.

A *Gift Shop* sells embroidered, wooden and woven items and jewelry with prices from $1 to $125. Greeting cards from 25¢ to 40¢.

Hours: Wednesday–Sunday, 1 P.M.–5 P.M. *Closed:* Monday, Tuesday.

Admission: Adults, $1; senior citizens, students, children, 50¢.

WHITNEY MUSEUM OF AMERICAN ART
945 Madison Ave.
New York, NY 10021
Tel: (212)570–3600

The museum, the most active institution devoted to the art of the United States, emphasizes works of the 20th century. Over 5,500 rich and diverse examples of paintings, sculptures, and drawings compose the collection. The museum, established in 1930, was founded by Gertrude Vanderbilt Whitney, whose own collection was the seminal source. After outgrowing its original quarters on West 8th Street, it moved to West 54th Street in 1954, where it remained until the construction of the present building in 1966. Designed by Marcel Breuer, the gray granite structure is entered by a bridgelike span from which one looks down on a small sculpture court. The permanent collection provides a setting against which new art in the changing exhibitions can more easily be interpreted.

SAMPLING THE COLLECTION

The works listed below are sometimes on loan or otherwise unavailable for viewing at the museum.

MAURICE PRENDERGAST
Canadian/American, 1859–1924

Central Park 1901
1901
Watercolor on paper

Prendergast, a member of "The Eight,"painted with a softer brand of Realism than the others. Although influenced by Cézanne, he applied colors laterally and more crudely, in a less-structured manner.

GEORGE BELLOWS
1882–1925

Dempsey and Firpo
1924
Oil on canvas

Bellows is mainly known for his scenes of prizefighters, this being his final rendition. His own bald head is visible at the far left of the canvas.

MARSDEN HARTLEY
1877–1943

Painting, Number 5
1914–1915
Oil on canvas

While working in Germany, Hartley often memorialized in paintings a young German friend, decorated and killed in the war. This, the most abstract rendition, was influenced by Cubism, Delaunay's work with color and German Expressionism.

PATRICK HENRY BRUCE
1881–1936

Painting
ca. 1930
Oil on canvas

Bruce's paintings presage the advent of the Hard Edge Abstractionists of the 1930s. Influenced by Cézanne and Matisse, they illustrate in their color and form a boldness and clarity derived from the Colorists and Purists that preceded him.

CHARLES DEMUTH
1883–1935

My Egypt
1927
Oil on composition board

The whimsical title refers to the grain elevators once standing in Demuth's hometown, Lancaster, Pennsylvania. This agricultural community fostered his attachment to the land resulting in many renditions of flowers, fruits, vegetables and still lifes.

GEORGIA O'KEEFFE
b. 1887

The White Calico Flower
1931
Oil on canvas

Early in her career O'Keeffe painted a series of magnified flowers in a semiabstract style. This one was inspired by the cloth flowers worn by New Mexican women.

EDWARD HOPPER
1882–1967

Early Sunday Morning
1930
Oil on canvas

Hopper's widow made a large bequest of his work to the museum at her death in 1968. This particular scene was acquired from him soon after its completion. His poetic paintings are composed in a simple geometric style contrasting light and shadow.

RALSTON CRAWFORD
Canadian/American, 1906–1978

Steel Foundry, Coatesville, PA
1936–1937
Oil on canvas

Crawford was a Precisionist whose work was grounded in Cubism. His most consequential paintings were executed during this time and are reductive architectural depictions drawn from agricultural, commercial and industrial sources.

ALEXANDER CALDER
1898–1976

The Brass Family
1929
Brass wire

Calder's wire sculptures illustrate his attraction to the circus. Its force and continuous activity find release in his later mobile inventions.

GASTON LACHAISE
French/American, 1882–1935

Standing Woman
1912–1927
Bronze

With his wife-to-be his original inspiration, Lachaise began this sculpture, later expanding on it. Exhibited in 1918 in plaster; lack of funds prevented him from casting it in bronze until 1927.

ISAMU NOGUCHI
Japanese/American, b. 1904

Humpty Dumpty
1946
Ribbon slate

Noguchi uses natural materials in his simple yet elegantly finished sculptures. This one, of a series of sculptures in marble and slate, is curvilinear, consisting of connected abstract shapes.

ARSHILE GORKY
Armenian/American, 1904–1948

The Betrothal, II
1947
Oil on canvas

Alexander Calder, The Brass Family. *Photographer, Geoffrey Clements; Collection of Whitney Museum of American Art, New York*

Gorky helped pave the way from Surrealism to Abstract Expressionism. The symbolic meaning of this painting is in doubt although it possibly refers to the betrothal of representation and abstraction.

DAVID SMITH   *Hudson River Landscape*
1906–1965   1951
                                   Steel

Many of Smith's sculptures have been likened to "drawings in space." This last, and most inspiring landscape, demonstrates his superior welding technique along with an enthusiastic appreciation of his theme.

JACKSON POLLOCK   *Number 27, 1950*
1912–1956   Oil on canvas

Pollock, the foremost Action Painter, commented, "I want to express my feelings rather than illustrate them." He allowed the subconscious to surface expelling explicit conventions adhered to in Renaissance and modern painting.

LOUISE NEVELSON   *Dawn's Wedding Chapel II*
b. 1900   1959
                                   Painted wood

Nevelson executed all her pieces in black until *Dawn's Wedding Feast* from which this sculpture was reconstructed. It was painted white, the single color unifying the found objects arranged in intricate compartmentalized design.

STUART DAVIS   *The Paris Bit*
1894–1964   1959
                                   Oil on canvas

Davis painted modern city life. His work, influenced by the Cubists, was executed in more simplified, stylized composition. Lettering and vivid color combined with commercial themes to presage certain elements of Pop Art.

WILLEM DE KOONING   *Door to the River*
b. 1904   1960

De Kooning was a leader of the Abstract Expressionist movement. This large-scale landscape abstraction was rapidly created with no evidence of the constant reworking of earlier efforts.

ROY LICHTENSTEIN   *Little Big Painting*
b. 1923   1965
                                   Oil on canvas

Commencing his career as an Abstract Expressionist, Lichtenstein turned to "re-presenting" works by celebrated painters as a Pop artist. This witty take-off on de Kooning capitalizes on and conventionalizes the energies of Abstract Expressionism.

JASPER JOHNS   *Three Flags*
b. 1930   1958
                                   Encaustic on canvas

This painting composed of three successively smaller canvases of the American flag placed one on top of the other is a singular statement arising from the dominance of abstract expressionism.

FACILITIES

Gallery Talks on current exhibitions are presented Thursday, Saturday and Sunday afternoons by museum curators or informed lecturers.

Changing Exhibitions are regularly featured.

The *New American Film Makers Series* presents daily screenings or installations of independently produced avant-garde films and videotapes.

The *Garden Restaurant* is adjacent to the sculpture court and displays paintings and sculpture. It provides light meals and other refreshments and offers a full bar. Hours: Tuesday, 11:30 A.M.–7:30 P.M.; Wednesday–Saturday,11:30 A.M.–4:30 P.M.; Sunday, 12 P.M.–5 P.M. (Also special summer hours.)

The *Sales Desk* offers, among its most popular items, posters, catalogs and books from current and past exhibitions, postcards and notepaper illustrating works from the permanent collection; Calder T-shirts and Whitney tote bags. Prices range from 20¢ postcards to $50 and over for some books, posters, and reproductions of sculpture.

The *Downtown Branch* at 55 Water Street, (212) 483–0011, features a variety of changing exhibitions. Monday–Friday, 11 A.M.–3 P.M. Admission is free.

Hours: Tuesday, 11 A.M.–8 P.M.; Wednesday–Saturday, 11 A.M.–6 P.M.; Sunday, holidays, 12 P.M.–6 P.M. *Closed:* Mondays, Christmas.

Admission: Adults, $2. Tuesday evening, 5 P.M.–8 P.M. free through a grant from Mobil; senior citizens, free; children under 12, free, made possible by Manufacturers Hanover Trust; college students with current I.D. free, made possible by Helena Rubinstein Foundation.

MOUNTAINVILLE

STORM KING ART CENTER
Old Pleasant Hill Rd.
Mountainville, NY 10953
Tel: (914)534-3115

Storm King Art Center was established in 1960 as an outdoor sculpture museum. The 200 acres of gardens and rolling fields provide a splendid setting for the collection of European and American sculptures, which includes 13 works by David Smith. The French Normandy-style museum was built in 1935 as a private residence.

SAMPLING THE COLLECTION

DAVID SMITH   *XI Books 111 Apples*
American, 1906–1965   1959
                                 Stainless steel
Smith's early sculptures were calligraphic silhouettes depicting a troubled, uneasy world. After the late 1950s he abandoned this style and until his death produced monumental works, simpler and more geometric.

ALEXANDER LIBERMAN   *Eve*
American, b. 1912   1970
                                 Steel
Liberman turned from Minimal painting, in which he concentrated on the circle, to monumental sculptures, which further explored his fascination with curvilinear forms.

HENRY MOORE   *Reclining Connected Forms*
British, b. 1898   1969
                               Bronze
Since 1945 Moore has worked in bronze. The reclining figure, a recurrent theme, is usually executed in two or three separate pieces which when viewed from certain angles appears as a whole.

ISAMU NOGUCHI   *Momo Taro*
Japanese/American, b. 1904   1977–1978
                               Granite
Noguchi was influenced by Brancusi. His late work combines both the fluidity and weightlessness of Brancusi's sculpture with heavier, weighted surfaces.

FACILITIES

Tours with a lecturer for groups of 15–50 adults may be arranged in advance. Weekdays, except Tuesday, 2 P.M.–5:30 P.M.

Hours: *Mid-May–October:* Daily except Tuesday, 2 P.M.–5:30 P.M. *Closed:* Tuesdays, except legal holidays, then open Tuesdays, closed Wednesdays. Grounds open from mid-April to Thanksgiving.

Admission: Suggested donation, $2.

OGDENSBURG

REMINGTON ART MUSEUM
303 Washington St.
Ogdensburg, NY 13669
Tel: (315)393-2425

The Parish Mansion, built in 1809–1810 and occupied by Remington's widow until her death, is now the Remington Art Museum. It houses the largest collection of original artwork by Remington, who is recognized as the foremost artist of the Old West.

SAMPLING THE COLLECTION

FREDERIC REMINGTON   *Artwork*
American, 1861–1909
Included in the collection are oils, watercolors, sketches and bronzes. The re-creation of the artist's last studio is on view with most of the original furnishings.

PARISH COLLECTION OF BELTER FURNITURE, 1809–1850s

Furniture acquired by a succession of Parish relatives plus other mementoes are on display.

FACILITIES

Guided Tours, Lectures and *Gallery Talks* are available.

The *Sales Shop*'s most popular offerings are reproductions of Remington's work which range in price from 15¢ to $55. Also available are books, cards and colored slides.

Hours: Monday–Saturday, 10 A.M.–5 P.M. (open all year); Sunday 1 P.M.–5 P.M.
(June–October only). *Closed:* Legal holidays.
Admission: Adults, $1; students 12 and over, 50¢; under 12, free.

POUGHKEEPSIE

VASSAR COLLEGE ART GALLERY
Poughkeepsie, NY 12601
Tel: (914)452-7000, ext. 2645

The gallery is located in Taylor Hall. The collection includes Renaissance, Baroque and modern paintings; paintings by the Hudson River School; Rembrandt and Dürer prints; a well-rounded collection of drawings, watercolors and prints; sculpture and a Classical collection.

SAMPLING THE COLLECTION

The permanent collection is rotated throughout the year, therefore the works listed may not always be on view.

MARSDEN HARTLEY   *Indian Composition*
American, 1887–1943   ca. 1914–1915
                             Oil on canvas
Beginning as an Impressionist, Hartley later worked in Germany investigating Cubism. On his return to Europe after exhibiting in the United States, he shifted toward more abstract designs.

MARK ROTHKO   *No. 18, 1948*
American, 1903–1970   1949
                             Oil on canvas
Rothko's early paintings were affected by Surrealism. His Abstract Expressionist canvases are more serene than those of other artists of similar bent. The fuzzy-edged colored rectangles float in space.

HUBERT ROBERT   *The Octavian Gate and Fish*
French, 1733–1808   *Market*
                             1784
                             Oil on canvas
During a sojourn in Italy Robert became friends with Piranesi and Panini, who were known for their prints and paintings of architectural ruins. Robert followed their lead and once back in Paris painted many romantic views of Paris street scenes. He particularly caught the crowded, bustling atmosphere of the moment.

EDWARD MUNCH   *The Sick Girl*
Norwegian, 1863–1944   1895
                             Drypoint etching with roulette
Munch, a forerunner of Expressionism, made his work a vehicle for a highly emotional and psychological content. His themes inevitably dealt with basic human feelings of love, fear, anxiety and loneliness.

FRANCIS BACON   *Study for a Portrait of a*
British, b. 1910   *Pope IV*
                             1953
                             Oil on canvas

Marsden Hartley, Indian Composition. *Courtesy Vassar College Art Gallery, Poughkeepsie*

This painting is one of many which Bacon did of the figure of the Pope. His technique of barely covering the canvas with paint and his sketchlike, abstract treatment of figure and background serve to itensify the figure's anguish.

ALEXANDER CALDER
American, 1898–1976

The Circle
1935
Metal, ceramic, wood and string

This 20th-century artist has created sculpture of simple color and form which is uniquely his. He has also pushed the once limited meaning of sculpture to include stabiles and mobiles which add a new dimension of movement to interacting color and form.

FACILITIES

A *Sales Desk* carries postcards, 10¢; writing cards, 35¢; and catalogs, $1–$10.

Hours: *School year:* Monday–Saturday, 9 A.M.–5 P.M.; Sunday, 1 P.M.–5 P.M.
             Closed: School holidays and sometimes for installation.
Admission: Free.

PURCHASE

NEUBERGER MUSEUM
STATE UNIVERSITY OF NEW YORK
Purchase St.
Purchase, New York
Tel: (914)253-5087

The museum was completed in 1972, the first building erected on the Purchase
campus. It was designed by Philip Johnson and conceived as a teaching museum. The burnt brick two-story building is located on the grounds of a former
estate. Five courtyards relieve the building's mass, providing a pleasant setting
for sculpture. The museum's interior is completely flexible. Lighting, wall space
and color are easily adapted to varied exhibitions. The permanent collection
contains primarily 19th- and 20th-century American art and primitive art from
New Guinea and Africa.

SAMPLING THE COLLECTION

JACKSON POLLOCK   *Number 8*   **2nd Floor**
American, 1912–1956   1949
                                    Oil, enamel and aluminum
                                    paint on canvas
Pollock expressed his emotions directly on huge unstretched canvases on which
he dripped and poured paints. Bustling activity marked his work, giving it the
name of Action Painting.

EDWARD HOPPER   *Barber Shop*   **2nd Floor**
American, 1882–1967   1931
                                    Oil on canvas
Hopper painted typically American subjects: small towns and city life. His work
is pervaded by a haunting melancholy and his canvases are frequently peopled
by alienated solitary figures.

MARK ROTHKO   *Old Gold over White*   **2nd Floor**
American, 1903–1970   1956
                                    Oil on canvas
Rothko's early Abstract Expressionist paintings were influenced by Surrealism.
Typical of his later work is this canvas of fuzzy-edged rectangular forms placed
against a single-colored background.

WILLEM DE KOONING   *Marilyn Monroe*   **2nd Floor**
American, b. 1904   1954
                                    Oil on canvas
In the 1950s de Kooning became one of the foremost Action Painters. His series
of *Women* paintings were marked by slashing brushwork and elemental color
with figures blended into the background.

HENRY MOORE   *Large Two Forms*   **On the Mall**
British, b. 1898   1967–1970
                                    Bronze

Moore's later works are mostly bronze and are composed of shapes hollowed from a solid mass to expose the inner form.

FACILITIES

Guided Tours of the collection are available.

Lectures by prominent authorities are offered.

Changing Exhibitions are regularly featured.

The *Sales Desk* carries postcards, posters and catalogs from 25¢ to $15.

Hours: Tuesday–Saturday, 11 A.M.–5 P.M.; Sunday, 1 P.M.–5 P.M. *Closed:* Mondays.

Admission: Free.

ROCHESTER

INTERNATIONAL MUSEUM OF PHOTOGRAPHY
900 East Ave.
Rochester, NY 14607
Tel: (716)271-3361

The museum is situated in the George Eastman House, an architectural landmark, set on 10 acres of landscaped gardens. Although the 50-room house is now a museum it still retains its warmth with some of the original furnishings. Modern exhibition galleries have been constructed on the second floor and in the garage and stables. The museum contains more than three million objects representing more than half the extant items of the history of photography in the entire world.

SAMPLING THE COLLECTION

INTERNATIONAL   *Photographs*
                                 19th c., 20th c.

Changing exhibitions, spanning more than 130 years, are culled from the collec-

Exterior view. Courtesy International Museum of Photography, Rochester

tion of photographs that have scientific, documentary or artistic interest. Examples range from daguerreotypes made in minutes to action photographs taken in a thousandth part of a second.

FRENCH   *Daguerreotypes*
                          19th c.

The museum houses between one-third and one-half of all the French daguerreotypes in the world. Daguerreotypes are a photographic technique invented by a French painter, Louis Daguerre (1787–1851), in collaboration with Nicéphore Niepce. His secret was purchased by the French government and made public in 1839. It was then improved so that exposures, at first minutes long, were reduced to seconds.

THE MOTION PICTURE STUDY COLLECTION

An international collection of over 3,000 titles are stored in fireproof vaults. Many of these are rare or unique such as the only known print of the first film in which Paul Robeson acted, *Body and Soul,* made in 1924.

FACILITIES

Concerts of chamber music are presented from time to time. Individual admissions are available.

The *Dryden Theater* offers vintage and foreign films throughout the year. Admission $2.

A *Senior Citizens* matinee is held every Thursday at 1:30 P.M. followed by a social hour. No fee.

A *Library* of photographic history may be used by appointment.

Hours: Daily, 10 A.M.–4:30 P.M. *Closed:* Mondays, New Year's, Christmas.

Admission: Adults, $1.50, children, students, 75¢; senior citizens, 50¢.

MEMORIAL ART GALLERY OF
THE UNIVERSITY OF ROCHESTER
490 University Ave.
Rochester, NY 14607
Tel: (716)275-3081

The gallery serves the public as well as the university community. It was opened in 1913 with "two paintings, four plaster casts and a lappet of lace." The main façade, constructed in limestone, features a Palladian entrance repeated in relief on either side. It was enlarged in 1926 to contain the expanding collection and includes a Fountain Court fashioned after a medieval Great Hall with clerestory windows. In 1968, a new wing, of the same limestone, almost doubled the capacity of the existing gallery, adding to it a Sculpture Garden and an auditorium. Strongest in its possession of medieval, Renaissance and 17th-century art; American painting; contemporary prints; classical glass and textiles, the gallery also houses examples of early Chinese sculptures and paintings; Japanese and Indian art; medieval antiques; English and continental silver; early Delftware; Old Masters; Master drawings and prints; contemporary sculpture; drawings and prints and Boehm porcelains. It attempts to display the finest examples of art from all major world cultures.

Exterior view. Courtesy Memorial Art Gallery of the University of Rochester

SAMPLING THE COLLECTION

At most times the following works are on view on the second floor.

PETER PAUL RUBENS
Flemish, 1577–1640

Reconciliation Between Henri III and Henri of Navarre
ca. 1630
Oil on panel

Rubens painted this preliminary study for one of a mural series commissioned by Marie de Medici for the Luxembourg Palace on the life of Henry IV. The Uffizi Gallery, Florence, houses the only two completed ones.

PIETRO PAOLINI
Italian, 1603–1681

Portrait of a Man Holding a Dürer Woodcut
1637
Oil on canvas

Paolini worked in Rome and in Lucca, where he established an academy. He invented an instrument which placed perspective views in true proportion.

WINSLOW HOMER
American, 1836–1910

The Artist's Studio in an Afternoon Fog
1894
Oil on canvas

Homer executed this scene in Prout's Neck, Maine, where he painted many seascapes in a style likened to that of Courbet for its realistic treatment of light.

CLAUDE MONET
French, 1840–1926

Waterloo Bridge, Soleil Voile
1903
Oil on canvas

Monet often painted in series attempting to capture the evanescent atmosphere on canvas. His paintings of the Thames are rendered in broken brush strokes and employ a very individual feeling for color.

THOMAS HART BENTON
American, 1889–1975

Boom Town
1928
Oil on canvas

Benton was a Regionalist who painted scenes of Midwestern life. His sinuous figures, harmoniously arranged in controlled composition, display great vitality.

FACILITIES

Guided Tours of the collections are regularly scheduled on Sunday, 2 P.M.

Art à la Carte featuring an important object from the gallery's collection are lunchtime talks. Thursday, 12:15 P.M.

Changing Exhibitions are regularly featured.

Concerts of chamber music are offered from time to time.

Films on art are screened on Sunday, 3 P.M.; Tuesday, 7:30 P.M.

Art Demonstrations are held on Sunday, 3 P.M.

The *Gallery Shop* stocks jewelry, books, paintings, sculpture and ceramics by regional artists, some of national repute.

The *Lending and Sales Gallery* sells additional works but they may only be rented by members.

The *Creative Workshop* is a school providing a variety of art experiences and is open to the public. A passageway connects the two buildings. **Cutler Union Building**

Hours: Tuesday, 2 P.M.–9 P.M.; Wednesday–Saturday, 10 A.M.–5 P.M.; Sunday, 1 P.M.–5 P.M.

Admission: Free.

SOUTHAMPTON

PARRISH ART MUSEUM
25 Job's Lane
Southampton, NY 11963
Tel: (516)283-2118

Exterior view. Courtesy Parrish Art Museum, Southampton

An arboretum and outdoor sculpture garden adjoin the museum, founded in 1898 and built in the style of the "Latin cross." A collection of 2,000 works range from ancient Tibetan tankas (painted scrolls) and Chinese earthenware tomb figures to the contemporary world of the Abstract Expressionists. The museum boasts the largest public collection of the works of William Merritt Chase, who established a summer art colony nearby.

SAMPLING THE COLLECTION

Most of the collection is not on permanent display but is shown from time to time.

STUDIO OF NICCOLO DI PIETRO
GERINI   *Virgin and Child in Glory*
Italian, Florentine, act. 1368–1415   *(The Throne Madonna)*
                                          Tempera and gilding on wood
Niccoló di Pietro Gerini perpetuated the traditions of Giotto, who moved from Byzantine forms to three-dimensional figures in natural action. He used living models and real landscapes in religious paintings instead of imitating previous paintings.

CHINESE   *Camel and Groom*
T'ang Dynasty, A.D. 618–907   Glazed earthenware
During this period in China extensive foreign contact was made and is reflected in the exotic subject matter of the pottery. Multicolor glazes, dripped and splashed, created vivid results in the tomb figurines.

WILLIAM MERRITT CHASE   *The Bayberry Bush (Chase*
American, 1849–1916   *Homestead, Shinnecock Hills)*
                                          ca. 1895
                                          Oil on canvas
One of over 40 of Chase's works in the collection, this scene portrays three of his daughters on the grounds of their summer home. Chase is known for Impressionistic still lifes.

THOMAS COLE   *Point Merion (Point on the*
American, 1801–1848   *Hudson)*
                                          Oil on canvas
Cole is the best known artist of the Hudson River School, a group of painters who praised the magnificence of nature in their highly romantic landscapes.

LARRY RIVERS   *Boy in Blue Denim*
American, b. 1923   1955
                                          Oil on canvas
Rivers's work shifts from semiabstract to more figurative expressions, yet he is always prompted by realistic subjects. This portrait is of his son.

FACILITIES

Gallery Talks, Lectures, a *Film Series* and *Concerts* are all offered. Call for schedule.

Changing Exhibitions are regularly featured.

A *Library* of art and rare books includes the personal library of Aline B. Saarinen and is available for use on the premises.

The *Sales Shop* carries books, cards, posters, craft kits, glassware, ceramics, imported toys and small sculptures. Although prices range from 50¢ to $50, most items are under $10.

Hours: Tuesday–Saturday, 10 A.M.–5 P.M.; Sunday, 2 P.M.–5 P.M. *Closed:* Mondays, New Year's, Easter, Memorial Day, July 4, Labor Day, Thanksgiving, Christmas.
Admission: Free.

STATEN ISLAND

JACQUES MARCHAIS CENTER OF TIBETAN ART
338 Lighthouse Ave.
Staten Island, NY 10306
Tel: (212)987-3478

Jacques Marchais was a woman whose interest in Tibetan art led her to establish a peaceful setting where people might enjoy the Oriental treasures she had amassed. Two stone buildings, opened in 1947, and designed to resemble a Tibetan monastery, overlook terraced gardens, a lotus pond and a view of New York's Lower Bay. The center houses one of the largest collections of Tibetan art in the Western Hemisphere and is intended as a miniature Potala. (The Potala is the monastery and residence of the Dalai Lama in Lhasa.) Inside is a collection of Buddhist art including over 1,000 Tibetan bronze images, paintings, ritual objects, artifacts, musical instruments and examples of Chinese, Japanese, Nepalese, Indian and Southeast Asian art.

SAMPLING THE COLLECTION

TIBETAN   *Dorje*
                                        18th c.
                                        Bronze
A dorje is a bell-shaped stand. The double dorje symbolizes the indestructible Knowledge of Buddhism. The bell stand symbolizes the Void. The two are joined in a rite representing the illumination of the initiate.

TIBETAN   *Vajra-dhara*
                                        18th c.
                                        Tanka (painted scroll)
Vajra-dhara is an Adi-Buddha, representing the creative energy of the cosmos, shown here in union with his female consort. He holds the dorje and the bell symbolizing the union of compassion and wisdom.

TIBETAN   *Trumpet*
                                        18th c.
                                        Conch shell on a silver mount
The trumpet produces a sound like the sacred syllable "om." It is heard during religious ceremonies where it heralds the pure qualities of the Buddhist Saints.

FACILITIES

Lectures and *Performances* are occasionally presented during the year.

The *Library* houses works on Oriental philosophy, art and history.

The *Shop* sells rugs, Tibetan wares, clothing, buttons, incense, and reproductions from the collection. Prices range from 50¢ to $250.

Hours: *April–November:* Saturday–Sunday, 1 P.M.–5 P.M. *June–August:* Thursday–Sunday, 1 P.M.–5 P.M.

Admission: Adults, $1; Children under 12, 50¢.

SYRACUSE

EVERSON MUSEUM OF ART
401 Harrison St.
Syracuse, NY 13202
Tel: (315)474-6064

Although the museum was founded in 1896, it was not until 1968 that it opened in its present quarters. Designed by I. M. Pei, who received two awards for this project, it stands on urban renewal land, beautifully proportioned to the plaza and to the urban complex surrounding it. The building, of reinforced concrete, contains three exhibition levels with four separate upper galleries cantilevered over the plaza. An impressive circular staircase rises from the Gifford Sculpture Court and bridges link the skylit galleries. The permanent collection is strongest in American art. The museum was the first to house a completely American paintings collection. It also possesses the widest ranging assemblage of 20th-century ceramics in the country along with English porcelains and Oriental examples. The collection of Chinese art spans 2,000 years from the Han Dynasty (206 B.C.-A.D. 220) to the Ch'ing Dynasty (1644–1912) and includes sculpture, painting, porcelain, wood, ivory and jade.

SAMPLING THE COLLECTION

The works listed below without locations are rotated for exhibition and may not always be on view.

Main Sculpture Court and/or Lobby. *Courtesy Everson Museum of Art, Syracuse*

GILBERT STUART   *Portrait of George Washington*
American, 1755–1828   1810
Oil on canvas
Over 50 successful versions of Washington established Stuart as the leading American portraitist of the Federal era. Washington usually closed his lips tightly to lessen the pain from his wooden teeth.

EDWARD HICKS   *The Peaceable Kingdom*
American, 1780–1849   1835–1844
Oil on canvas
Hicks was a coach and house painter before becoming an itinerant artist. Over 25 versions exist, of this his favorite theme, from Isaiah 11:6, in which the animals lie down together.

EASTMAN JOHNSON   *Corn Husking*
American, 1824–1906   1860
Oil on canvas
Johnson was a portrait and genre painter of American scenes whose traditional Dutch style was straightforward and simple.

MORRIS LOUIS   *Alpha-Delta*   **Main Lobby**
American, 1912–1962   1961
Acrylic on canvas
Louis, a Color Field painter, used thin paint to stain his nonobjective canvases, tilting them to achieve the desired effect against a blank background.

HENRY MOORE   *Two-Piece Reclining Figure*   **Outdoor**
British, b. 1898   *No. 3*   **Sculpture**
1961   **Court**
Bronze
Moore now works mainly in bronze. The reclining figure, a recurrent theme, is usually executed in two or three separate pieces which when viewed from certain angles appears as a whole.

FACILITIES

Guided Tours may be arranged by calling the Guide Office Tuesday–Friday, 9:30 A.M.–1 P.M.

The *Library* is open to the public on Saturday–Sunday, 1 P.M.–5 P.M. but books are not circulated.

The *Luncheon Gallery* is open for lunch Tuesday–Friday, 12 P.M.–2 P.M.; Saturday–Sunday, 12 P.M.–4 P.M. and displays changing exhibitions of the work of different artists.

The *Sales Gallery* stocks books, cards, posters, calendars, inexpensive miniature reproductions, toys and puzzles, and features one artist's work each month. The most popular items are pottery and reproductions of the museum's permanent collection. Prices range from $1 to $100.

Temporary Exhibitions culled from the museum's collection or *Loan Exhibitions* from other institutions are regular features of the museum's program.

Lectures on art or of concern to the regional public are presented regularly. **Auditorium**

Poetry Readings and *Dramatic Presentations* are also regularly scheduled. **Auditorium**

Musical Programs feature prominent artists, followed by questions and answers. **Auditorium**

Films both classic and avant-garde are screened on Friday evenings. **Auditorium**

Hours: Tuesday–Friday, 12 P.M.–5 P.M.; Saturday, 10 A.M.–5 P.M.; Sunday,
12 P.M.–5 P.M. *Closed:* Mondays, New Year's, July 4, Thanksgiving,
Christmas.
Admission: Free.

JOE AND EMILY LOWE ART GALLERY AND UNIVERSITY ART COLLECTION
Sims Hall, Syracuse University
Syracuse, NY 13210
Tel: (315)423-4097

The strength of the gallery's collection lies in its 19th- and 20th-century American paintings, its sculpture and its print collection. It also contains decorative
arts and Indian and African sculpture and textiles.

SAMPLING THE COLLECTION

**Art
Collection
Exhibition
Area**

SAMUEL F. B. MORSE
American, 1791–1872

Exhibition Gallery of the Louvre
1832–1833
Oil on canvas

Not long after he executed this canvas Morse abandoned the painting of Romantic landscapes and portraits to work on inventions. His most famous, the
telegraph, was invented in 1832.

**Lowe Art
Center,
Exterior
Court**

IVAN MESTROVIC
Yugoslavian/American, 1883–1962

Job
1945
Bronze

Meštrović's style emanated from antique influences and was expressed in
figurative sculpture having Cubist qualities.

**Heroy Hall,
Lobby**

RICO LEBRUN
Italian/American, 1900–1964

Crucifixion
1950
Oil on gypsum board

Lebrun's work combines a violent Expressionism in a modern Baroque style.
This crucifixion triptych is the culmination of a series begun in 1947.

**Crouse Hall,
East Wall**

BEN SHAHN
Lithuanian/American, 1898–1969

Passion of Sacco and Vanzetti
1967
Mosaic

Shahn was attracted by the School of Paris. His realistic style, depicting themes
of social protest, often contains elements of semiabstraction.

**Crouse Hall,
East Court**

CHAIM GROSS
Austro-Hungarian/American, b. 1904

Dancing Mother
1956
Bronze

Gross is interested in the figure. Witness his repeated themes, mothers with
children and circus performers. The subject matter of his delicately balanced
essential figures are secondary to their form.

**Newhouse
Communica-
tions Center,
Interior
Court**

JACQUES LIPCHITZ
Lithuanian/American, 1891–1973

Birth of the Muses
1964
Bronze

Lipchitz was influenced by El Greco. Thus his early Cubist sculpture had Mannerist overtones. His later "sculptures transparentes" or openwork sculptures
are typified by Baroque Expressionism.

Jacques Lipchitz, Birth of the Muses. *Courtesy Joe and Emily Lowe Art Gallery and University Art Collection, Syracuse*

JEAN-ANTOINE HOUDON	*George Washington*	**Maxwell**
French, 1741–1828	ca. 1795	**Hall,**
	Bronze	**Foyer**

Houdon is recognized for his talented portrait sculpture. His rather ordinary torsos are crowned with realistic and insightful heads.

FACILITIES

Hours: Tuesday–Sunday, 12 P.M.–6 P.M. *Closed:* Monday, national holidays.

Admission: Free.

UTICA

MUNSON-WILLIAMS-PROCTOR INSTITUTE
310 Genesee St.
Utica, NY 13502
Tel: (315)797-0000

The institute emerged through the union of three prominent Utica families. It consists of the Museum of Art, opened in 1960 and designed by Philip Johnson; the School of Art, Fountains Elms, which is a house-museum; and a Meetinghouse. Cited for its excellence, the granite museum building appears to float above slightly recessed glass walls. The cantilever design results in large, uncluttered galleries and a sculpture court without obstructions. Primarily American, the collection consists of approximately 6,000 items including paintings, drawings, prints, sculpture and decorative art.

Exterior view. Courtesy Munson-Williams-Proctor Institute, Utica

SAMPLING THE COLLECTION

Main Floor JACKSON POLLOCK   *No. 2, 1949*
American, 1912–1956   Oil, duco and aluminum paint
on unsized canvas
Pollock is best known for his totally Abstract works, giving a material quality to
painted surfaces. His drip paintings featured texture almost exclusively.

Auditorium, JOHN QUIDOR   *Anthony Van Corlear Brought*
Gallery   American, 1801–1881   *into the Presence of Peter*
Level   *Stuyvesant*
1839
Oil
Much of Quidor's work has been lost or destroyed. Most of his paintings had
literary ties, especially to James Fenimore Cooper and Washington Irving. He
interpreted their work in imaginative and often grotesque ways.

2nd Floor   THOMAS COLE   Voyage of Life:
American, 1801–1848   *Childhood*
1839

Youth
1840

Manhood
1840

Old Age
1840
All oil on canvas
The founder of the American landscape school, Cole painted this series of four
allegories while continuing to do more profitable realistic landscapes.

ALEXANDER CALDER
American, 1898–1976

Three Arches
1963
Metal sculpture

**In Front of
Museum**

Calder, trained as an engineer, moved on to painting and sculpture, doing figures and animals of wire and wood. He invented the "mobile" with its airiness and charm and the "stabile," stationary and frequently awesome.

FACILITIES

Fountain Elms is an Italian villa-style house built in 1850. The building contains examples of furniture and decorative arts from the Early American period through the Victorian.

Performing Artists of international reputation appear each year.

Temporary Exhibitions culled from the museum's collection or *Loan Exhibitions* from other institutions are regular features of the museum's program.

The *Reference Library* of books, exhibition catalogs, pamphlets, color slides and current periodicals are available for reference.

The *Music Library* consists of a Listening Library and a Circulating Library. The Listening Library contains a large collection of long-playing records for use on the premises.

Lectures by prominent members of the worlds of art, architecture, history and music are often open to the public.

**Auditorium
Level**

The *Children's Room* contains a variety of interesting toys appealing to children from the ages of 3 to 10. The room is constantly supervised leaving parents free to view the exhibitions.

**Sculpture,
Court Level**

Hours: Tuesday–Saturday, 10 A.M.–5 P.M.; Sunday, 1 P.M.–5 P.M. *Closed:* Mondays, holidays.

Admission: Free.

YONKERS

HUDSON RIVER MUSEUM
511 Warburton Ave.
Yonkers, NY 10701
Tel: (914)963-4550

Founded in 1948 as a general museum of arts, science and humanities, the museum is housed in "Glenview," an 1876 châteaulike mansion set on a bluff overlooking the Hudson River. There is evidence in the architectural details and furnishings of the influence of Charles Eastlake.

SAMPLING THE COLLECTION

The items listed below may not always be on view.

RED GROOMS
American, b. 1937

The Bookstore
1979
Environmental sculpture
Painted wood, stuffed vinyl,
fabric, metal

Bookstore

Exterior view. Courtesy Hudson River Museum, Yonkers

Grooms, noted for his artistic comic comments on culture, was inspired by the Morgan Library and the Mendoza Book Store to create the environment for *The Bookstore.*

Exhibition DAN FLAVIN   *Untitled*
Building American, b. 1933   1979
                                               Blue, green, pink and yellow
                                               fluorescent light
Flavin uses fluorescent light to complement and enhance the spaces.

Glenview HIRAM POWERS   *Eve Disconsolate*
Mansion American, 1805–1873   1871
                                               Marble
Powers was recognized for his sculptures in the Neoclassical style.

FACILITIES

Guided Tours and *Lectures* are offered.

Special Changing Exhibitions culled from the museum's collection or *Loan Exhibitions* from other institutions are regular features of the museum's program.

The *Andrus Planetarium* features changing programs Wednesday–Friday, 4 P.M.; Saturday–Sunday, 2 P.M. and 4 P.M. Adults $1.50; children, senior citizens, $1.00. Call for special group rates.

The *Bookstore,* in addition to a broad range of specially selected items, carries children's items from 75¢ up.

Hours: Wednesday–Saturday, 10 A.M.–5 P.M.; Sunday, 1 P.M.–5 P.M. *Closed:* Mondays, Tuesdays, Thanksgiving, December 24–25, New Year's.

Admission: Voluntary contribution.

PENNSYLVANIA

ALLENTOWN

ALLENTOWN ART MUSEUM
**Fifth at Court St.
Allentown, PA 18105
Tel: (215)432-4333**

In 1975, a modern wing was added to the Neoclassical building of 1906. It tripled the size of the museum. The first floor houses changing exhibitions and permanent installations of American paintings and sculpture; the Max Hess, Jr. Gallery is devoted to revolving educational exhibitions. The second level exhibits European paintings, sculpture, prints and drawings.

SAMPLING THE COLLECTION

FRANK LLOYD WRIGHT	*The Library from the Francis*	**1st Floor**
American, 1869–1959	*W. Little Residence*	
	1914 Minnesota	

This reception room is from the last of Wright's Prairie-style houses. Twentieth-century residential architecture is founded on this style in which the major rooms flow together in uninterrupted space that is even carried to the outside.

Exterior view, Allentown Art Museum. *Photography by John Kress Bachman*

2nd Level REMBRANDT HARMENSZ VAN RIJN *Portrait of a Young Woman*
Dutch, 1606–1669 1632
Oil on panel
This portrait is typical of Rembrandt's early work with its fine drawing. The wide range of color he employed during these years decreased with the chiaroscuro of his later work.

2nd Level JAN STEEN *Soo de Ouden Songen*
Dutch, ca. 1625–1679 ca. 1668
Oil on oak panel
This typically crowded tavern scene, a fusion of complex gaiety and melancholy, exhibits Steen's mastery of the rich and intricate use of color with subtle variations of hue.

2nd Level HANS SUSS VON KULMBACH *The Adoration of the Magi*
German, ca. 1480–1522 1512–1513
Mixed technique on panel
A master of Dürer's monumental style, von Kulmbach was one of the major artists active in Nuremberg in the first quarter of the 16th century.

2nd Level ANTON WOENSAM VON WORMS *The Suitors of Mary*
German, before 1500–1541 before 1520
Oil on oak panel
There are only two works by this Cologne master in American museums. Von Worms was the major book illustrator in Cologne. This work exhibits his Netherlandish Mannerist sources.

FACILITIES

Gallery Tours are available on Wednesdays at 1 P.M..

Lectures, some followed by lunch, are frequently offered.

Concerts and *Classic Films* are scheduled regularly.

The *Library* contains books on general art subjects.

The *Museum Shop* sells art books, catalogs, cards, craft items and reproductions ranging in price from $1 to $50.

Hours: Tuesday – Saturday, 10 A.M.–5 P.M.; Sunday, 1 P.M.–5 P.M. *Closed:* Mondays, national holidays.

Admission: Free, but contributions are always welcome.

BETHLEHEM

ANNIE S. KEMERER MUSEUM
427 North New St.
Bethlehem, PA 18018
Tel: (215)868–6868

The museum offers the visitor a glimpse into Bethlehem's gracious past in combination with a modern art gallery. The collection consists of 17th- and 18th-century furniture, Oriental rugs, glass, porcelain, Currier and Ives prints, early Bethlehem oils and a group of fine locally made grandfather clocks.

SAMPLING THE COLLECTION

Fire Engine	**Fire Annex,**
1698	**Off Museum**

This fire engine, the oldest in the United States, began servicing Bethlehem in **Patio**
1763.

Cameo Glass	**Glass Gallery**
19th c.	

Bohemia, comprised of Germany, Austria and Czechoslovakia, set up glass-making houses in medieval days. Innovative decorations were introduced in the glass of the 19th century.

Victorian Parlors	**2nd Floor**

These double parlors are rich with ornate carpet, red and gold wallpaper and Belter-type rose-carved furniture.

GUSTAVUS GRUNEWALD	*Delaware Water Gap*	**Drawing**
19th c.	Oil	**Room**

Grunewald painted romantic canvases of nature which he considered to be realistic because he painted what he saw.

FACILITIES

Tours are offered to clubs, organizations and school groups.

An *Illustrated Lecture* on the museum collection is available.

The *Museum Shop* features items made by local craftsmen. Leaded glass ornaments, painted tin and wooden ware and ceramics which copy old patterns are but a few.

Hours: Monday–Saturday, 1 P.M.–4 P.M.; second and fourth Sundays, 2 P.M.–4 P.M. *Closed:* National holidays.

Admission: Free, but there is a contribution box. Small fee for groups. Call for appointment.

CHADDS FORD

BRANDYWINE RIVER MUSEUM
U.S. 1, just west of PA 100
Chadds Ford, PA 19317
Tel: (215)459–1900

The museum opened in 1971 in a renovated 19th-century grist mill close to the famous Revolutionary War battle site. Entered through a cobblestone courtyard ornamented with patterns of old millstones, the three-level building combines the original hand-hewn beams with rough white plaster walls, a pleasantly contrasting background for the art it displays. Dramatic glass areas provide a view of the terraces and river below. The museum houses a collection of work by Howard Pyle, known as the father of American illustration, and some of his 120 students, including Maxfield Parrish, Harvey Dunn, Frank Schoonover and

Jessie Wilcox Smith. Always on view are the paintings of three generations of the Wyeth family, N. C. Wyeth (Newell Convers), illustrator for such books as *Kidnapped, Treasure Island* and *The Last of the Mohicans;* his son, Andrew; and his grandson, Jamie.

SAMPLING THE COLLECTION

ANDREW WYETH
American, b. 1917

Erickson's Daughter Series:
The Sauna, 1968, Tempera
The Virgin, 1969, Tempera
Siri, 1970, Tempera
Indian Summer, 1970, Tempera
Black Water, 1972, Watercolor
Seabed, 1972, Tempera

These paintings of Siri Erickson, a young Maine neighbor of Wyeth's, are his only female nudes. She was fourteen when he caught her first stirrings of sensuality; by eighteen this blossomed into bold maturity.

Roasted Chestnuts
1956
Tempera

Wyeth, noticing a young neighbor by the highway on cold winter afternoons, drove by him several times. He replaced the whizzing automobiles and modern road with a scene of haunting timelessness.

FACILITIES

Guided Tours are offered. Group discounts are available.

Concerts and *Plays* are scheduled.

Special Annual Events are the spring Memorial Day *Antique Show* and the autumn *Harvest Market* held in the museum courtyard and featuring local produce and crafts.

Changing Exhibitions are regularly featured.

The *Library* is available by appointment.

The *Tea Room* serves sandwiches, salads and homemade pastries in a brick-lined room overlooking the river. Open daily, 11:30 A.M.–3 P.M.

The *Bookstore* carries the latest Wyeth reproductions, framed and unframed, art books for children and adults, plus a wide selection of environmental books. Unframed Wyeth reproductions cost $8–$20.

Hours: Daily, 9:30 A.M.–4:30 P.M. *Closed:* Christmas.

Admission: $1.75; senior citizens, children (6–12), students with I.D., $1.

GREENSBURG

WESTMORELAND COUNTY MUSEUM OF ART
221 North Main St.
Greensburg, PA 15601
Tel: (412)837–1500

Andrew Wyeth, Siri. *Copyright © 1979 by the Brandywine Conservancy*

The museum, which overlooks the town, was opened in 1959 in a Georgian building of native brick enhanced by a stone portico. Included in the collection are American paintings, sculpture, decorative arts, prints and drawings; 18th-century English rooms; silver; paintings; furniture and Victorian period rooms.

SAMPLING THE COLLECTION

REMBRANDT PEALE   *Portrait of George Washington*   **1st Floor,**
American, 1778–1860   Oil on canvas   **Foyer**
Peale is most celebrated for his porthole-type portraits of George Washington. He produced about 80 replicas. The original is in the Capitol Building in Washington, D.C.

FACILITIES

Lectures are offered by visiting authorities.

Changing Exhibitions are regularly featured.

Concerts of classical music are scheduled several times a year.

Films of high quality are featured once a month on Sundays at 2 P.M.

The *Museum Shop* has recently been reorganized and offers a variety of goods.

Hours: Tuesday–Saturday, 10 A.M.–5 P.M.; Sunday, 1 P.M.–5 P.M. *Closed:* Mondays, national holidays.

Admission: Free.

LORETTO

SOUTHERN ALLEGHENIES MUSEUM OF ART
St. Francis College Mall
Loretto, PA 15940
Tel: (814)472–6400

The museum is located in a former gymnasium in a rural campus setting, the only art repository in a six county area. The permanent collection is hung in flexible exhibition space and is on view from December through February. It contains 19th- and 20th-century American art.

SAMPLING THE COLLECTION

1st Floor   MARY CASSATT   *The Somber One*
American, 1845–1926   1872
                              Oil on canvas
Cassatt painted *The Somber One* early in her career while studying in Paris. She was still influenced by academic artists before commencing her long association with the Impressionists.

1st Floor   CHARLES BURCHFIELD   *The Lonely Chimney*
American, 1893–1967   1918
                              Watercolor
Between 1916 and 1918 Burchfield painted romantic, ominous landscapes set in small-town America. In these he depicted imagined terrors from his childhood through an invented set of pictographs.

1st Floor   JOHN SLOAN   *Fifth Avenue Critics*
American, 1871–1951   1905
                              Etching
This print was executed early in his career when Sloan worked as a magazine illustrator. His portrayals of city life, done with dexterity, were nonetheless restrained in detail.

                              Bright Rocks
                              1914–1915
                              Oil on canvas
Sloan founded "The Eight" which became the Ashcan School. Summer sojourns at this time provided him with a wider variety of subjects which he expressed in brighter colors than heretofore.

THOMAS HART BENTON
American, 1889–1975

From the Top of James Peak
1952
Ink and watercolor

1st Floor

Benton was a Regionalist whose paintings of Midwestern and Southern rural life were executed in a romantic, stylized manner revealed in vivid colors.

FACILITIES

Guided Tours and/or luncheon can be arranged by calling in advance.

Lectures and *Symposia* are offered during the year.

Temporary Exhibitions culled from the museum's collection or *Loan Exhibitions* from other institutions are regular features of the museum's program.

Special Events feature dance programs, concerts and multimedia presentations.

Hours: Wednesday, Thursday, Friday, 10 A.M.–5 P.M.; Saturday, Sunday, 1:30 P.M.–5:30 P.M. *Closed:* Mondays, Tuesdays, holidays.

Admission: Free.

MERION

BARNES FOUNDATION
**300 North Latch's Lane
Merion Station, PA 19066
Tel: (215)667–0290**

The Barnes Foundation was established in 1922 as an educational institution. Its gallery and buildings are located on a 12-acre arboretum in which specimen trees, shrubs and flowers thrive. Its unique collection and facilities are primarily utilized as teaching instruments and only secondarily does it permit visitors on a limited schedule. The gallery houses a collection of paintings and sculpture. Over 1,000 paintings include Old Masters works by Giorgione, Titian, Tintoretto, Paolo, Veronese, El Greco, Claude Lorrain, Chardin, Daumier, Delacroix, Courbet and Corot. There are also paintings by Renoir, Cézanne, Manet, Degas, Seurat, Rousseau, Picasso, Matisse, Soutine, Modigliani, Pascin, Demuth, Glackens, Charles and Maurice Prendergast, Pippin, Klee, Miró, Rouault and Afro. Dutch painters and Italian, French, Spanish, German and Flemish primitives are also represented. Additionally, Chinese, Persian, Greek, Egyptian, Hindu, American Indian art and primitive African Negro sculpture is exhibited. Along with the paintings and sculpture are choice pieces of antique furniture and early handwrought iron. In all of these mediums it is possible to trace the evolution of the traditions and methods indigenous to past epochs and personalities.

FACILITIES

Restrictions include children under 12 not being admitted. Children between 12 and 15 must be accompanied by and remain with an adult.

Reservations are limited to 100 on Friday and Saturday; 50 on Sunday afternoons. Call or write for reservations allowing time for mail acknowledgment.

Group Reservations can be made for Friday and Saturday only. Limited to 25 in the morning and 25 in the afternoon.

Visitors on Nonreserved-Basis are limited to 100 persons on Friday and Saturday; 50 on Sunday afternoons.

Hours: Art Collection open to the public: Friday, Saturday, 9:30 A.M.–4:30 P.M., Sunday afternoon, 1 P.M.–4:30 P.M. *Closed:* Legal holidays, July, August.

Admission: $1.

BUTEN MUSEUM OF WEDGWOOD
246 North Bowman Ave.
Merion, PA 19066
Tel: (215)664–9069

Founded in 1957, the museum is devoted to the study and exhibition of Wedgwood ware produced by Josiah Wedgwood and his successors from 1759 to the present. More than 10,000 examples are available for viewing making it one of the largest, most comprehensive collections of Wedgwood in the world.

SAMPLING THE COLLECTION

JOSIAH WEDGWOOD   *Pottery*
British, 1730–1795   1759 to the present

Wedgwood created three types of pottery. Earthenware, fired at the lowest temperature, is porous and must be glazed to be useful. Of the four varieties, Queen's Ware, Majolica, Variegated Ware and Pearl Ware, only Queen's Ware is still manufactured. Also manufactured today, is bone china, characterized by high firing which makes the body glassy and watertight requiring a glaze only esthetically. Stoneware, opaquelike earthenware, is fired at a higher temperature, watertight and usually unglazed. There are five varieties: Jasper, Black Basalt, Cane Ware, Rosso Antico and Parian. The first two are still produced. In his early career, Wedgwood created mostly functional pieces turning later to decorative works in the Neoclassical style. Usually ornamented with low relief figures, they were set against a dark background.

FACILITIES

Gallery Lectures and *Tours* by associate curators are given. Group visits by appointment.

The *Sales Desk* offers Wedgwood special issues, remainders, grade II wares, books and slides. Prices start at $1.

Hours: Tuesday – Thursday, 2 P.M.–5 P.M.; Saturday, 10 A.M.–1 P.M. *Closed:* Mondays, Fridays, Sundays, July, August, September.

Admission: $1.

NEW BRIGHTON

MERRICK FREE GALLERY
Fifth Ave. and 11th ST.
New Brighton, PA 15066
Tel: (412)846–1130

Wedgwood and Bentley figure of Autumn, *in black basalt,19" high. Courtesy Buten Museum of Wedgwood, Merion*

Established in the late 19th century in a former railroad depot building that was constructed in 1830, the collection comprises 249 19th-century European and American paintings. A gracious courtyard separates the annex from the main building.

SAMPLING THE COLLECTION

PIERRE PAUL PRUD'HON   *Head of a Girl*
French, 1758–1823   Oil on canvas
Prud'hon was painter to Napoleon's empresses. He portrayed mostly women in Rococo tradition although his interior decorations reflect the Neoclassical style made popular by David.

THOMAS SULLY   *Mother and Child*
American, 1783–1872   Oil sketch
Sully painted over 2,500 portraits, miniatures and other works concentrating
chiefly on portraiture. His style could be elegant but was often emotional and
lacked depth.

GUSTAVE COURBET   *Landscape*
French, 1819–1877   Oil on canvas
Courbet, a dedicated Realist, reacted to academic art and to French politics in
particular in such a vociferous manner that he was exiled to Switzerland.

FACILITIES

Hours: Tuesday–Saturday, 10 A.M.–5 P.M.; Sunday, 1 P.M.–5 P.M. *Summer
         hours:* Considerably shorter. Call for schedule. *Closed:* Mondays,
         New Year's, Good Friday, July 4, Thanksgiving, Christmas.
Admission: Free.

PHILADELPHIA

THE ATHENAEUM
219 South Sixth St.
East Washington Square
Philadelphia, PA 19106
Tel: (215)925–2688

The Athenaeum building is one of America's finest restored Victorian structures.
Erected in 1845, it is the first major Italianate Revival building in the country
and has been declared a National Historic Landmark. It is furnished with original
antiques and art (ca. 1810–1850). The Athenaeum is an independent research
institution specializing in the Victorian period.

SAMPLING THE COLLECTION

Bonaparte   MICHEL BOUVIER   *Sécretaire à Abattant*
Parlor   French/American, 19th c.   ca. 1820
                                                 Mahogany
Bouvier, a French cabinetmaker, emigrated to New Orleans after the French
Revolution. This piece, in Philadelphia High Empire style, was made for Napo-
leon's brother, Joseph Bonaparte, King of Spain.

Main Hall   ANTONIO CANOVA   *Pauline Bonaparte Borghese*
                 Italian, 1757–1822   ca. 1811
                                                 Marble
Canova was the most successful Neoclassical sculptor of his time. He executed
many pieces for Napoleon such as this sensuous statue of the emperor's sister.
He favored glossy finishes.

Grand Stair   CHARLES ROBERT LESLIE   *The Stag Hunt*
                  British/American, 1794–1859   Oil on canvas

News Room   *Timon of Athens*
Gallery   Oil on canvas

Interior view. Courtesy The Athenaeum of Philadelphia

The Stag Hunt was painted after Benjamin West, who influenced Leslie's style when he lived and worked in London. *Timon of Athens* was one of many literary themes Leslie painted.

FACILITIES

Guided Tours are available daily at 10:30 A.M. and 2 P.M.

The *Sales Desk* offers books published by The Athenaeum on Victorian architecture and decorative arts, slides and postcards.

Hours: Monday–Friday, 9 A.M.–5 P.M. *Closed:* Saturday, Sunday, legal holidays.

Admission: Free.

INDEPENDENCE NATIONAL HISTORIC PARK
Visitor Center
3rd and Chestnut Sts.
Philadelphia, PA 19106
Tel: (215)627–1776

The park contains historic buildings and sites from 1732 to 1834 including Independence Hall, Congress Hall and the Second Bank of the United States. The historic objects in the park's collection are used to interpret the park's themes of the American Revolution; Philadelphia, the Capital City; and Franklin, Man of Ideas. The Bank, constructed in Greek Revival style, between 1819 and 1824, has been restored by the National Park Service and adapted to house a collection of American portraits from the Colonial and Federal periods.

SAMPLING THE COLLECTION

Officers of the Revolution Gallery

WILLIAM RUSH
American, 1756–1833

George Washington
ca. 1814
Painted wood

Rush, sometimes called the "father of American sculpture," carved this life-size piece in imitation of a marble statue of Classical antiquity. The detailed handling typifies Rush's best work.

Pennsylvania Galleries

ROBERT FEKE
American, ca. 1705–1752

William Allen
ca. 1751

Although they were sometimes wooden in appearance, Feke captured the likenesses demanded by his prominent patrons. The earliest portrait in the collection, of Pennsylvania's Chief Justice, typifies mid-18th-century Colonial painting.

Signers' Gallery

RALPH EARL
American, 1751–1801

William Floyd
1793
Oil on canvas

This forceful portrait of a signer of the Declaration of Independence was imaginatively composed. Earl usually included a backdrop identifying the subject's occupation or social standing, in this case, Floyd's Long Island homestead.

Signers' Gallery

CHARLES WILLSON PEALE
American, 1741–1827

Thomas Jefferson
1791
Oil on canvas

Exterior view, Second Bank of the United States. *Courtesy Independence National Historic Park, Philadelphia*

Peale framed many of the portrait busts he executed with oval gilt spandrels. This is the only life portrait of Jefferson that shows his natural auburn hair.

JAMES SHARPLES	*James Madison*	**American**
British, 1751–1811	ca. 1796	**Statesmen**
	Pastel on paper	**Galleries**

This painting, completed when Madison was a member of the United States House of Representatives, exemplifies Sharples's realistic portraiture. He depicted many notables in similar style.

FACILITIES

The *Eastern National Park and Monument Association* sells interpretive materials at two sales facilities within the park.

Hours: Daily except Christmas, 9 A.M.–5 P.M.

Admission: Free.

INSTITUTE OF CONTEMPORARY ART
UNIVERSITY OF PENNSYLVANIA
34th and Walnut Sts.
Philadelphia, PA 19104
Tel: (215)243–7108

Agnes Martin installation. *Courtesy Institute of Contemporary Art, University of Pennsylvania, Philadelphia*

The institute, founded in 1963, presents a program of changing exhibitions of contemporary art during the year. It seeks to familiarize the public with current trends in the world of art.

FACILITIES

A full program of *Lectures, Films, Concerts, Children's Activities* and *Artists' Performances* are offered.

The *Sales Desk* carries catalogs of exhibitions held at the institute.

Hours: Tuesday, 10 A.M.–7:30 P.M.; Wednesday–Friday, 10 A.M.–5 P.M.; Saturday–Sunday, 12 P.M.–5 P.M.. *Closed:* Mondays, Christmas, Thanksgiving, Easter.

Admission: Free.

PENNSYLVANIA ACADEMY OF THE FINE ARTS
Broad and Cherry Sts.
Philadelphia, PA 19102
Tel: (215)972–7600

Founded in 1805, the academy is the oldest art museum and school in the United States. The third and present building was erected to coincide with the Centennial celebration of 1876. Designed by architect Frank Furness, it is constructed of polychrome brick and stained and gilded glass and ornamented with floral motifs of bronze and stone. It departed from the Classical tradition of most public edifices. Built in a variety of styles it is considered a masterpiece of Victorian architecture. Well-lit galleries lay behind and above a Grand Stair Hall. The individuality of its style in no way detracts from its functionalism. It was restored for the Bicentennial and declared a Registered National Historic Landmark. The collection includes major examples of American art from the 18th century to the present.

SAMPLING THE COLLECTION

The collection is frequently rotated so that it is not possible to list gallery locations for the artwork.

Interior Staircase. *Courtesy Pennsylvania Academy of Fine Arts, Philadelphia*

WASHINGTON ALLSTON
1779–1843

*Dead Man Restored to Life by
Touching the Bones of the
Prophet Elisha*
1811–1813
Oil on canvas

Allston was one of the first important Romantic artists of the 19th century in America. He also painted religious and historical works in the European academic tradition. The academy purchased its Allston in 1816 in a pioneering spirit.

CHARLES WILLSON PEALE
1741–1827

Washington at Princeton
1779
Oil on canvas

While Philadelphia was the nation's capital, this painting hung in Independence Hall. Charles Willson Peale, ablest of the prominent family of painters, represented Washington as a youthful and victorious general.

The Artist in His Museum
1822
Oil on canvas

Trained in England, Peale eschewed English Neoclassical portraiture for clear-cut narrative. An energetic, inquisitive man who tried many occupations, he retired from painting to become a museum proprietor.

Self-Portrait
1824
Oil on canvas

Peale returned to his narrative style, combining with it a trompe-l'oeil device. He had temporarily adopted a painting system based on imaginary ideals conceived by his son, Rembrandt Peale.

WILLIAM RUSH
1756–1833

Self-Portrait
ca. 1822
Terracotta bust

Marquis de Lafayette
1824
Terracotta bust

Rush, the first native American sculptor, was one of only three artists, and the only sculptor, among the 71 founders of the academy.

THOMAS EAKINS
1844–1916

Walt Whitman
1887
Oil on canvas

The Cello Player
1896
Oil on canvas

At odds with other members, and also because he posed a nude male before his class, Eakins was forced to resign from the academy as board member and teacher. His later works were mostly portraits. *Walt Whitman* met with criticism when exhibited; *The Cello Player* was immediately successful. Eakins was a Realist who demanded scientific accuracy in his paintings. He died largely unacclaimed.

GILBERT STUART
1755–1828

*The Lansdowne Portrait
of Washington*
1796
Oil on canvas mounted on wood

Stuart created several replicas of this standing portrait, but the academy's version is the only signed and dated one. It was painted in Philadelphia during Washington's second term as President.

BENJAMIN WEST   *William Penn's Treaty with*
1738–1820   *the Indians*
                                 1771
                                 Oil on canvas

Early in his career West settled in England. His contemporary historical paintings were executed realistically. Although his subjects were clothed in modern dress, they were arranged in classical compositions.

Christ Rejected
ca. 1814
Oil on canvas

Death on a Pale Horse
1817
Oil on canvas

West's paintings progressed from Classicism to Realism to Romanticism, echoing the styles of the past. He influenced many American painters, among them Allston, Peale and Stuart.

WINSLOW HOMER   *The Fox Hunt*
1836–1910   1893
                                 Oil on canvas

The Fox Hunt was painted in Homer's later years in a vigorous, well-organized style. Living in the Northeast, he sought to portray man's struggle against nature.

FACILITIES

Guided Tours are scheduled weekdays leaving from the main desk at 12 P.M. and 2:00 P.M. Foreign-language tours can be arranged. Call Director of Museum Education at (215)972–7608.

Changing Exhibitions are regularly featured.

The *Museum Shop* carries an interesting assortment of merchandise, all with a focus on American art. Some of the most popular items are the Book of Unicorns, unique craft and illustrated calendars; T-shirts and tote bags; art books ranging from *John Twachtman* by Academy Director Richard J. Boyle to the *Grammar of Color* and from *Travel Sketches* of Louis I. Kahn to *Learning to Look* by Joshua Taylor. Distinctive greeting cards, 35-mm slides and reproductions from the academy collection are also for sale in the charming Museum Shop.

Parking is available in four lots in the vicinity of the museum: one in the 1300 block of Cherry, two in the 1400 block of Cherry and one on the west side of Broad Street between Cherry and Race.

Wheelchairs are available. Persons requiring them are asked to call in advance. The academy is a fully accessible facility.

Hours: Tuesday – Saturday, 10 A.M. – 5 P.M.; Sunday, 1 P.M. – 5 P.M. *Closed:* Mondays, Thanksgiving, Christmas, New Year's.

Admission: Adults, $1; children under 12, students, senior citizens, 50¢.

PHILADELPHIA MUSEUM OF ART
26th St. and the Parkway
Philadelphia, PA 19130
Tel: (215)763–8100

Founded in 1876 as an art gallery for the Centennial Exposition, the museum, first known as the Pennsylvania Museum, was located in Memorial Hall in West Fairmount Park. Outgrowing its quarters during the early part of this century, a new building of Greek and Roman design was erected on its present 10-acre site in 1928. It houses more than 200 galleries with upward of 500,000 works of art. Truly it is one of our country's great museums. Among its most notable holdings are the John G. Johnson Collection of Western European Paintings, the Arensberg Collection of 20th-century art; outstanding period rooms; the Kretzschmar von Kienbusch Collection of Arms and Armor; Medieval European art; Near Eastern and South Asian art; Far Eastern art; European art from 1400 to the 20th century; English art from 1700 to 1850; American art and a Print and Drawing collection that rotates its holdings for exhibition.

SAMPLING THE COLLECTION

Entrance   CLAUDE MICHEL CLODION   *Dancing Nymphs*
Hall   French, 1738–1814   18th c.
                                           Plaster

Clodion's playful interpretation of Classical themes made him a popular sculptor with French society. This was one of a group of four. It was originally in the dining room of a French town house.

Great   AUGUSTUS SAINT-GAUDENS   *Diana*
Stair Hall American, 1848–1907   1892
                                           Copper sheets

Created as a weathervane for New York's Madison Square Garden, this nude figure caused quite an outcry from the prudish Victorian public until its later achievement of landmark status.

1st Floor *JOHN G. JOHNSON COLLECTION*

JAN VAN EYCK   *Saint Francis Receiving the*
Flemish, ca. 1380–1441   *Stigmata*
                                15th c.
                                Oil on panel

Although this work is only six inches wide, Van Eyck used slow-drying oils and created a scene with many details and warm colors.

PIETRO LORENZETTI   *Virgin and Child Enthroned*
Italian, Sienese, fl. 1320–1344 1320–1329
                                Oil on panel

Religious paintings of the Renaissance more and more mirrored human experience with their increasing warmth and vigor.

ROGIER VAN DER WEYDEN   *Crucifixion with the Virgin*
Flemish, ca. 1399–1464   *and Saint John*
                                15th c.
                                Oil on two panels

This religious masterpiece brings to the canvas the impact of three-dimensional sculpture. The sorrow of the mourners is exquisitely felt in the details of its portrayal. The life of Christ was a continuing theme in Van der Weyden's work.

EDOUARD MANET
French, 1832–1883

The Alabama and the Kearsarge
19th c.
Oil on canvas

Manet painted the sinking of the Confederate ship, *Alabama,* outside the harbor of Cherbourg in 1864. Interested in experimenting with light and color, his work helped pave the way for Impressionism.

20TH-CENTURY ART

1st Floor

PABLO PICASSO
Spanish, 1881–1973

The Musicians
1921
Oil on canvas

Here with every Cubist device, Picasso defies the tradition of older paintings. He was one of the most productive and innovative geniuses in 20th-century art.

JOAN MIRO
Spanish, b. 1893

Dog Barking at the Moon
1926
Oil on canvas

This is a dreamlike canvas by this Surrealist painter that was not taken seriously when first on view. His work is more abstracted than most Surrealists and he is partial to curved forms and fields of color.

TOM WESSELMANN
American, b. 1931

Bedroom Painting, No. 7
1967–1969
Oil on canvas

Wesselmann was inspired by the mass media. This larger-than-life nude conveys the allure of its subject though only the toes appear. He is known as a Pop artist.

STUART DAVIS
American, 1894–1964

Something on the 8 Ball
1953
Oil on canvas

Davis foresaw the future of Pop Art. Here he abstracts a city scene.

ARENSBERG COLLECTION

1st Floor

MARCEL DUCHAMP
French, 1887–1968

Nude Descending a Staircase, No. 2
1912
Oil on canvas

Duchamp's work was based on Cubist and Futurist concepts. The idea for this painting, one of the most controversial of this century, came from photographic studies of motion. When first on view, it was met with derision.

CONSTANTIN BRANCUSI
Rumanian, 1876–1957

The Kiss
1912
Limestone

In his early work Brancusi was influenced by African art. His late pieces are distinguished by simplicity and the finest craftsmanship. He used *The Kiss* six times as a theme in his sculptures.

JUAN GRIS
Spanish, 1887–1927

Man in the Café
1912
Oil on canvas

Gris was one of the original Cubists. Here is an example of structured forms in space, the beginning of Abstract art.

SALVADOR DALI
Spanish, b. 1904

Soft Construction with Boiled
Beans (Premonition of Civil
War)
1936
Oil on canvas

Dali's technical skills combine with an unreal setting to give us a masterful Surrealist painting.

South Wing,
1st Floor

AMERICAN ART

WILLIAM RUSH
1756–1833

Comedy and Tragedy
1808
Pine

These sculptures were made to grace a Philadelphia theater. They were originally painted gray to give them the appearance of stone. Rush based his representation on the art of the Greeks and Romans.

JOHN EAST
British, act. 1704–1737

Flagon
1708
Silver

PHILIP SYNG, SR.
1676–1739

Flagon
1715
Silver

These two flagons, part of the ceremonial silver of Christ Church in Philadelphia, are still used in the church on important holy days. The Syng flagon was a replica of the East, made in England and presented to Christ Church by Queen Anne in 1708.

MAKER UNKNOWN

Secretary Bookcase
ca. 1765
Mahogany, poplar and cedar

Mahogany accommodates carving well, having a lovely wood grain and warm tones. It was much used by 18th-century American cabinetmakers. Most furniture in that period was custom-made.

CHARLES WILLSON PEALE
1741–1827

Staircase Group
1795
Oil on canvas

After Copley departed for England, Peale became the foremost American portraitist. This painting, placed within a doorframe and having a wooden step before it, was so lifelike that upon viewing it George Washington bowed to the figures.

PENNSYLVANIA
Philadelphia

Side Chairs
ca. 1825–1830
Black ash, poplar and pine
painted

Empire art seemed especially meaningful to Americans in their new republic, based on the traditions of Greek democracy. Much of the structure and ornamentation of these chairs derive from a Greek chair of the 5th century B.C.

RANDOLPH ROGERS
1825–1892

The Lost Pleiad
ca. 1882
Marble

Rogers made plaster casts from clay models. They were reproduced in marble. This method enabled him to be more prolific. There are at least nine replicas of *The Lost Pleiad,* a Greek mythological tale.

FRANK FURNESS 1839–1912

Desk
ca. 1875
Walnut, white pine and poplar

Furness was an architect whose furniture designs resembled the architecture of his buildings. This desk, with three vertical sections, is quite like the Pennsylvania Academy of Art which was also his work.

WINSLOW HOMER 1836–1910

The Life-Line
1884
Oil on canvas

Homer became increasingly interested in painting scenes of unbridled nature, particularly the sea. This canvas of a lifeline rescue from ship to shore was inspired by activities he observed at a modern lifesaving station in Atlantic City, New Jersey.

THOMAS MORAN 1837–1926

The Grand Canyon of the Colorado
1892, reworked 1908
Oil on canvas

Moran traveled in the West independently and as the artist on government-sponsored expeditions. Combining on-the-spot sketches and photographic material with his memory and imagination he synthesized vast scenes onto relatively small canvases.

MARSDEN HARTLEY 1877–1943

Painting No. 4 (Black Horse)
ca. 1915
Oil on canvas

Hartley, caught up by German Expressionism while working in Europe from 1912 to 1915, incorporated this style into many works inspired by American Indian themes.

ANDREW WYETH b. 1917

Ground-Hog Day
1959
Egg tempera on masonite

Wyeth works in tempera. His paintings are carefully crafted portrayals of life in rural Pennsylvania and Maine. This painting is of the corner of the kitchen of his Pennsylvania neighbors.

ALEXANDER CALDER
American, 1898–1976

Ghost
1963
Painted sheet metal and
metal rods

2nd Floor,
Great Stair
Hall
Balcony

Calder combined his engineering and artistic skills to create a new form of "mobile" sculpture.

DESIGNED BY PETER PAUL RUBENS *Seven Tapestries*
Woven in Paris, Flemish, 1577–1640   Wool, silk, gold, silver
One of seven tapestries presented by King Louis XIII to Cardinal Francesco Barberini while he was a guest at the French Court.

2nd Floor,
Great Stair
Hall
Balcony

KRETZSCHMAR VON KIENBUSCH COLLECTION

2nd Floor

Housed in five galleries, this extraordinary collection of arms and armor (15th c.–16th c.) includes examples from as long ago as the Bronze Age. However, it is predominantly Gothic and Renaissance and contains both battle and parade equipment.

MEDIEVAL EUROPEAN ART

2nd Floor

SPANISH

Pax
1480
Gold

The pax was held by the priest during the celebration of the Mass. This one portrays the Pietà.

FRENCH   *Statue of a Knight*
                                          13th c.
                                          Stone

This statue originally stood in a niche over the knight's tomb in the chapel of La Merlerault.

FRENCH   *Holofernes Army Crossing the*
                                          Euphrates
                                          13th c.
                                          Stained and painted glass

A panel from one of the 15 windows in the Sainte-Chapelle Chapel in Paris built by Saint Louis.

FRENCH   *Cloister from Saint-Genis-des*
                                          Fontaines
                                          ca. 1160–1180

Founded in 819 and deserted in the 18th century, the cloister is the setting for the marble fountain of the same style.

Cloister from Saint-Genis-des-Fontaines. *Courtesy Philadelphia Museum of Art, Philadelphia*

NEAR EASTERN AND SOUTH ASIAN ART 2nd Floor

SPANISH | *Carpet*
15th c.

Woven for an admiral of Castile, this Oriental rug reflects the Moorish influence existing in Spain after the 8th-century invasion.

SOUTH INDIAN | *Pillared Temple Hall from Madura*
16th c.

This reconstructed temple interior is the only example of Indian stone architecture in an American museum. Its interior contains life-size figures of heroes, sages and divine beings along with epic carvings from the Ramayana.

INDIAN | *Nandi*
Mysore | 13th c.
Indurated potstone

The sacred bull Nandi ("Joy"), a favored theme in South Indian sculpture, indicated the presence of the god, Shiva.

CAMBODIAN | *Avalokiteshvara*
Khmer Empire | 7th c.
Sandstone

An unknown but devout Buddhist modeled this statue of the Lord of Mercy.

FAR EASTERN ART 2nd Floor

CHINESE | *Chamber from the Main Reception*
Peking | *Hall from the Palace of Duke Chao*
17th c.

The wooden roof of this chamber where visitors were received is exposed and decoratively painted with traditional Chinese symbols. In the Far East, attention was often focused on roof structure.

CHINESE | *Hexagonal Lantern*
Ch'ing Dynasty, 1644–1912 | 18th c.
Porcelain

This lantern is one of a pair adorned with floral designs.

CHINESE | *Red Camellia*
Ming Dynasty, 1368–1644 | 15th c.
Watercolor on silk

Masterly floral paintings are typical of Chinese art. Chinese painters preferred watercolors and ink to oils, and silk or paper to canvas. Because of its delicate nature, this painting and similar ones are rotated for exhibition.

JAPANESE | *Ceremonial Teahouse*
Tokyo | ca. 1917

Using natural materials as a background, the teahouse offers serenity in the midst of daily activity.

EUROPEAN ART, 1400–1700 2nd Floor

LUCA DELLA ROBBIA | *Virgin and Child*
Italian, ca. 1400–1482 | 15th c.
Glazed terracotta

ANDREA DELLA ROBBIA
Italian, 1435–1525

The colors of this roundel are as vibrant today as when it was painted because of a method invented by Luca della Robbia for glazing terracotta sculptures.

Pillared Temple Hall from Madura. *Courtesy Philadelphia Museum of Art, Philadelphia*

FRENCH
Dijon

Choir Screen from the Chapel of the Château of Pagny
ca. 1535–1540

This choir screen was a Renaissance addition to a Gothic chapel in the château of a 16th-century French admiral.

PETER PAUL RUBENS
Flemish, 1577–1640

Prometheus Bound
ca. 1611–1612
Oil on canvas

This Greek myth is eminently suited to the Baroque style in which it is painted, appealing to our emotions with its vitality.

NICHOLAS POUSSIN
French, 1594–1665

The Birth of Venus
ca. 1635
Oil on canvas

Harmony and balance are the hallmarks of this classical masterpiece. Painted for Cardinal Richelieu, it was also owned by Catherine the Great.

EUROPEAN ART, 1700–1870   **2nd Floor**

FRENCH
Paris

Salon from the Hotel Letellier
1789

Classical architectural decoration adorns this salon which was completed just two weeks prior to the fall of the Bastille.

FRANCOIS-THOMAS GERMAIN
French, 1726–1791

Tureen with Cover and Tray
1759
Gilded silver

This Rococo tureen was ordered by Elizabeth of Russia and was part of a service of 300 pieces.

JOSEPH MALLORD WILLIAM
TURNER
British, 1775–1851

*Burning of the Houses of
Parliament*
19th c.
Oil on canvas

Turner experimented with light and atmosphere in this dramatic work, bursting with color and achieved with rapid brilliant brush strokes.

JEAN FRANCOIS MILLET
French, 1814–1875

Meridian
19th c.
Pastel drawing

Millet, a leader of the Barbizon School of landscapists, painted mainly figures at work in pastoral settings. Although his subjects were thought to be revolutionary his technique was academic.

ENGLISH ART, 1700–1850   **2nd Floor**

ENGLISH

*Drawing Room from Lansdowne
House*
1765–1773

Outstanding craftsmen were employed to execute this design of Robert Adam (1728–1792), the renowned English architect of Neoclassical style.

GRINLING GIBBONS
1648–1721

The First Oak Room
18th c.
Fruitwood

Carved by the foremost woodcarver in England, this room from a great country house holds many of the museum's English paintings.

THOMAS CHIPPENDALE
ca. 1718–1779

Commode from Raynham Hall
18th c.
Mahogany

The floral design of this splendid commode resembles the architectural decoration of the room.

THOMAS GAINSBOROUGH
1727–1788

Anne, Lady Rodney
18th c.
Oil on canvas

Although his preference was for painting landscapes, Gainsborough is best known for his portraits of superb technique and opulent color.

2nd Floor   EUROPEAN ARTS AFTER 1870

CLAUDE MONET   *Poplars*
French, 1840–1926   1891
                                     Oil on canvas
One of a series of canvases Monet painted in his continuing investigation of light and atmosphere.

VINCENT VAN GOGH   *Sunflowers*
Dutch, 1853–1890   1888
                                     Oil on canvas
In his later work, van Gogh created a highly personal style seeming to produce a light of its own in addition to the piercing light and color of southern France.

PAUL CEZANNE   *The Large Bathers*
French, 1839–1906   1898–1905
                                     Oil on canvas
Cézanne was interested in the underlying geometric forms of his subject. In modeling with color to express the geometric forms beneath the surface, he laid the groundwork for Cubism.

HENRI ROUSSEAU   *Carnival Evening*
French, 1844–1910   1886
                                     Oil on canvas
Rousseau had no formal training. He began painting in his forties and relied on his own sense of color and design.

FACILITIES

Temporary Exhibitions culled from the museum's collection or *Loan Exhibitions* from other institutions are regular features of the museum's program.

Free *Museum Tours* are offered Wednesday–Sunday on the hour, 10 A.M.–3 P.M. Foreign-language tours by appointment.

At the *Art Sales and Rental Gallery,* members only may rent original art on consignment from galleries with an option to purchase. Anyone can buy.

The *Museum Shop* carries an excellent variety of items including cards, art books, needlepoint kits, jewelry, and reproductions with a large price range from 50¢ to $1,800—something for everyone.

Cafeteria serves cold salads, hot and cold sandwiches. Open 10 A.M.–3:45 P.M.

The *Restaurant* serves luncheon Wednesday–Sunday, 11:30 A.M.–2 P.M.

For the Handicapped an entrance with ramp is on the south side of the building. Restrooms have special facilities.

Wheelchairs and *Strollers* are available in the coat rooms.

Hours: Wednesday–Sunday, 10 A.M.–5 P.M. *Closed:* Monday, Tuesday, legal holidays.

Admission: Adults, $1.50 (groups of 20 or more, $1.25); children under 18, 75¢; children under 5, free; students with I.D. cards and senior citizens, $1. Free to everyone on Sundays from 10 A.M.–1 P.M.

RODIN MUSEUM
Benjamin Franklin Parkway at 22nd St.
Philadelphia, PA 19101
Tel: (215)763–8100

The Rodin Museum houses the largest collection outside of Paris of works by the 19th-century French sculptor, Auguste Rodin. It is administered by the Philadelphia Museum of Art.

AUGUSTE RODIN   *Sculpture and Drawings*
French, 1840–1917
Rodin was the most famous sculptor of the 19th century. Much influenced by Michelangelo, he created a new kind of sculpture, the fragment as a total work. Like Michelangelo he would finish parts of the uncompleted work very finely while leaving other parts barely touched. This lent great feeling and fluidity to his work which, combined with the use of symbolism and exaggeration, made an especially strong statement. Although artistically successful, most of his public commissions were failures. From 1880 until the end of his life, he worked on *The Gates of Hell* for the Ecole des Arts Decoratifs. Still unfinished at his death it was, nevertheless, a source of inspiration for a number of his best-known figures such as *The Kiss* and *The Thinker.*

FACILITIES

Guided Tours and *Lectures* are available.

The *Sales Desk* offers books and postcards.

Hours: Wednesday–Sunday, 10 A.M.–5 P.M.   *Closed:* Monday, Tuesday, national holidays.

Admission: Pay-what-you-wish donation.

ROSENBACH MUSEUM AND LIBRARY
2010 Delancey Pl.
Philadelphia, PA 19103
Tel: (215)732–1600

Founded in 1954 in the former 19th-century town house of the Rosenbach brothers, the museum houses the treasures they collected in the first half of this century. Much of the house remains as they left it. There are 18th-century examples of Chippendale, Vile, Adam, Hepplewhite and Sheraton furniture; English silver and gold of the 17th to the mid-19th centuries; over 1,000 portrait miniatures; 18th-century porcelain, glass; paintings; drawings; sculpture and, of course, rare books and manuscripts. The latter collection now numbers about 30,000 volumes and over 130,000 pieces of manuscript primarily devoted to Americana, British and American literature and book illustration.

SAMPLING THE COLLECTION

MADE FOR CHARLES II	*Treasure Chest*	**1st Floor,**
British, 1630–1685	ca. 1660	**Parlor**
	Olivewood veneer with	
	silver-gilt mounts	

This box or casket, done during a period of brilliance in English literature and art, was recorded in the inventories of Windsor Castle until 1830.

Interior view. Courtesy Rosenbach Museum and Library, Philadelphia

| 1st Floor, Parlor | WILLIAM SAVERY American, 1721–1788 | *Highboy* 3rd quarter of 18th c. Mahogany |

Savery, a Philadelphia cabinetmaker, is best known for his simply wrought furniture executed in the Chippendale style.

| 1st Floor, Library | SAMUEL MCINTIRE American, act. 1757–1811 | *Sofa* ca. 1810 Mahogany |

McIntire was a prominent master carpenter, architect and builder in Salem, Massachusetts. His Classical carvings were inspired by the excavations taking place at Pompeii and Herculaneum.

| 1st Floor, Hallway | JAMES JOYCE Irish, 1882–1941 | *Manuscript of Ulysses* 1917–1921 |

The complete manuscript of *Ulysses* numbering 837 handwritten pages is owned by the museum.

MAURICE SENDAK	*Original Drawings*	**2nd Floor,**
American, b. 1928		**Exhibit**

The Rosenbach Museum is the repository for Sendak's collection, and owns over 2,000 drawings by the children's book author and illustrator.

MARIANNE MOORE	*Apartment*	**3rd Floor**
American, 1887–1972		

The poet's Greenwich Village apartment is reconstructed and houses Moore's manuscripts, correspondence, library and personal effects.

FACILITIES

Guided Tours are conducted for individuals or groups. Group Tours are also available by telephoned reservation, weekdays 9 A.M.–5 P.M.

Changing Exhibitions are regularly featured.

The *Library* is open for scholars Monday to Friday by appointment.

For *Sale* are adult and children's books, facsimiles, manuscripts and periodicals.

Hours: *September–July:* Tuesday–Sunday, 11 A.M.–4 P.M. *Closed:* August, national holidays.

Admission: Tours: Adults, $1.50; group rate $1; students with I.D. and children, 75¢. Exhibits only, 75¢.

UNIVERSITY MUSEUM OF
THE UNIVERSITY OF PENNSYLVANIA
33rd and Spruce Sts.
Philadelphia, PA 19104
Tel: (215)243–4000

This museum of archeology and anthropology houses collections representative of the life and works of primitive and ancient man. Since its founding in 1889, the museum has been engaged in more than 275 expeditions and continues to send archeologists and anthropologists all over the world. The most important collection of native American gold in existence and the most representative collection of West African art in the United States are on view here.

SAMPLING THE COLLECTION

EGYPTIAN	*Sphinx from the Sanctuary*	
Memphis	*of Ptah*	
	3rd millennium B.C.	

Ptah was the local deity of Memphis and the patron of craftsmen, especially sculptors. Today only traces remain of the temple of Ptah, once one of the greatest in Egypt.

MESOPOTAMIAN	*The Ram in the Thicket*	**Near East**
Ur	ca. 2500 B.C.	**Hall**
	Gold and lapis lazuli	

This world-famous object may have been made for a piece of royal furniture.

Mesoamerican Hall	GUATEMALAN Piedras Negras	*Stela 14* A.D. 761 Stone

Stelae, vertical stone slabs, were erected to commemorate important ceremonials which concluded certain calendrical periods. Elaborate figures were carved on front while glyphs recorded the date and other information on the back and sides.

Peruvian Hall	PERUVIAN Chavín Culture	*Jaguar* ca. 1000 B.C. Stone

Stone, the most readily available material in the Peruvian highlands, predominated in this culture's architecture and sculpture. The prevailing feline motif seems to indicate that the society was a theocratic one.

North American Hall	AMERICAN A.D. 800–1400	*Deer Head Mask* Wood

A ceremonial mask used by the Indians of Key Marco. The realistic carving was unmatched by northern carvers.

Alfred Hall	AFRICAN Nigeria, Benin City	*Bronzes and Ivories* ca. A.D. 1600

The Benin people, technically able with bronze, produced realistic ancestor heads as well as works in praise of the ruler and his court. The bronzes, ivories and wood carvings often accentuate the head and abound with geometric motifs.

Oceania	HAWAIIAN Oceania	*Cloak* Feathers

Ancestor worship was very important to this culture and was often expressed in its art. Feather cloaks, capes and helmets were manifestations of these people's artistry.

China	CHINESE T'ang Dynasty, A.D. 618–906	*Relief of Horses*

These are two of the six reliefs ordered by Emperor T'ai'tsung to be set up around the interior walls of his mortuary chamber in 644. They depict the horses he rode in the battles to secure China's frontiers.

FACILITIES

Guided Tours Wednesdays, Saturdays, 11 A.M. and 1:30 P.M. Sundays, 1:30 P.M. (Donation suggested.) Other times, French, German, Spanish and American sign language by appointment.

Free Lectures by museum curators, Wednesdays at 3 P.M. from March to October.

Free Movies and *Concerts* for adults, Sundays, 2:30 P.M. from October to May.

Free Movies for children, Saturdays, 10:30 A.M. from October to May.

The *Nevil Gallery for the Blind and Sighted* presents changing exhibitions with Braille legends. Children are especially enthusiastic when learning they may touch everything.

The *Library* is open fall and spring semesters: Mondays, Fridays, Saturdays, 9:30 A.M.–4:45 P.M.; Tuesday–Thursday, 9:30 A.M.–9:30 P.M.; Sunday, 1 P.M.–4:45 P.M. Holidays, Summer: Tuesday–Friday, 9:30 A.M.–4:45 P.M.; Saturday, 9:30 A.M.–12:45 P.M. *Closed:* Sunday, Monday.

The *Potlatch Restaurant* serves hot lunches, sandwiches, salads, desserts and beverages in cafeteria style, Tuesday–Saturday, 10 A.M.–4 P.M.; Sunday, 1 P.M.–5 P.M.

The *Museum Shop* and the *Pyramid Shop* (for children) carry a variety of books, jewelry, gifts and contemporary crafts from around the world with a price range from $5 to $1,000.

Hours: Tuesday–Saturday, 10 A.M.–5 P.M.; Sunday, 1 P.M.–5 P.M. *Closed:* Monday, national holidays. *Summer:* Tuesday–Saturday, 10 A.M.–5 P.M. *Closed:* Sunday, Monday.

Admission: A contribution of $1 is suggested but not required.

PITTSBURGH

FRICK ART MUSEUM
7227 Reynolds St.
Pittsburgh, PA 15208
Tel: (412)371–7766

The Frick Art Museum, built in 1970, is an Italian Renaissance-style building containing a collection of Italian, Flemish and French paintings from the Early Renaissance to the 18th century. Included is a French 18th-century period room with furniture made for Marie Antoinette and the family of Louis XV. Among other decorative arts are Chinese 18th-century porcelains, Italian Renaissance bronzes, French and Flemish tapestries and 17th- and 18th-century Russian parcel gilt silver. Sculpture is represented by works by Jean Antoine Houdon and Claude Michel (called Clodion).

Exterior view, south façade. Collection of the Frick Art Museum, Pittsburgh

Italian Gallery	SCHOOL OF LUCCA Italian	*Madonna and Child Enthroned with Four Scenes of the Passion*

ca. 1270
Tempera on panels (triptych)
The influence of the conventionalized formal Byzantine style is clearly apparent in this painting with the elongated figures and linear treatment of drapery. But a certain tenderness of expression suggests the more emotional approach of the Renaissance.

Italian Gallery	STEFANO DI GIOVANNI (SASSETTA) Italian, Sienese, ca. 1400–1450	*Madonna and Child with Two Angels*

Tempera on panel
Sassetta was an outstanding painter of the 15th-century Sienese school. This painting is an excellent example of the delicate handling of line expressing the courtly style of the international school and the spiritual quality of Sienese painting.

French and Flemish Gallery	ANTOINE LE NAIN French, 1588–1648	*Le Bénédicité* Oil on copper

Le Nain was one of three brothers working in the 17th century in France. This painting reflects the delightful realism of the Dutch and Flemish genre painters, accomplished without social commentary or sentimentality.

French and Flemish Gallery	PETER PAUL RUBENS Flemish, 1577–1640	*Princesse de Condé, Elenore de Bourbon* Oil on canvas

Rubens, foremost Baroque painter, expresses in this painting his skill in portraiture. As an early work, it is characteristic of his outstanding ability to portray with remarkable realism the splendor of the court of Flanders.

FACILITIES

Guided Tours may be arranged for groups.

Concert and *Lecture* programs are offered throughout the year free of charge, with admission by ticket.

The *Sales Desk* carries color art postcards of the collection (winners of the First Prize Award by the Printing Industries of America), 10¢ each; books pertaining to the museum, notably a handsome publication entitled *Treasures of the Frick Art Museum,* $17.50 plus handling and tax if applicable.

Ample *Parking* is free.

Hours: Wednesday–Saturday, 10 A.M.–5:30 P.M.; Sunday, 12 P.M.–6 P.M. *Closed:* Monday, Tuesday, Memorial Day, July 4, Labor Day, Thanksgiving, Christmas.

Admission: Free.

MUSEUM OF ART, CARNEGIE INSTITUTE
440 Forbes Ave.
Pittsburgh, PA 15213
Tel: (412)622–3200

The Museum of Art, Carnegie Institute, was founded in 1896. Located on the edge of Schenley Park, the institute—a gift to the city of Pittsburgh from Andrew

Carnegie in 1890—was planned as a cultural center complete with a library and music hall. The Neoclassical building designed by Longfellow, Alden and Harlow, dedicated in 1895, and its extension of 1907, houses not only the exhibition galleries, ancient and decorative arts collections, but also the Carnegie Museum of Natural History. In 1974 the Museum of Art opened a new wing, with an open sculpture court, by architect Edward Larabee Barnes, built in memory of Sarah M. Scaife for the permanent collection of painting, sculpture and graphic arts. The collection has been secured largely through the international exhibitions and the efforts of private donors such as the Scaife family. The collection includes European paintings and sculpture from the Renaissance to the 20th century, with an important concentration of Impressionist, Post-Impressionist and 19th-century American works. Contemporary art is well represented, as are drawings, watercolors and prints. There is also a growing collection of photographs and films.

The section of Antiquities, Oriental and Decorative Arts consists of a choice selection of ancient Egyptian, Greek, Roman and Near Eastern objects; a survey of Chinese works of art from Neolithic period through the 20th century; Southeast Asian sculptures; African, pre-Columbian and American Indian objects; and an international collection of objects and decorative arts with emphasis in the area of European works from the Collection of Ailsa Mellon Bruce, including silver, porcelain and especially French furniture.

SAMPLING THE COLLECTION

CHINESE
Kansu Province, Neolithic Period, Yang-shao Culture, Pan-shan Type, ca. 7000–2205 B.C.
Jar
Earthenware with painted designs
Decorative Arts Hall

The Neolithic period in China produced the finest in early decorated pottery as is demonstrated in this jar. It was among the vessels excavated from a cemetery in the Pan-shan Hills.

EGYPTIAN
Old Kingdom, Middle Dynasty IV, 2780–2280 B.C.
Relief from Mastaba of Mery
Stone
Decorative Arts Hall

The mastaba, in use before the pyramid, was a rectangular tomb with stone facing, a flat top and sloping sides inside which the mummy rested.

EGYPTIAN
New Kingdom, 1567–1085 B.C.
Anubis, Jackal-Headed God of Embalming
Wood
Decorative Arts Hall

This figure, depicting the soul of a pre-Dynastic pharaoh, may have been painted and inlaid with semiprecious jewels or faïence (glaze) channels. Remains of linen and gesso are present.

CHINESE
T'ang Dynasty, A.D. 618–906
Figure of a Horse
"Three-Color" glazed pottery
Decorative Arts Hall

This large noble horse was a replica buried in its master's tomb along with clay models of other animals, servants and articles thought useful in afterlife.

ATT. TO DAVID ROENTGEN, MASTER
1780–1807 (perhaps in collaboration with Heinrich Gambs)
Secretary-Medal Cabinet
ca. 1790
Mahogany, gilt bronze mounts
Decorative Arts Hall

This piece, in the style of Louis XVI, has two fall fronts, one for a writing desk and one for a sitting desk. Behind the fronts and a tier of three drawers are hidden mechanically spring-loaded locks which trigger opening mechanisms.

Decorative Arts Hall

PAINTING ATT. TO ADAM
FRIEDERICH VON LOWENFINCK   *Pair of Vases*
(After engraving by Peter Schenck)   ca. 1730–1735
                                        Meissen

These vases, in early Meissen full Baroque style, are baluster-shaped with necks sunken into the shoulders. A yellow ground with two reserves on each one depict visions of the imaginary Cathay.

Pair of Vases, Meissen. *Courtesy Museum of Art, Carnegie Institute, Pittsburgh. Purchase: Ailsa Mellon Bruce Collection (by exchange)*

Decorative Arts Hall

ENGLISH   *Secretary-Bookcase*
                                        ca. 1715–1720
                                        Walnut, walnut veneers, box
                                        stringing

This piece, in full Queene Anne Baroque style, with an arched broken pediment is subtly inlaid and has gilded detail.

Decorative Arts Hall

ATT. TO JOHN COGSWELL   *Chest of Drawers*
American, Boston, Massachusetts,   ca. 1765–1775
1738–1818   Mahogany

This typically bold American chest has a widely overhanging top and robustly carved ball and claw feet. It exhibits a richly grained finish.

Decorative Arts Hall

JOHN BODDINGTON   *Queen Anne Cup and Cover*
British, 18th c.   1702
                                        Silver

This cup and cover contrast richly decorated areas of cut card work, gadrooning and curved handles with bright shiny undecorated areas typical of the early Queen Anne Baroque period of English silver.

FRANCESCO TRAINI
Italian, Pisan, act. 1321–1363

*Allegorical Representation of
the Crucifixion with Saints
Andrew and Paul*
ca. 1350–1360
Tempera, gesso and gold leaf on
wood panel

Gallery 1

The emotionality of this painting combined with its texts suggest that this was
executed after 1348 when Tuscany had been devastated by the plague.

MASTER OF THE STRAUS
MADONNA
Italian, Florentine, ca. 1350–1420

*Diptych: Madonna and Child and
Crucifixion*
ca. 1380
Tempera and gold leaf on panel

Gallery 1

The two hinged panels, created as a small, portable "altarpiece" for private
worship in the home, could be kept closed when not in use. The Virgin Mary
is represented as Queen of Heaven, with the Christ Child holding a goldfinch.

TINTORETTO (JACOPO ROBUSTI)
Italian, Venetian, 1518–1594

Allegory of Winter and Autumn
ca. 1575–1585
Oil on canvas

Gallery 2

Allegory of Spring and Summer
1575–1585
Oil on canvas

Renaissance painters often expressed themselves in allegorical form, as in masculine and feminine personifications of the seasons. The muscular *Winter* and
the vigorous *Autumn* reveal Michelangelo's influence on Tintoretto. The
broadly painted brush strokes derive from Titian.

GEORGE CATLIN
American, 1796–1872

Ambush for Flamingoes
ca. 1857
Oil on canvas

Gallery 3

Catlin is the hunter camouflaged among the Argentine salt marshes. This subject
was commissioned by the Colt Firearms Company for advertising purposes. The
scene is animated by flamingoes nesting and in flight.

FREDERIC EDWIN CHURCH
American, 1826–1900

The Iceberg
1891
Oil on canvas

Gallery 3

Church spent the summer of 1859 "chasing" and depicting icebergs. Many
years later, he returned to the theme in this version, compatible with his respect
for the awesomeness of nature.

WINSLOW HOMER
American, 1836–1910

The Wreck
1896
Oil on canvas

Gallery 4

This painting was the earliest acquired for the institute's art collection, when
Homer was honored at the first Carnegie International. Man against nature was
a favorite theme of the artist.

JEAN FRANCOIS MILLET
French, 1814–1875

The Sower
1850
Oil on canvas

Gallery 4

Millet's painting of this lone figure symbolizes the peasant and his difficult way
of life. The controversial theme brought him fame. His work greatly influenced
19th-century painters interested in the human condition.

JEAN-BAPTISTE CAMILLE COROT
French, 1796–1875

Early Spring near Mantes
1855–1865
Oil on canvas

Gallery 5

Francesco Traini, Allegorical Representation of the Crucifixion with SS. Andrew and Paul. *Courtesy Museum of Art, Carnegie Institute, Pittsburgh. Gift of the Martha Edwards Lazear Foundation*

Corot was interested in the accurate portrayal of the landscapes he painted. He used an oil glaze to impart a silvery tone which was close to the natural light of northern France.

Gallery 5   HILAIRE GERMAIN EDGAR DEGAS   *Henri Rouart*
French, 1834–1917   ca. 1875
Oil on canvas

Degas believed that the modern portrait should integrate the person and his daily life. Therefore, the industrialist Rouart, a friend and benefactor, is represented with his factory in the background.

Le Bain
1890
Oil on canvas

Around 1886 Degas painted many pastel nudes of women in the bath. This oil stems from that series. The abstract use of color and design is characteristic of Post-Impressionism.

CAMILLE PISSARRO   *Le Carrefour, Pontoise*   **Gallery 5**
French, 1830–1903   1872
                           Oil on canvas

This sunny landscape belies the fact that Pissarro had recently lost all his possessions in the Franco-Prussian War. The somewhat whitened colors, created by bright light, brings unity to the scene.

Street in Pontoise
1872
Oil on canvas

This village scene painted out-of-doors typifies Impressionism. A haze pervades the day. Nothing dramatic occurs, and the few definitive linear elements do not overwhelm the Impressionist effect.

PIERRE AUGUSTE RENOIR   *The Garden in the Rue Cortot,* **Gallery 5**
French, 1841–1919   *Montmartre*
                           ca. 1878
                           Oil on canvas

One of the museum's Impressionist masterpieces, the spectacle of dahlias in full

Camille Pissarro, Le Carrefour, Pontoise. *Courtesy Museum of Art, Carnegie Institute, Pittsburgh. Acquired through the generosity of the Sarah M. Scaife family*

bloom makes this an impressive garden subject. Renoir loved rich colors and the abundance of nature expressed with an overall contentment. The cool and warm colors create a mosaic effect.

Bathers with Crab
1890–1892
Oil on canvas

Later in his career, Renoir returned to more traditional painting with figures more positively drawn, culminating in his *Bathers* series.

Gallery 5   ALFRED SISLEY   *Village on the Shore of*
             French, 1839–1899   *the Marne*
                                          1881
                                          Oil on canvas

A close inspection of one of the museum's earliest Impressionist acquisitions reveals that Sisley has given substance to the forms and shapes of this painting in a manner approaching Post-Impressionism.

Gallery 5   PAUL GAUGUIN   *Landscape with Three Figures*
             French, 1848–1903   1901
                                          Oil on canvas

This is one of the few remaining works from Gauguin's last period in the Marquesas Islands. He was interested in religious beliefs and folklore, and created a style in accord with his primitive subject matter, painting for emotional effect rather than visual accuracy.

Gallery 5   PAUL CEZANNE   *Portrait of the Artist*
             French, 1839–1906   ca. 1883–1887
                                          Oil on canvas

This self-portrait, suggestive of Cézanne's feelings about himself at a time when he had not yet achieved recognition, was painted from a photograph taken ten years earlier. The isolated figure against a green background creates an aura of the loneliness of his past, present and future.

Gallery 5   *Landscape near Aix, the Plain*
                                          of the Arc River
                                          ca. 1892–1895
                                          Oil on canvas

Cézanne sought to resolve the problem of capturing nature truthfully on his canvases by studying the same motif from different angles. This complex work shows great solidity of forms, yet the brushwork is vibrant.

Gallery 5   VINCENT VAN GOGH   *The Plain of Auvers*
             Dutch, 1853–1890   1890
                                          Oil on canvas

Painting in France in July before his suicide, van Gogh experienced a brief period of relative calm enabling him to commit to canvas the vast wheat fields after rain.

Gallery 5   HENRI DE TOULOUSE-LAUTREC   *Portrait of Dr. Henri Bourges*
             French, 1864–1901   1891
                                          Oil on cardboard mounted on panel

For five years Lautrec shared an apartment with Bourges, who once saved the artist's life. A great draftsman, Lautrec added little color to his insightful pictures mostly of the Parisian demimonde.

Gallery 5   PAUL SIGNAC   *Place des Lices, St. Tropez*
             French, 1863–1935   1893
                                          Oil on canvas

This painting, a fine example of Pointillism, combines cool and warm color dots resulting in strong outlines. The style, though evolved from Impressionism differs in that the artist exercises strict control in accordance with color theories.

EDOUARD VUILLARD French, 1868–1940

Interior with Women **Gallery 5**
1900
Oil on canvas

Vuillard's mature style, Intimism, signified a decorative arrangement of color patterns, balanced and contained by a subdued emotional content using familiar, intimately known subject matter.

CLAUDE MONET French, 1840–1926

Waterloo Bridge **Gallery 5**
1903
Oil on canvas

Waterloo Bridge is from Monet's series of London views of 1899–1905. This view over the Thames shows the effect of sunlight through opalescent veils of fog, mist and smoke.

Nymphéas (Water Lilies) **Gallery 6**
1920–1921
Oil on canvas

Water Lilies, one of Monet's famed series completed toward the end of his life, incorporates all of his skills as an Impressionist.

HENRI ROUSSEAU French, 1844–1910

La Maison, Environs de Paris **Gallery 5**
ca. 1905
Oil on canvas

Rousseau's unnaturalistic paintings were akin to the Post-Impressionists. Naïve but carefully detailed, they were endowed with a certain mysticism and magic.

ODILON REDON French, 1840–1916

Flowers in Green Vase **Gallery 5**
1905
Oil on canvas

This work communicates the otherworldly quality of Redon's late paintings. These flowers of the imagination are both real and unreal; they are Redon's unique creation.

PABLO PICASSO Spanish, 1881–1973

Head of a Boy
1906
Oil on canvas

The primitive element in this pre-Cubist painting (possibly a self-portrait) reflects the influence upon Picasso of ancient Iberian sculpture.

PIERRE BONNARD French, 1867–1947

Nude in Bathtub **Gallery 5**
1941–1946
Oil on canvas

Bonnard's primary concern seems to be with color and pattern which he handles abstractly. The subject itself is secondary to the enjoyment of the painting.

HENRI MATISSE French, 1869–1954

The Thousand and One Nights **Gallery 6**
1950
Gouache on cut-and-pasted paper

This major paper cut-out dates from Matisse's most abstract period. It is a twelve-foot frieze of brilliantly colored rectangles and semiabstract motifs with forms arranged in horizontal sequence.

ARTHUR DOVE American, 1880–1946

Tree Forms **Gallery 6**
ca. 1928
Pastel on wood

Essentially a landscape painter, Dove's imaginative forms were inspired by nature. After 1911, he experimented with abstraction in pastels. His imaginative forms were derived from nature.

Gallery 6 GEORGIA O'KEEFFE *Gate of Adobe Church*
American, b. 1887 1929
Oil on canvas
The adobe church, with its simple geometric forms, was a theme frequently painted and well-suited to O'Keeffe's Precisionist style.

Gallery 6 ELIE NADELMAN *Circus Performer*
Polish/American, 1882–1946 ca. 1919
Painted wood
Nadelman combined the influence of American folk art, Classical art, Cubism and Art Nouveau with humor and sophistication to execute *Circus Performer.* It is one of four versions.

Gallery 7 WILLEM DE KOONING *Woman VI*
American, b. 1904 1953
Oil on canvas
Women have been a favorite theme of de Kooning's. He seldom painted completely abstract works but made, of bland subjects, challenging paintings that grated, shocked and were difficult to behold.

Gallery 7 JOAN MIRO *Queen Louise of Prussia*
Spanish, b. 1893 1966
Oil on canvas
Miro is a Surrealist whose paintings are completed in two stages. The first is free and often accidentally inspired, sometimes by hallucinations, while the second is thoughtfully considered.

Gallery 7 ALBERTO GIACOMETTI *Man Walking*
Swiss, 1901–1966 1960
Bronze
Giacometti's attenuated, isolated figure is roughly finished. The existential quality in his work is particularly compatible with an increasingly alienated society.

FACILITIES

Gallery Talks and *Guided Tours* are conducted daily by museum guides on both the permanent collection and special exhibitions.

The *Film Section* exhibits films as an art form, in series based on the esthetics and history of film, and maintains a study collection of avant-garde films.

The *Education Section* offers various children's programs and art classes, as well as tours and outreach lectures.

The *Gallery Café* serves from Tuesday to Saturday, 11 A.M.–4 P.M. Sunday, 1 P.M.–5 P.M.

The *Museum of Art Shop* sells original prints, postcards, posters, jewelry, rugs, fabrics, clothing, china, pottery, books and sculpture.

Lower Level The *Cafeteria* is open Monday–Saturday, 10 A.M.–4 P.M.

Hours: Tuesday–Saturday, 10 A.M.–5 P.M.; Sunday, 1 P.M.–6 P.M. *Closed:* Mondays, national holidays.

Admission: A contribution of $1.50 is suggested for adults, 75¢ for children and students. Saturday is free to all. This admits to Museum of Art and Museum of Natural History.

UNIVERSITY PARK

MUSEUM OF ART
THE PENNSYLVANIA STATE UNIVERSITY
Curtin Rd.
University Park, PA 16802
Tel: (814)865–7672

The permanent collection of this university museum is strongest in American art with special regard for Pennsylvania artists. It also boasts an Oriental collection in which Chinese art and Japanese prints predominate. These, in addition to Baroque art and some 19th-century French paintings and drawings, are the major emphasis of the collection.

SAMPLING THE COLLECTION

The permanent collection is rotated and cannot all be seen at one time. Any item not currently displayed may be viewed upon request.

CHU TA (PA-TA-SHAN-JEN)
Chinese, 1625–1706

Lotus
1705
Ink on paper

Chu Ta is considered one of the most spirited painters of the school of Individualists or Eccentrics of the Early Ch'ing Dynasty. His innovative, dramatic and spontaneous brushwork contrasted with the rigidity of the literati.

CHINESE
Chou Dynasty, ca. 1027–256 B.C.

Earth Symbol (T'sung)
Carved jade

The *T'sung,* an earth symbol used in burials in ancient China, is a squared tubular form. Its lines are simple and geometric.

CHINESE
Lung-ch'uan , Ming Dynasty,
1368–1644

Vase
Celadon glaze

Jade was much valued by the Chinese. The potters of Lung-ch'uan were able to create a glaze that assumed many of the characteristics of jade.

HENDRIK HONDIUS, THE ELDER
Dutch, 1573–1649

Portrait of a Man, after
Lucas van Leyden
1640
Pencil and chalk

Like van Leyden, Hondius was influenced by Dürer as well as the Italian Renaissance.

AMERICAN

Portrait of a Woman
ca. 1840
Oil on canvas

This unsophisticated painting executed by an anonymous limner is typical of the charming folk portraits done at this time.

FREDERICK CARL FRIESEKE
American, 1874–1939

Baby in Pram
ca. 1914
Oil on canvas

Frieseke was an American Impressionist much influenced by Renoir as is evidenced in this light-filled canvas.

EMILE BERNARD
French, 1868–1941

Mlle Antoinette
ca. 1888
Oil on canvas

Chu Ta, Lotus. *Courtesy Museum of Art, Pennsylvania State University, University Park*

Bernard pioneered a style called *Cloisonnisme* which lent his work an enameled effect. Gauguin received the credit for inventing this method which led to a quarrel between the two men.

FACILITIES

Museum Tours are available on Sunday.

Varied programs of *Gallery Talks, Lectures* and *Concerts* are offered. Call for schedule.

Changing Exhibitions are regularly featured.

The *Museum Store* carries books, notepaper, original and reproduction prints and sculpture, folk objects, toys and gifts.

Hours: Daily, 12 P.M.–5 P.M. *Closed:* Mondays, national holidays.

Admission: Free.

RHODE ISLAND

NEWPORT

NEWPORT HISTORICAL SOCIETY
SABBATARIAN MEETING HOUSE
82 Touro St.
Newport, RI 02840
Tel: (401)846–0813

The society was founded in 1853 and was originally quartered in the Sabbatarian Meeting House, the earliest Seventh Day Baptist Church in America, built in 1729. It was the first 18th-century building to be restored in Newport and is now protected by a brick veneer. The society's collections contain paintings, decorative arts, graphics, glass, silver, costumes, a marine display and numismatic material. Archives date back to Newport's earliest days. The society also owns the Wanton-Lyman-Hazard House (1690) and the Friends Meeting House (1690).

SAMPLING THE COLLECTION

JOHN TOWNSEND	*Newport Furniture*	**1st Floor,**
American, 1732–1809	18th c.	**Newport**

JOHN TOWNSEND   *Newport Furniture*   **1st Floor,**
American, 1732–1809   18th c.   **Newport**
John Townsend, one of the Townsend and Goddard families, with his relatives **Room** produced some of the finest furniture in Newport. Many pieces were done in Santo Domingo mahogany, a prominently grained wood.

NEWPORT ARTISANS   *Silver and Pewterware*   **1st Floor**
American   18th c.
American pewter was functional, decorative and of fine quality duplicating the appearance of silver. The surface of American 18th-century silver is quite plain.

ROBERT FEKE   *Portraits*   **2nd Floor,**
American, ca. 1705–1752   18th c.   **Gallery**
Feke, an itinerant artist, was one of Colonial America's finest painters. His lively portraits are dignified and elegant although quite stylized. He was adept at handling fabrics.

FACILITIES

Changing Exhibitions are regularly featured.

The *Library* is available to nonmembers at a fee of $1 per day. It contains works on Newport and Rhode Island genealogy and history and a collection of reference works on the decorative arts.

The *Reception Desk* sells postcards and some prints as well as the Society Bulletins and other publications.

Hours: Tuesday–Friday, 9:30 A.M–4:30 P.M.; Saturday, 9:30 A.M.–12 P.M. During the summer the museum is additionally open on Saturday until 4:30 P.M., Sunday, 1 P.M.–5 P.M. *Closed:* Mondays.

Admission: Free. Donations are welcome.

REDWOOD LIBRARY AND ATHENAEUM
50 Bellevue Ave.
Newport, RI 02840
Tel: (401)847–0292

The library was established in 1947 with 1,300 books purchased from England. The following year a miniature Roman temple with a Tuscan portico was erected to accommodate the collection which has grown to over 138,000 books. Over 100 portraits by important American artists hang in the Marquand Room and in the original Library Hall where busts and statues of literary figures may also be seen. On the south side of the library lies a pleasant garden with a flagstone walk leading to a garden house.

SAMPLING THE COLLECTION

GILBERT STUART
American, 1755–1828

Self-Portrait
1778
Oil on canvas

Stuart, the greatest portraitist of the Federal period, is best known for his portraits of George Washington. He painted faces with dexterity and insight, but was less successful at other kinds of paintings.

ROBERT FEKE
American, ca. 1705–1750

Mrs. Joseph Wanton
Oil on canvas

Feke was an itinerant painter. With adroit handling of color and material he managed to express Colonial sentiments in his somewhat wooden portraits.

CHARLES WILLSON PEALE
American, 1741–1827

William Bradford, Jr.
Oil on canvas

Peale fathered a family of American painters who flourished during the Colonial and Federal periods. A self-taught painter whose work was well regarded, he abandoned painting for alternative interests.

FACILITIES

Sales Desk carries publications about Newport and the Library.

Hours: Monday–Saturday, 10 A.M.–6 P.M. *August:* 10 A.M.–5 P.M. *Closed:* Sundays, holidays.

Admission: Free.

PROVIDENCE

MUSEUM OF ART
RHODE ISLAND SCHOOL OF DESIGN
224 Benefit St.
Providence, RI 02903
Tel: (401)331–3511

The Museum of Art, Rhode Island School of Design, serves the general public, an art school and a university audience. Founded in 1877, it contains treasures of ancient art (jewelry, sculpture, bronzes and Greek vases), 19th-century French paintings, graphics and the John D. Rockefeller Collection of Japanese

Birds and Flower Prints. It also displays 20 centuries of Oriental art, master-pieces of older European art, American painting and contemporary art. Pendle-ton House, with its American furniture and decorative arts, is the earliest example of an "American Wing" in the United States. These collections are complemented by major holdings in graphics, costumes and textiles.

SAMPLING THE COLLECTION

THE PROVIDENCE PAINTER *Red-Figured Amphora*
Greek, 5th c. B.C. Ceramic
An excellent example of a red-figure vase from the 5th century B.C., this vase is a prime specimen of the work of an anonymous painter known as the Providence Painter.

CLAUDE MONET *Bassin d'Argenteuil*
French, 1840–1926 ca. 1872
  Oil on canvas
Argenteuil was a favorite site of the French Impressionist painters of the 1870s, where they experimented with the treatment of light and color. This is one of four works by Monet in the museum's collection.

JAPANESE *Buddha*
  10th–15th c.
  Wood
The museum's towering Buddha (nine feet high) is the largest wooden Buddha outside Japan.

AUGUSTE RODIN *Balzac*
French, 1840–1917 1893
  Bronze

This is an important early study for Rodin's *Monument to Balzac.*

EDOUARD MANET   *Le Repos*
French, 1832–1883   ca. 1872
                                 Oil on canvas

Berthe Morisot, herself a recognized artist, was Manet's model for this painting, considered to be one of the most important Manet paintings in this country.

WINSLOW HOMER   *On a Lee Shore*
American, 1836–1910   1900
                                 Oil on canvas

This seascape is typical of a later period in Homer's life during which he withdrew to the coast of Maine to paint scenes of the sea.

BABYLONIAN   *Lion*
                                 6th c. B.C.
                                 Glazed ceramic brick

Over 120 of these glazed brick reliefs originally lined the walls of the processional way to the Ishtar gates of ancient Babylon; this is one of only seven in the United States.

AMERICAN   *Bombé Chest of Drawers*
Boston, Massachusetts   Mahogany, wood

Bombé, or kettle-base, chests of drawers were much favored in Boston in the middle of the 18th century. Beautiful use of figured mahogany enhances the curved silhouette, which is the tour de force of the cabinetmaker's art.

FACILITIES

Guided Tours may be arranged by calling (401)331–3511, ext. 279.

A program of *Lectures, Concerts* and *Films* is offered. Call for schedule information (401)331–6363.

Changing Exhibitions are regularly featured.

The *Library* of art history books is available for use on the premises.

The *Museum Shop* carries a fine selection of jewelry, crafts, unusual gift items, postcards, stationery, art books, catalogs, and original works of art.

Hours: *Winter:* Tuesday, Wednesday, Friday, Saturday, 11 A.M.–5 P.M.; Sunday, holidays, 2 P.M.–5 P.M.; Thursday, 1 P.M.–7 P.M. *Summer:* Tuesday–Saturday, 11 A.M.–4:30 P.M.; Sunday, holidays, 2 P.M.–4:30 P.M. *Closed:* Mondays, Thanksgiving, Christmas, New Year's, July 4, month of August.

Admission: Adults 19 and over, $1; children 5–18, 25¢; children 4 and under, free. Saturday, free with voluntary admission donation.

VERMONT

BENNINGTON

BENNINGTON MUSEUM
West Main St.
Old Bennington, VT 05201
Tel: (802)442–2180

The north wing of the museum, founded in 1876, was originally the first Roman Catholic Church in southern Vermont. The collection in this regional museum includes Bennington pottery; American blown and pressed glass; a gallery of Grandma Moses paintings, the Grandma Moses Schoolhouse Museum moved to Bennington from Eagle Bridge, New York; furniture; rare documents, costumes and uniforms; firearms and swords, toys and dolls; Early American household items; contemporary Vermont and other European paintings, and sculpture and the Bennington flag.

SAMPLING THE COLLECTION

SIMEON SKILLEN, JR. American, ca. 1756–1806	*Carved Eagle* Wood	**Military Gallery**

JOHN SKILLEN
American, 1746–1800
The Skillen brothers were sons of America's first woodcarver. Simeon executed the first figurehead for the U.S.S. *Constitution.* From 1870 on, they worked in partnership.

RALPH EARL American, 1751–1801	*Captain Elijah Dewey* 1798 Oil on canvas	**Military Gallery**

Earl was a portraitist whose forthright early work was influenced by Benjamin West while visiting England. His later portraits were stiffer and more studied.

GRANDMA MOSES (ANNA MARY ROBERTSON MOSES) American, 1860–1961	*Paintings*	**1st Floor, Moses Gallery**

Grandma Moses's naïve paintings first gained prominence when she was over seventy years old. Her carefully detailed landscapes, with the figures added afterward, are done from memory, and depict scenes of the four seasons.

BENNINGTON POTTERY American, Vermont	*Toilet Set* ca. 1850–1858 Stoneware	**2nd Floor, Johnson Gallery**

Factories imitating English ware were established in Vermont in the 1830s. Decorated in gold and the traditional blue of Bennington pottery, the owner's name appears in gold on each piece of this set.

FACILITIES

The *Genealogical Library* contains comprehensive town and county histories and many family genealogies of the area. Consultation services are available with the librarian. Library hours: Monday–Friday, 9:30 A.M.–12 P.M.; 1:30 P.M.–4:30 P.M.

Exterior view. Courtesy Bennington Museum, Bennington

The *Gift Shop* features books, Grandma Moses prints and books, museum-related gifts, Parian ware, gifts by local craftsmen and Bennington Museum souvenirs.

Hours: *Winter:* Open 7 days a week and holidays, 9:00 A.M.–5:00 P.M. *Summer: End of May,* 9 A.M.–5 P.M. *Closed:* December, January, February.

Admission: Adults, $2; children 12–17, $1; under 12, free, if accompanied by an adult; unaccompanied, 25¢. Tour groups of more than 10 are half-price if notified in advance.

BURLINGTON

ROBERT HULL FLEMING MUSEUM
University of Vermont
Colchester Ave.
Burlington, VT 05405
Tel: (802)656–2090

The museum opened in 1932 in a McKim, Mead and White building of Neoclassical design with a collection which originated as a "cabinet" of curiosities in 1826. Two floors containing eight galleries surround a gracious Marble Court. The museum once housed collections of natural history, archeology and art but was divided in the 1950s and is now a fine arts museum covering all periods and parts of the world. Its strongest holdings are in American art of the 19th and early 20th centuries, Native American art and African art. Of special interest also are the Ancient and Medieval Galleries and the Oriental Gallery. Additionally there are 19th-century European paintings, furniture and artifacts; pre-Columbian ceramics and textiles; prints; and costumes exhibited in rotation.

SAMPLING THE COLLECTION

American Gallery	WINSLOW HOMER American, 1836–1910	*The Tent or Summer by the Sea* Oil on academy board

Homer lived for a time in rural New England painting cheerful naturalistic scenes of the life around him. He experimented with light but not so intensively as did the Impressionists.

AFRICAN	*Head*	**Ethnographic**
Nigeria, Benin City	18th c.	**Gallery**
	Bronze	

(Not always on display as exhibits are rotated.)
This head of a queen mother was made for the ceremonial altar. It was cast in the lost-wax process which the artists of Benin handled with great proficiency.

ASSYRIAN	*Winged Genie Mural Relief*	**Marble**
	ca. 880 B.C.	**Court**
	Alabaster	

This relief was carved for the Northwest Palace of Ashurnasirpal II in Nimrud in northern Mesopotamia. Alabaster murals of repeated designs of the king, deities and an inscription adorned the palace walls.

FACILITIES

Changing Exhibitions are regularly featured.

Special Events are scheduled, such as lectures, gallery talks and concerts. For program information inquire at the Information Desk.

The *Education Room* has a "hands on" area for children.

The *Wilbur Room Library* is noncirculating. Open for reading and research Monday–Friday, 9 A.M.–12 P.M. Tuesday, Thursday afternoons, 1 P.M.–5 P.M.

The *Sales Desk* carries mainly cards and catalogs.

Hours: Monday–Friday, 9 A.M.–5 P.M.; Saturday–Sunday, 1 P.M.–5 P.M. *Closed:* Most major holidays.

Admission: Free.

ST. JOHNSBURY

ST. JOHNSBURY ATHENAEUM
30 Main St.
St. Johnsbury, VT 05819
Tel: (802)748–8291

The library was founded in 1871 and the art gallery in 1873. The Athenaeum building is a fine example of Victorian architecture. The gallery itself is a period piece having been maintained as a 19th-century gallery. It is the oldest to remain in its original form in the United States. The permanent collection contains approximately 100 works primarily of 19th-century Americans.

SAMPLING THE COLLECTION

ALBERT BIERSTADT	*Domes of the Yosemite*
1830–1902	1867
	Oil on canvas

Bierstadt was instantly successful. His huge, dramatically lit canvases depicted the wilderness of Western America.

Albert Bierstadt, Domes of the Yosemite. *Courtesy St. Johnsbury Athenaeum, St. Johnsbury*

SAMUEL COLMAN
1832–1920

The Emigrant Train, Colorado
1872
Oil on canvas

Colman's early works were Northeastern landscapes. After the Civil War he produced paintings of westward-moving emigrants. Both his oils and watercolors were brightly colored with strong chiaroscuro effects.

WORTHINGTON WHITTREDGE
1820–1910

On the Plains, Colorado
1877
Oil on canvas

Whittredge was a member of the Hudson River School who, after studying in Europe, returned to paint landscapes of the American West.

SANFORD GIFFORD
1823–1880

The Views from South Mountain in the Catskills
1873
Oil on canvas

Gifford captured the light and air in detailed scenic views. His finished canvases were coated with a semitransparent substance that corresponded with the natural veil of the atmosphere.

FACILITIES

A catalog of the art gallery collection, $1, and postcards of the museum building and Bierstadt painting *Domes of the Yosemite,* 10¢, are available for purchase.

Hours: Monday, Friday, 9:30 A.M.–8 P.M.; Tuesday, Wednesday, Thursday, Saturday, 9:30 A.M.–5 P.M. *Closed:* Sunday, national holidays.

Admission: Free.

GLOSSARY

ABSTRACT EXPRESSIONISM was a name given to the post-World War II art movement that was nonrepresentational and feeling and in which the subconscious was given free reign. It comprised two methods: Action Painting and Abstract-Image Painting. See **COLOR FIELD PAINTING**.

ABSTRACT-IMAGE PAINTING. See **COLOR FIELD PAINTING**.

ACTION PAINTING. A term describing a brand of Abstract Expressionism practiced by Jackson Pollock, Willem de Kooning, etc. Paint is dripped and splashed on the canvas in an unrestrained manner, the accidental being used to advantage.

ANALYTICAL CUBISM was the first phase of Cubism. It was explored by Picasso and Braque from 1907 to 1912 and based on Cézanne's handling of nature "in terms of the cylinder, the sphere and the cone." They sought to convey subjects in the round as a totality without diminishing the value of the picture's flat surface.

ART DECO is a design and decorative arts style associated with the 1920s and 1930s. Exotic decorations and streamlined geometric designs, influenced by Cubism, permeated architecture, interior and industrial design, graphics and crafts.

ART NOUVEAU was an international style popular in the 1890s in architecture, the applied arts and interior design. Highly stylized, it emphasized intricate organic themes.

ASHCAN SCHOOL. See **THE EIGHT**.

BARBIZON SCHOOL was composed of a group of French landscapists who settled at the edge of the forest of Fontainebleau in the village of Barbizon and fostered landscape painting as an expression of art important in its own right.

BAROQUE ART, originating in Italy, especially Rome, was dominant in Western Europe, ca. 1580–ca. 1720. It is marked by dynamic, intensely emotional expression, dramatic lighting, asymmetry and compositions that seemingly extend into space. Individual effects are dominated by the whole.

CHAMPAGNE SCHOOL appeared in Champagne, France, toward the close of the 15th century and the opening of the 16th century. It favored the simple, serious Gothic style of earlier times and was especially popular among the rich middle class.

CHIPPENDALE is a furniture style of the mid-18th century that mirrors the French Rococo. Mahogany chairs with pierced complex splats typify these designs as does ornately carved furniture of Chinese and Gothic influence, some of which are carved, japanned or gilded. Commencing in the 1760s luxuriously carved pieces became classical in design.

CLASSICISM in art implies reason, order, restraint and harmony based on models and principles descended from ancient Greece and Rome.

CLOISSONNISME. See **SYNTHETISM**.

COLOR FIELD PAINTING evolved in the 1950s and is known interchangeably as Post-Painterly Abstraction, Cool Art and Abstract-Image Painting. Rejecting drawing, optical illusion, motion, light and figuration these artists were concerned with simple, flat, brilliantly colored areas and general form concentrating on the act of painting itself.

CONSTRUCTIVISM, essentially a nonobjective, three-dimensional art most commonly seen in sculpture, also appears in paintings and graphics. Originating in Russia in the 1920s, its proponents employed modern technological materials such as plastic, iron and wire.

CUBISM, begun by Picasso and Braque about 1907, became the watershed from which many abstract styles developed. It was derived from Cézanne's later work in which he attempted to control space and light in geometric forms and from African sculpture with its faceted surfaces, stylization and simple forms. Cubism consists of two phases—**ANALYTICAL CUBISM** and **SYNTHETIC CUBISM.**

DADAISM was a precursor of **SURREALISM**, an international movement popular from about 1916 to 1923. Its center was in Zurich but it was also developed in New York and Paris. Disillusioned by World War I, these artists attacked tradition in all forms, expressing themselves with irreverence and absurdity.

THE EIGHT were artists Arthur Davies, William Glackens, Ernest Lawson, George Luks, Maurice Prendergast, Everett Shinn, John Sloan, led by Robert Henri. In 1907, they defected from the National Academy of Design to exhibit together. Most of them painted realistic pictures of the sordid life of the city, although some conveyed its pleasant aspects. Even though their styles were individual, they used predominantly dark colors and unidealized subjects, hence they were referred to in the 1930s as the **ASHCAN SCHOOL.**

EMPIRE STYLE in furniture and decoration was created in France in the early 19th century. It combines Neoclassicism with archeological details made popular after Napoleon's Egyptian campaign.

EXPRESSIONISM is an art form characterized by distortion and exaggeration because the artist concerned themselves with emotional expressions stemming from their inner feelings, rather than depictions of nature or rational subject matter. Greatly influenced by van Gogh, it began in France about 1905 but appeared in other European countries at about the same time. It reached its climax in movements that flourished in Germany.

LES FAUVES, meaning "the wild beasts," was a sobriquet bestowed on a group of artists whose work was shown in 1905 at the Salon d'Automne. Their paintings were distorted, executed in vivid color and composed of bold brush strokes.

FRENCH RESTORATION refers to the restoration of the Bourbons to the French throne in 1815 after the downfall of Napoleon. Neoclassicism yielded to Romanticism. In painting, dramatic lighting, color and contemporary subject matter were featured as exemplified by work of Baron Antoine Jean Gros.

FUTURISM, an early 20th-century movement in literature and art, flourished mainly in Italy commencing in 1910. The painters, in revolt against the past, tried to convey the excitement and motion of the scientific present. Their subjects were things of motion—wheels, legs, fast-moving vehicles. They painted multiple images and used color to achieve a feeling of motion.

GENRE refers to paintings whose subject matter is everyday life. It was a particularly popular mode of expression with 17th-century Dutch painters.

GEORGIAN STYLE applies to architecture, furniture and decorative work produced in England from 1714 to 1820. Organic, unified forms were employed on a small scale. About 1750 the French influenced the simpler English designs introducing Rococo decorations.

GOTHIC predominated in art and architecture in Northern Europe from about 1140 until the 16th century. In Italy it was replaced by the **RENAISSANCE** in the 14th century. Some of its main architectural features are the pointed arch, vaulting buttresses and flying buttresses, stained glass and slender vertical piers, the combination resulting in a soaring skyward monumentality. Humanism and spatial effects appeared in painting.

GOTHIC INTERNATIONAL STYLE was a phase of Gothic art, and appeared in the late 14th and early 15th centuries. It emphasized naturalism, often in secular subjects, refined color and graceful lines.

HUDSON RIVER SCHOOL of painters were 19th-century landscapists who painted romantic interpretations of American scenery concentrating mostly on the Catskill Mountains fringing the Hudson River. They varied in their outlooks from intimate poetic expressions to lofty imaginative ones.

IMPRESSIONISM orginated in the 1870s in France in opposition to academicism. Middle-class subjects were portrayed in broken brush strokes of pure color. The Impressionists sought to capture the evanescence of light and atmosphere on canvas while projecting the greatest naturalism.

INTIMISM is a type of painting practiced in the late 19th century concerned with mainly intimate interior scenes and objects providing a feeling of warmth and security.

MANNERISM, a painting style prominent from about 1520 to 1600, revolted against the classicism of High Renaissance art. Its emotional expression appears in often violent color, elongated figures and distorted exaggerations.

MINIMALISM is an impersonal, precise and restrained art style relying on color and form for its expression.

MUNICH SCHOOL was founded in the second half of the 19th century under the patronage of King Ludwig I of Bavaria. In an effort to enhance the prestige of German art, the school imitated the monumental mural painting of the Italian Renaissance.

NEOCLASSICISM is an artistic and architectural style that predominated ca. 1770–ca. 1830. With the unearthing of Pompeii and Herculaneum and the ensuing interest in antiquity, a reaction against Baroque and Rococo styles occurred. This ordered and restrained style paid attention to accurate detail gleaned from material yielded by the excavations.

NEW YORK SCHOOL. See **ABSTRACT EXPRESSIONISM.**

OP (OPTICAL ART), a movement of the 1960s, uses graphic devices and the placement of line, pattern and color to create visual distortions that result in illusions to the eye.

POINTILLISM was invented by Seurat in the 1880s. It is a scientifically based method of painting in which small dabs of pure complementary color are placed next to each other and fuse in the eye of the beholder.

POP ART, a movement of the 1960s, originated in England somewhat earlier than the more dynamic American version. It deals with popular and commercial subjects, isolating them in a way that demands that the observer reinspect his surroundings.

POST-IMPRESSIONISM is a loose term generally used to describe the art of Cézanne, Gauguin, van Gogh and others whose varied styles succeeded French Impressionist painting.

PRECISIONISM employs a realistic, often photographic style with flat areas of color and smooth finishes. It evolved in the 1920s, influenced by the geometry and frugal detail of Cubism.

PRE-RAPHAELITE BROTHERHOOD was a group who aimed to study nature and portray events in all honesty regardless of how undecorative the results. They tried to recapture the purity of art before the Renaissance and Raphael who was, they considered, too scientific in his approach.

QUEEN ANNE is a furniture and architectural style that was popular in the first half of the 18th century and originated in England. Marked by Oriental and Classical influences, it is simply carved in mahogany or walnut. Its curved legs end in ornamental feet.

REGIONALISM refers to the work of American painters of the 1930s who depicted life in particular geographical sections. A large number of these artists were from the Midwest and produced pictures of small rural communities there.

RENAISSANCE art began in 14th-century Italy and was adopted throughout Europe yielding, in the early 16th century, to the beginning of modernism.

The Early Renaissance, prior to about 1500, was distinguished by humanism and an interest in realism. The climax of the High Renaissance, ca. 1495–ca. 1520, added to these the Classical ideals of harmony and balance.

REPRESENTATIONAL ART, unlike Abstract and Nonobjective art, seeks to duplicate an object or figure fairly closely.

ROCOCO art and decoration originated in 18th-century France and was disseminated throughout Europe. Marked by elegance, gaiety, animation and high color, it is also distinguished by curves, scrollwork and asymmetry.

ROMANESQUE STYLE appeared about the middle of the 11th century and began to decline at the end of the 12th century. It was an eclectic style that drew from Byzantine, Roman, Carolingian and barbarian sources. The details of its architecture are best observed in its massive monasteries that were simple and ordered. The sculpture was linear and angular, often distorted to allow the architecture to accommodate it. Paintings of the period were mostly murals that reflected the same influences as the sculpture and architecture.

ROMANTICISM first emerged in the late 18th century and attained its greatest popularity in the first third of the 19th century. Appearing in art and literature it was fed by the imagination and emotions. It could be subjective and rebellious or manifested in a love of nature and primitive or common man. It often showed an interest in the exotic.

SCHOOL OF FONTAINEBLEAU. The more illustrious First School of Fontainebleau, ca. 1530–ca. 1560, refers to the Mannerist paintings and decorations executed by Italian artists who worked in France for Francis I on the Palace of Fontainebleau. The Second School, during the second half of the century, saw an effort by mainly French artists to continue this work.

SCHOOL OF PARIS refers to the international artists who worked in Paris from about 1900 on. Attracted by the freedom offered by the city for discussion and exhibition, in comparison to other European cities, their art was avant-garde and generally abstract.

SPONTANEOUS STYLE. A popular style of painting at the close of the Sung Dynasty (1127–1279) which combined the shorthand techniques of earlier scholar painters and calligraphers with the older Lyric Style. It added a feeling for nature and man derived from Taoism and Ch'an Buddhism.

SURREALISM emerged ca. 1922 and owes its origins partly to Dadaism and Cubism. It attempts to fuse the dream world with the real one demanding that the artist free himself from his usual means of expression and devote himself to his subconscious and the irrational.

SYNCHROMISM was developed in 1913 in Paris by the Americans Stanton MacDonald-Wright and Morgan Russell. It depended on planes of color and their relationships.

SYNTHETIC CUBISM, the second phase of Cubism, incorporated printed and other collage material on its plane surfaces reintroducing color and subject.

SYNTHETISM, or Cloisonnisme, is a painting method that expresses the emotions rather than duplicating the observable. Its artificial appearance helps to convey the intangible. Flattened, two-dimensional areas are encompassed by broad curved outlines of high color resembling stained glass painting or cloisonné enamel.

THE TEN were a group of American, mostly Impressionist painters, who exhibited together from 1895 on.

VICTORIAN art and architecture were so named for the style popular during the reign of England's Queen Victoria (1837–1901). Rococo and Renaissance styles were adapted to mass production manifested in showy, ornamented pieces.

WASHINGTON COLOR PAINTERS were a group who exhibited in the Washington, D.C. Gallery of Modern Art in 1965. Interested in the optical effects of color that could be achieved through geometric, largely hard-edged repeated designs, they usually painted in series to stress the changeability and property of the colors.

WILLIAM AND MARY period of furniture design, popular ca. 1690–ca. 1730, echoed the Baroque style of the earlier 1600s. Contrasting wood grains were used and columnar supports became more delicate.

INDEX OF ARTISTS

73